Manufacturing Technology in the Electronics Industry

Manufacturing Technology in the Electronics Industry

An introduction

Phillip R. Edwards

Principal Scientific Officer, British Rail Research, Derby, UK.

CHAPMAN & HALL

London · New York · Tokyo · Melbourne · Madras

Published by Chapman & Hall, 2–6 Boundary Row, London SE1 8HN

Chapman & Hall, 2–6 Boundary Row, London SE1 8HN, UK

Van Nostrand Reinhold Inc., 115 5th Avenue, New York NY10003, USA

Chapman & Hall Japan, Thomson Publishing Japan, Hirakawacho Nemoto Building, 7F, 1-7-11 Hirakawa-cho, Chiyoda-ku, Tokyo 102, Japan

Chapman & Hall Australia, Thomas Nelson Australia, 102 Dodds Street, South Melbourne, Victoria 3205, Australia

Chapman & Hall India, R. Seshadri, 32 Second Main Road, CIT East, Madras 600 035, India

First edition 1991

© 1991 Phillip R. Edwards

Typeset in 10/12pt Palatino by Columns Design & Production Services Ltd.

Printed in Great Britain by St Edmundsbury Press, Bury St Edmunds, Suffolk

ISBN 0 412 37130 8   0 442 31362 4 (USA)

A catalogue record for this book is available from the British Library

Library of Congress Cataloging-in-Publication Data
Edwards, Phillip R., 1958–
    Manufacturing technology in the electronics industry : an introduction / Phillip R. Edwards.
        p.   cm.
    Includes bibliographical references and index.
    ISBN 0–442–31362–4 (pbk.)
    1. Electronic apparatus and appliances—Design and construction.
2. Electronic industries.   3. Printed circuits—Design and
construction.   I. Title.
TK7836.E39   1991
621.381—dc20   91–2819
                                                                          CIP

⑧ Printed on permanent acid-free text paper, manufactured in accordance with the proposed ANSI/NISO Z 39.48–199X and ANSI Z 39.48–1984

Contents

Preface

The sequence of events which led to the writing of this book started at a seminar on Manufacturing Technology in the Electronics Industry given by the Institution of Production Engineers in 1987. The seminar identified that the field of manufacturing engineering for the electronics industry was effectively missing from the vast majority of production engineering degree courses. The reason for this was that production engineering departments typically spring from mechanical engineering departments. This leads to a mechanical bias in the practical aspects of such courses.

The consequence of this was that electronics companies could not recruit graduates with both relevant production engineering and electronic engineering backgrounds. This necessitated either recruiting production engineering graduates and giving them the necessary electronic engineering training, or giving production engineering training to electronic engineering graduates. A consequence of the lack of courses in a subject is that there is also a lack of relevant textbooks in the area, as most textbooks are intended to tie into courses. In the field of manufacturing technology for the electronics industry, existing textbooks tend to be highly specialized and mainly concerned with the fabrication of semiconductor devices.

The book assumes no previous knowledge of electronics and keeps the actual electronic theory to a minimum. Where electronic components are introduced, the emphasis is placed on their handling and packaging. The main subject areas addressed by this book are components, design, semiconductor device fabrication, printed circuit board manufacture, surface mount components, and non-standard devices and their associated technologies. Each area is viewed with respect to its impact on the manufacture of electronic devices.

One of the major problems associated with any textbook which addresses the field of electronics is that technology is continually advancing at such a rapid pace that sections can rapidly become obsolete. The manufacturing aspect of the electronics industry is not in practice changing as rapidly as the component technology. Many processes can accommodate changes in technology by operating on a smaller scale. The principles are the same except that process control needs to be much better. Processing faults which were tolerable on a larger scale can become unacceptable on a smaller scale.

Modern society has an increasing requirement for cheap, reliable and increasingly complex electronic devices. This makes the efficient application of manufacturing technology to the electronics industry an important and challenging subject area which will be in great demand for the foreseeable future.

Dr Phillip R. Edwards

1
Introduction to the electronics industry

The electronics industry encompasses a wide range of different manufacturing processes and products. The most visible products of the electronics industry are consumer goods such as television sets, music reproduction systems and computers. These visible products represent a tip of the iceberg situation as a large part of the electronics industry is concerned with the manufacture of the component parts of products. The manufacture of switches, printed circuit boards, semiconductor devices and the assembly of complex computer systems are all aspects of the electronics industry. The fact that each of these activities would typically be performed by different organizations shows that there are few common factors across the electronics industry's component companies.

An electronic product (excluding its packaging or casing), whether it be a simple transistor radio or a complex supercomputer, consists of two basic parts – the electronic components (transistors, resistors etc.) and the interconnections between the components. The electronics manufacturing industry is primarily concerned with interconnection technology – the methods of electrically joining the inputs and outputs of electronic components to form working circuits. Even the companies which manufacture the actual electronic components have to provide methods of connecting them to other devices.

This book is primarily concerned with the manufacturing aspects of the electronics industry. In general a knowledge of the theory of electronics is not necessary for many manufacturing processes used for the manufacture of electronic products. The only exceptions to this are when a device's performance is sensitive to manufacturing-related parameters.

This chapter is concerned with the global aspects of the electronics industry. A historical perspective is used to show the impact of rapidly changing technological progress on the industry. The increasing demands imposed by the market for electronic products is examined with respect to its effect on the electronics manufacturing industry. In order to appreciate the differing requirements and the resulting compromises which need to be reached for a typical product, the departmental structure and the interaction between departments are discussed for a typical manufacturing company. The functions of quality assurance and test engineering are so intimately entwined with almost every other function that they cannot be considered in isolation. An overview of the quality and test functions, and their interactions with other activities, is given. The actual quality and test activities are described alongside the descriptions of the individual manufacturing processes where appropriate.

Chapter 2 is concerned with the individual electronic components. Components are grouped into families with related electrical or physical characteristics where appropriate. From the manufacturing point of view, the most important aspects of electronic components are those of their physical dimensions, their terminal connections, and their quality.

Chapter 3 is concerned with the design processes, in particular the design of electronic circuits and the layout of circuits using computer-aided design where appropriate.

Chapter 4 describes the fabrication of semiconductor devices. Processing from design through to manufacture is covered completely.

Chapters 5, 6 and 7 are concerned with the manufacture of complete printed circuit boards. Chapter 5 is concerned with the manufacture of the bare printed circuit board. Chapter 6 is primarily concerned with the assembly of conventional leaded components into printed circuit boards. Chapter 7 discusses the introduction of surface-mounted components and their impact on printed circuit board manufacture.

Chapter 8 completes the discussion by describing some of the non-standard electronic devices and interconnection methods.

1.1 A HISTORY OF THE ELECTRONICS INDUSTRY

The electronics industry has evolved very rapidly since its beginnings. The enormous advances in technology, particularly since the late 1950s, have imposed considerable pressures towards change. In fact the progress of change is itself increasing, which makes obsolescence a serious problem.

A good perspective of this rapid evolution, and how it has

Table 1.1 Chronological table of electronic advances

Year	Event
1801	Jacquard loom
1833	Semiconductor effect discovered
1835	Rectifier effect discovered
1879	Telephone invented
1906	Cat's whisker radio
1920	Valve radios mass produced
1926	Band theory describes semiconductor effect
1937	Atanasoff computer
1940s	Strowger exchange
1940	First printed circuit board
1943	Colossus computer
1949	First transistor fabricated
1959	First integrated circuit fabricated
1970s	First electronic exchange
1976	8 μm IC geometries
1980s	8-bit microprocessors
1981	5 μm IC geometries
1985	3 μm IC geometries
1987	1.5 μm IC geometries
1989	1 μm IC geometries
1990s	32-bit microprocessors

influenced the industry, can be obtained by looking from a historical point of view. A history of electronic devices highlights the rapid progress of technology. The effect of this progress on the different components of the electronics industry can be shown by looking at two consumer product manufacturing industries, the telecommunications industry and the computer manufacturing industry. The telecommunications industry is examined because it is a long-standing industry to which sophisticated electronics is a fairly recent introduction which has subsequently dominated the industry. The computer industry, by contrast, is still fairly young but has had to keep up with the leading edge of technology. Table 1.1 shows the major events of advances in electronic device technology, advances in the telecommunications industry and advances in computer technology in chronological order.

1.1.1 A history of electronic devices

A fundamental building block of electronic devices is the rectifier junction. This is the simplest solid state switching device, consisting of two different materials in contact, which allows an electric current to pass more easily one way than the other. The rectifier effect was originally discovered, as a laboratory curiosity, in 1835 by Munck Roschenschold. It was not exploited until 1906 when the carborundum and cat's whisker rectifier was developed which formed a principal component of early crystal radios.

The earliest true electronic devices made use of the thermionic valve. The simplest valve, a rectifier, consisted of two non-contacting metal electrodes encapsulated in an evacuated glass tube. One of the electrodes, the cathode, was heated by an electric coil to produce a supply of free electrons. An electric current flows if the anode is electrically more positive than the cathode. Thermionic valves by definition are very hot and power consuming. They operated at high voltages and were very unreliable.

The thermionic valve radio receiver was one of the earliest electronic devices to be mass produced and dates back to the 1920s. The circuits were generally constructed upon a metal chassis onto which components were fixed. The electrical connections were created by means of wiring which utilized the metal chassis as a ground return and for shielding. Insulating strips with metal contacts, known as tag strips, were used in addition to component terminals for wiring support. Bundles of wires which had the same routeing were often bound together with lacing cord to form a wiring harness. This provided mechanical support and could also be attached to the chassis using insulated clips. All wiring was performed by hand, which necessitated the use of trimming components to compensate for wiring variations which could adversely affect a circuit's performance.

Semiconductors, from which many modern electronic devices are fabricated, were first discovered by Faraday in 1833. The semiconductor effect was not fully explained until the development of band theory in 1926. As a semiconductor material for the manufacture of electronic devices there is nothing special about silicon. There are many different semiconductor materials from which electronic devices can be constructed. Silicon happens to be a very commonly occurring substance (our beaches are covered in it, because sand is silicon dioxide) with the right properties.

In 1949 the first bipolar (p–n) junction transistor (TRANSfer resISTOR) was invented by William Shockley, working at Bell Research Laboratories. This revolutionized the electronics industry. Active electronic components could be made much smaller and cheaper. They required much less power and hence less cooling, and were much more reliable.

The transition between transistors and valves was very dramatic – a whole new concept. In particular it required a great deal of adaptability from electronics engineers, some of whom considered that a device is not electronic unless it can deliver burns and electric shocks. Many people mourned the loss of the 'valve sound' when high fidelity amplifiers were transistorized (although the more recent use of field effect transistors, which have similar characteristics to valves, has restored this).

Early transistors were made from the semiconductor material germanium (germanium oxide can be extracted from coal ash). Silicon, which is much more abundant, has largely taken over from germanium for today's devices.

The first silicon chip, or integrated circuit (IC), as we know it today, consisting of many transistors fabricated on the same piece of silicon, was made at Fairchild in 1959. More recent developments have been towards miniaturization – packing more and more active components or gates onto a single chip of silicon. The level of device complexity is usually referred to as a scale of integration. The evolution from small-scale integration (SSI), through large-scale integration (LSI), to very-large-scale integration (VLSI) has already occurred, and the scale is running out of adjectives. The scale of integration is based on the number of logic elements that constitute a device. An alternative method of defining device complexity is to specify the dimensions of device features in microns. The latter method was used to show increasing device complexity in Table 1.1.

An example of the increasing complexity of integrated circuits is the memory chip. In the early 1980s, the largest commercially available memory devices could store about 1000 bits of information. In 1990, memory chips with a capacity of 1 000 000 bits are readily available and are three times faster. Microprocessor chips which were state-of-the-art in 1980 are now so cheap that they are used in applications that greatly underutilize their capabilities. 1990s state-of-the-art microprocessors are more powerful than 1980s minicomputers. Table 1.2 shows how the complexity of the Intel range of microprocessors has increased since 1979. It also shows how a microprocessor's speed of operation has increased in millions of instructions per second (MIPS).

In parallel with the evolution of components from the thermionic valve to the transistor, interconnection technology evolved from chassis wiring to the printed circuit board. The printed circuit board, often abbreviated to PCB and sometimes referred to as a printed wiring board or PWB, was invented by Dr Paul Eisler in the early 1940s. It has since become an almost universal medium for electronic circuits. The

Table 1.2 The evolution of the Intel family of microprocessors

Year	Device	Transistors	Speed (MIPS)
1979	8088	29 000	0.2
1982	80286	120 000	2.3
1985	80386	275 000	7.0
1989	80486	1 200 000	25.0

printed circuit board offers many advantages over chassis wiring; in particular, printed circuit board assembly can be automated, thus reducing human error and offering a consistent quality. Following the invention and the subsequent widespread adoption of the junction transistor, which is much more suited to printed circuit board mounting than the thermionic valve owing to its smaller size, the printed circuit board has gained almost universal acceptance.

Although component technology has evolved rapidly, interconnection technology is still widely based on printed circuit boards. Advances have been made in terms of component packing density and the ability to accommodate the more complex components but the principle remains the same. Some more advanced interconnection techniques have been developed, and are discussed in Chapter 8; however, the industry's reluctance to move away from the printed circuit board has limited their usage.

1.1.2 A history of the telecommunications industry

The examination of the telecommunications industry from a historical viewpoint gives a good example of how electronics has been introduced to, and has subsequently dominated, an industry that used predominantly electromechanical technology. The pattern of change is particularly noticeable as the industry had changed very little until the introduction of electronics. The post-electronic industry has been forced to keep pace with the frontiers of technology.

The telephone was invented by Alexander Graham Bell in 1879. The first telephone exchange followed in the early 1900s. This first exchange was an electromechanical device that utilized manual switching. Each telephone which was connected to the exchange had an indicator flag which signalled to an operator that the telephone handset had been lifted. The operator determined the call destination by plugging a handset into the flagged line and requesting the destination from the caller. Connection was then achieved by connecting the telephone lines by means of plugs and sockets, if the destination telephone subscriber was available.

In the 1940s Alman B. Strowger, an undertaker, was losing business because the local telephone operator was a cousin of a competitor. Whenever anybody telephoned for an undertaker, the operator referred them to the cousin. Strowger wanted a telephone system that allowed callers to select their own destination without using the services of an operator. This led to the development of the Strowger automatic telephone exchange. The development of an automatic telephone exchange required some difficult technical problems to be solved. For example, the telephone dial needs to deliver a series of dialling pulses (one for a one, nine for a nine). Correct exchange operation required that the pulses needed to be evenly spaced in time in order for it to be possible to determine when a number started and finished. The use of a simple return spring is not sufficient as the returning force, and hence pulse spacing, is proportional to the spring extension. The development of a return speed governor was required to overcome this difficulty.

The Strowger telephone exchange was a large electromechanical device. This by definition had a lot of moving parts in the form of relays and autoselectors. These moving parts were prone to frequent breakdown and were very labour intensive to maintain. This situation was acceptable when labour was relatively inexpensive, but expensive to run at today's rates. Strowger exchanges are essentially analogue devices and are very prone to noise pickup and hence poor quality voice links.

Strowger telephone exchanges revolutionized telecommunications in such a way that by 1960 only international calls required operator intervention in the United Kingdom. The Strowger exchanges were only superseded in 1982 by digital exchanges and still have not yet been fully replaced.

Digital exchanges as typified by System X which started development in the 1970s are rapidly replacing the old Strowger exchanges and have themselves revolutionized the telecommunications industry. The use of digital electronics has made the switching operations much faster and more reliable. One of today's 'smart exchanges' can reroute partially connected calls to make optimal use of the available equipment. The digital encoding of speech allows noise-free transmission over large distances. Many of today's major trunk routes are served by fibre optic cabling which is more reliable and has a higher capacity than conventional wire-based cabling. The use of communications satellites allows international direct dialling to most countries.

Frequency shift keying (FSK) (push-button two-tone dialling) has replaced the pulse dialling system and enables virtually instantaneous connection of calls. An exchange can return a ringing tone on receipt of the final dialled digit – before the dialled subscriber's telephone starts to ring. Ironically, in the United Kingdom most telephones use the pulse dialling system even when the exchange supports the FSK system. Modern electronic telephones simulate their electromechanical predecessors by sending dialling pulses. This is a case of the tail wagging the dog – the telephones use, or simulate, an old technology which forces exchanges to use an old and inefficient interface.

Recent technological advances include cordless telephones, and the cellnet car and portable telephones which are not dependent on a single exchange.

1.1.3 A history of the computer industry

Although the computer industry does have its mechanical and electromechanical beginnings, true electronic computers are a relatively recent development which have had to keep pace with the progress of technology. Any discussion of the history of computers must start with the abacus – one of the earliest calculators. The Jacquard loom, which was invented in 1801 and used punched cards to define the weave patterns, is widely accepted as the first programmable machine. The British mathematician Charles Babbage invented the first computer according to modern principles – an electromechanical device.

The first truly electronic computer was invented by Dr John V. Atanasoff between 1937 and 1942 (Mackintosh, 1988). This computer, called ABC for Atanasoff–Berry computer, used thermionic valves to carry out computations and used capacitors as memory devices. The machine was designed to calculate the solutions of simultaneous equations of up to 29 variables. Until ABC gained recent recognition, the first electronic computer was considered to be the Colossus, developed in 1943 to decipher the German Enigma code of the Second World War. The next computer was the Electronic Numerical Integrator and Computer (ENIAC).

Early computers used thermionic valves as their active switching units. These were very large, hot, used very high voltages and were very unreliable. A mean time between failure (MTBF) of 20 min was not uncommon. Memory devices consisted of ferrite cores threaded with wires and stored information magnetically. These were referred to as core memories – a term which is anachronistically still used today to describe a large computer's main memory.

A large computer of the 1960s would occupy a building the size of a three-storey warehouse. The actual thermionic-valve-based circuitry was contained in a series of large cabinets on the middle floor. All the interconnections between circuits resided on the lower floor level. The upper floor level contained all the power connections. The systems required massive, usually water-based, cooling systems to remove the excess heat generated by the thermionic valves.

One of the major sources of problems was that of bad connections due to poor, or heat-damaged, solder joints. In many cases, systems had known bad connections which were not worth correcting as the operation would be very time consuming and very likely to introduce new, and hence unknown, bad connections. Often the best cure for a bad connection was the use of violence. The hitting of a faulty electronic device was sound practice in the days of valves as it often caused a poor connection to remake itself – this rarely works with modern equipment.

This form of fault repair is typified by the following true example. A computer system had a number of bad connections which caused intermittent failures. The electronic engineer responsible for the maintenance of the system had implemented a 'repair facility' consisting of a series of taped crosses on the casing of the machine and a large rubber mallet. Each cross marked the location of a bad connection – hitting the machine at such a location cured a known fault. Whenever a fault was reported the engineer would proceed to strike the machine with the mallet, on the positions marked with a cross, in a sequence dependent on the nature of the fault.

The developments in computing power have grown at a fantastic rate since the 1960s. Modern computers are also considerably more reliable, a faulty connection being totally unacceptable by today's quality standards. A typical minicomputer of the 1970s such as a DEC PDP 11/34 was a 16-bit machine with a maximum memory of 256 kbytes, costing in excess of £5000. A modern personal computer based on an Intel 80386 microprocessor is a 32-bit machine with a minimum memory of 1 Mbyte, costing from £1500. Microprocessors from the 1970s, such as the Intel 8080 and the Motorola 6800, are so cheap today that they can be used to give local intelligence to household devices such as washing machines. Electronic calculators, once only capable of simple arithmetic using reverse Polish logic, are now fully programmable and have become so commonplace that they have (sadly) rendered logarithm tables obsolete. The minicomputer is rapidly becoming obsolete in favour of networked microprocessor-based workstations. Supercomputers, for example the Cray II and the Cyber 205, are parallel processing machines which have been developed for very complex applications such as weather prediction and animation.

1.2 THE ELECTRONICS MARKET

The marketplace of the electronics industry encompasses a wide range of other industries and services. Typical customers for electronic products include the retail, finance and manufacturing industries, central government, general industries, local government, utilities, telecommunications, health systems and defence ministries. There are also a large number of electronic industries which supply components to other electronic industries. There are a number of distinct trends evident in the electronics marketplace. These have combined to make it fiercely competitive.

Product lifetimes are steadily declining; a period of five years is a long time in the electronics industry. Some modern products have lifetimes which can be measured in terms of months. Marketing strategies therefore have to be fairly short term in order to accommodate such short product lives.

Market forces are demanding that electronic products become available at steadily decreasing prices and at higher reliabilities. Product prices are typically reducing at a rate of 10–20% per annum.

The days of cost-plus products where the customer, usually a government on a defence project, pays all incurred costs on a yearly basis for an indefinite period are gone. Defence contracts are now bid for on a fixed cost basis. There are often penalty clauses when a product is late on delivery. This had a major impact on the larger organizations which specialized in defence work. The end of cost-plus contracts necessitated major streamlining operations.

Companies can no longer afford to make all the components of an electronic system as was previously the case. A company can now only afford to manufacture what it is good at. If a component, or a subsystem, can be bought for less than it can be manufactured by a particular company it is uneconomical to manufacture it. This has resulted in companies which specialize in certain subsystems, for example computer keyboards, and have captured a significant propor-tion of that aspect of the market. A typical cost breakdown for a commercially viable product is 72% materials, 25% overheads and 3%

labour. Hence materials is the crucial area from the costing point of view. The decision whether to make or buy individual components of a system can have an important impact on the cost breakdown. The traditional method of cost cutting by reducing labour costs is no longer applicable to many electronics companies as any reductions on 3% are unlikely to be significant.

Although the electronics market has a number of common characteristics, the wide range of actual products leads to implications which are specific to particular areas of the market. Two widely differing industries from the marketing point of view are the telecommunications and computer industries.

1.2.1 The telecommunications market

The main characteristic of the telecommunications market is that the products tend to be restricted to a small number of customers. A large telephone exchange would only be purchased for use with a large public network. Each country can only support a small number of public network companies, which limits the total number of potential customers. Smaller private telephone exchanges have a wider market but are largely restricted to large organizations. Although actual telephones have a large market, a telecommunications company would typically sell them through a small number of large retail outlets.

Public telephone companies often have rigorous standards to which all equipment which they purchase must conform. A company manufacturing telecommunications equipment must have quality assurance and test departments which are sufficiently flexible to test products to these customer-dictated standards.

A telecommunications company will also need to have the capacity for both high and low volume production. Large public exchanges and telephones may have components which need to be manufactured in high volumes. Smaller private telephone exchanges will need to be highly configurable to suit the customer's requirements and hence require small volume manufacture.

There has been a strong trend in recent years towards larger telecommunications manufacturing organizations. Many smaller companies have either merged or been taken over by larger organizations. It is now getting to the stage where it is recognized that the world can only support six major telecommunications companies. These six constitute two companies for each of the Far Eastern, European and North American world areas.

1.2.2 The computer market

In recent years the larger electronics companies have undergone a massive growth. This can be seen by examining the list of the top ten electronics companies. In 1987 the total world revenue of the electronics companies was $255 000 million and the top ten companies are shown in Table 1.3 (Datamation, 1988) in order of rank. In 1989 the world revenue was estimated at $268 000 million and the top ten companies are shown in Table 1.4 in order of rank. It can clearly be seen that IBM is a long way ahead of its competition, holding about 20% of the world market and being five times bigger than the second company, DEC. The remaining places in the top ten are fiercely competitive, with Japanese companies gaining ground. Few companies can compete directly against IBM and succeed, as can be shown by the example of the personal computer market.

Before the IBM PC, there was a proliferation of personal computers and their associated manufacturing companies. There was little in the way of standardization and compatibility between the different machines. Once the IBM PC was announced it became a long sought after industry standard; most other personal computers became obsolete. With the exception of some of the larger organizations, the majority of today's manufacturers produce personal computers which are compatible with the IBM PC. The current trend is for companies to produce customer 'solutions' rather than just the hardware. The proliferation of low cost PC clones shows that many companies have the capability of producing the hardware at ever-decreasing prices. A customer solution, on the other hand, is a combination of hardware and software which is customized to the particular customer's requirements.

Table 1.3 The top ten electronics companies in 1987

Rank	Company	Revenue (million $)
1	IBM (USA)	50485.7
2	Digital Equipment Corp. (USA)	10391.3
3	Unisys (USA)	8742.0
4	Fujitsu Ltd (Japan)	8740.0
5	Nippon Electric Corp. (Japan)	8230.5
6	Hitachi Ltd (Japan)	6273.7
7	Siemens AG (West Germany)	5703.0
8	NCR Corp. (USA)	5075.7
9	Hewlett-Packard Co. (USA)	5000.0
10	Ing.C Olivetti Co. SpA (Italy)	4637.2

Table 1.4 The top ten electronics companies in 1989

Rank	Company	Revenue (million $)
1	IBM (USA)	62700
2	Digital Equipment Corp. (USA)	12900
3	Fujitsu Ltd (Japan)	11200
4	Nippon Electric Corp. (Japan)	10500
5	Unisys (USA)	10100
6	Hitachi Ltd (Japan)	8700
7	Hewlett-Packard Co. (USA)	7600
8	Siemens AG (West Germany)	N/A
9	NCR Corp. (USA)	N/A
10	Group Bull (France, USA, Japan)	N/A

One of the major problems which computer users have encountered in the past is the lack of standardization. In particular, software written for one computer required a major conversion process to make it work on another type. This tended to tie users to a particular manufacturer's machines. This lack of standardization is slowly being overcome by large consumer companies insisting that all the equipment which they purchase is compatible. A good example of this is the recent MAP communications protocols for the networking of computers and machine tools.

1.3 ELECTRONICS MANUFACTURING COMPANY STRUCTURE

The electronics industry encompasses a wide range of company types. These company types include the following:

1. component manufacturers;
2. semiconductor device manufacturers;
3. printed circuit board bare board manufacturers;
4. printed circuit board assemblers for third parties;
5. high volume manufacturers which perform the assembly of printed circuit boards and the final assembly of printed circuit boards into complete systems (typical examples of high volume manufacture products are domestic appliances such as television sets);
6. low volume manufacturers which perform both printed circuit board assembly and product assembly (typical examples of low volume manufacture products are telephone exchanges and large computer systems);

7. assembly-only companies which build complete systems, often to customer specification, from complete printed circuit boards (an example of an assembly-only company is a personal computer manufacturer which buys in all the component printed circuit boards).

The apparent complexity of the manufacturing process associated with each of the above company types is in no way an indication of the complexity of the actual company. An assembly-only company can be as large as and as complex as a high volume manufacturer. In general, electronics companies will have a number of departments which is dependent on the nature and size of the individual company. All electronics companies will have test and quality assurance departments in order to maintain their product quality. As test and quality assurance interact with most other departments they will be discussed separately in section 1.4.

There are a number of departments which are particularly related to product manufacture and are common across many large companies. These are production, production test, industrial engineering, purchasing, materials control, design, and marketing, which has already been discussed. Each of the departments will be discussed in the context of a high volume manufacturing company.

1.3.1 Production

Production is the department which is responsible for the actual manufacture of products. Ultimately, all other departments either support or are supported by production. The functions of production departments are described with the associated processes in Chapters 4–7.

1.3.2 Production test

The production test department is responsible for performing all product testing operations which occur before, during and after production. Production test activities are integrated with many production processes in that they have fixed positions within the production cycle of a product. Product test operations are described alongside the production processes with which they are associated.

1.3.3 Industrial engineering

Industrial engineering, which is synonymous with manufacturing engineering and production engineering, is concerned with providing the manufacturing tools for the production department. Industrial engineers are responsible for the implementation of new technologies into the production facility. They are responsible for the diagnosis and reporting of faults and the implementation of fault cures. The industrial engineering functions are described alongside the descriptions of the manufacturing tools in Chapters 4–7.

1.3.4 Purchasing

The purchasing department has become increasingly important because more components are being purchased. This is a result of the trend towards a company only making what it is good at. The objectives of the purchasing department can be summarized by 'obtaining components of the right quality at the right time in the right quantity from the right source at the right price'.

Collaboration with suppliers is becoming increasingly prevalent in order to ensure quality standards and to reduce the need for incoming goods testing (this will be discussed in more detail in Chapter 2). The result of this collaboration is that companies have a preferred list of suppliers with which certain quality standards are agreed.

The increasing implementation of the just-in-time (JIT) strategy has had a big impact on purchasing activity. Components which are purchased too early tie up monies in the form of stock. Components which are purchased too late cause late delivery of products which delays payment and may invoke penalty clauses in contracts.

Compromises need to be reached when considering the quantity of components to purchase. Large quantity orders can result in considerable savings in terms of discounts. They can also lead to the need to stockpile components which are excess to requirements. These compromises also occur in the selection of suppliers. The use of a single supplier allows larger orders to be placed. This, however, eliminates competition and may lead to reduced bargaining power and having to purchase components from an unknown source if the supplier cannot deliver. A small number of preferred suppliers, which have been carefully selected, provides a good middle ground.

Component price is a complex issue which contains many factors. Prices are often negotiable; procedures vary considerably dependent on whether an individual, a company, a vendor company, a cartel or a monopoly is being dealt with. An individual can often be negotiated down on price whereas a cartel will often set a price. When considering the price of components, the hidden extras need to be examined. Factors such as transportation costs, handling charges, taxes, insurance and packaging may or may not be included. Another important factor is whether penalty clauses are included for late delivery of goods.

1.3.5 Materials control

The materials control department is concerned with ensuring that the correct materials are available at the correct time and place for manufacture. Materials control forms a link between the purchasing and manufacturing departments and must liaise with these departments in order to ensure that constraints imposed by suppliers, lead times and capacity are not violated. The materials control function can be divided into production planning, materials and inventory control and material requirements planning.

(a) Production planning

The production planning function needs to be able to integrate production resources with new and existing contracts. Once an order has been placed by a customer it is necessary to find a slot in the production schedule to accommodate the order. The factors which need to be considered when assigning a production slot are lead times, availability and flexibility of labour, and the capacity and available facilities of the factory.

Lead times can result from both the ordering of components and the manufacture of subassemblies. An order cannot be scheduled into production until all its component parts are available. The labour requirements for a product need to take into account factors such as skill and availability of the workforce. Labour requirements include the assembly of non-standard components, customer's test requirements and assembly into cabinets.

Factory facilities include the actual production capability and the availability of equipment such as test units.

(b) Materials and inventory control

The materials and inventory control department needs to know all the components and facilities required for the manufacture of a product. This is often facilitated by means of a company's coding system. Each product will have a high level code associated with it. This code can then be subdivided into codes for each individual subassembly and further subdivided down to codes for each of the individual component parts. The product codes contain information on the actual identities of components, whether they are to be purchased or manufactured, the required packaging style, the required quality standards, order times and minimum quantities, and the names of preferred manufacturers. The breaking down of a high level product code into its component subcodes is performed by creating a bill of materials. The product codes, which form a part code file, can be used to direct the purchasing of components and subassemblies and the manufacture of the finished product.

(c) Material requirements planning

A powerful tool which is used by the materials control department is a computer program called a material requirements planning system or MRP system. An MRP system is based on the concepts of component demand, lead times and component usage.

Component demand can be either dependent on or independent of other components. Independent demand components are typically spares and finished products and can be requested independently of other components. Dependent demand components are typically parts of other products and are requested in conjunction with other components.

Lead times fall into the two categories of ordering lead times and manufacturing lead times. Ordering lead times are associated with the acquisition of components from suppliers. These can be long if components are not in stock. Manufacturing lead times are associated with the manufacture of component subsystems of a product.

Component usage consists of information as to whether a particular component is used by several products. This information can be used to ensure that a large order for a component type is issued as opposed to several smaller orders.

The MRP program is input with the production schedule, the bill of materials files and an inventory record file for the time period under consideration – typically two weeks. The MRP program then runs (this will typically take many hours and would be run overnight) and produces a materials control report. The report contains recommendations as to which components need to be purchased. In some cases the

MRP program can automatically place an order with a supplier. Computerized stock control systems can be instructed to flag batches of components from 'in stock' to 'work in progress'. In some cases where components are out of stock the MRP program will need either to reschedule production or to bring forward an order from a supplier. As components are issued from stores they need to be labelled for use by production, i.e. R22 and IC3 etc.

One problem associated with an MRP system is that it makes little allowance for scrap. If a scrap allowance is incorporated into the MRP program it tends to cause a stock buildup. The alternative is to allow production to requisition replacement parts, which can cause problems if the stock of a component runs out.

1.3.6 Design

The design department is concerned with the production of new products. This takes the form of the design of new circuits and of new printed circuit board artwork. The function of the design department is described in Chapters 3 and 4.

1.4 TEST ENGINEERING AND QUALITY ASSURANCE

Two important aspects of manufacturing are those of quality assurance and testability. In many respects the two activities are interdependent – good quality assurance techniques can reduce the testing requirements. The implications of quality and testing manifest themselves in almost every department of an electronics company. These implications include the interfacing with suppliers towards zero defects on incoming goods and the integration of testability with the product design process. In fact the test engineering and quality assurance departments are themselves departmentalized, each subdepartment being concerned with one or more departments of an organization. For example, the production department will have its associated test and quality divisions.

1.4.1 Test development engineering

The test development engineering function provides the test equipment and test methods necessary to enable the effective testing of a product.

The main objective is to find all the failure modes of a product. In practice this identifies a large majority of all faults. A secondary objective is to diagnose the causes of failure in order to enable effective repair.

Test development engineering needs to interface to nearly every other department within an organization as described in the following subsections.

(a) Production

The production department needs to feed failure information back to test development engineering in order to improve performance. This information usually takes the form of assembly problems such as missing, wrong or damaged components, and operating problems such as bad soldering and reworking.

(b) Production test

The production test department is the area in which test development engineering has the greatest impact. Test development engineering has to provide the test documentation for both hardware and software products. Documentation is required for the following activities: incoming goods testing; in-circuit testing; functional tests; substitution tests; systems tests; stress failure testing; training and equipment. The production test department provides ideas for the improvement of test equipment. This includes information on ongoing faults and failures which need to be tested for by diagnostics.

(c) Industrial engineering

Test development engineering needs to provide industrial engineering with advice on products' test requirements. This includes information on floor space requirements for test equipment, power consumption, compressed air supply requirements, static electricity precautions etc. Test development engineering also needs to provide information on which tests are to be performed on a particular product and at what stage during production. This includes information on when test links need to be removed and on post-fit requirements – parts which are added out of normal production sequence in order to facilitate testing. Industrial engineering provides test development engineering with information on commonly occurring faults on board assemblies.

(d) Quality assurance

The quality assurance department needs to provide test development engineering with information such as BS 5750 documentation and functional specifications. Quality assurance also provides supplier evaluation material from incoming goods testing.

Test development engineering provides quality assurance with process monitoring information in order to produce statistical information on common faults. Quality assurance also needs to be provided with support for customer problems, supplier problems and quality test equipment. For example, in the telecommunications industry British Telecom have a requirement for a complex series of tests on telephones which take over an hour to execute which must be accommodated in production schedules.

(e) Customer and field support

Many customers now wish to buy a manufacturing facility rather than products. In effect a company's production facility is turned over to a third party's products. In order for this to be effective test development engineering needs to provide test backup. This can, however, lead to contractual complications such as royalty implications. Test development engineering needs to be able to provide technical backup on commonly occurring faults and to be able to conduct special investigations into newly occurring faults.

(f) Purchasing and materials control

Test development engineering needs to support the purchasing and materials control departments by assisting with the selection of preferred suppliers. It is necessary to be able to test new components to, and sometimes outside, their manufacturer's specifications on incoming goods testing. Support is needed for evaluating new suppliers and components by checking first piece examples and providing information for supply evaluation quality assurance. The purchasing department needs to be advised when test development engineering needs to buy new or replacement test equipment.

(g) Suppliers

Test development engineering needs to provide support for preferred suppliers in the form of incoming and outgoing goods testing for the purpose of quality assurance. This is particularly important as the industry trend is to transfer the emphasis from buyer's incoming goods testing to supplier's outgoing goods testing. When components are to be used outside their manufacturer's specifications, additional test methods need to be provided. Test development engineering needs to perform evaluations of new, improved or enhanced equipment.

(h) Sales

Test development engineering needs to provide support for the sales department in the form of assisting with the incoming goods testing performed on products by purchasers. In the case of technology transfer, it is important that the testing technology is transferred along with the product technology. Test development engineering also needs to support sales by providing facilities and technical backup for special customer trials, product demonstrations and factory tours.

(i) Contracts

Test development engineering provides support to the contracts department in the form of information on whether or not everything on a given order can be tested without overstretching available resources. Methods need to be provided for improving products' software and firmware and for implementing special software configurations. The contracts department provides test development engineering with information on product changes, new hardware and software configuration requirements and forecasted production volumes.

(j) Finance

Test development engineering provides the finance department with advance expenditure plans for the next one to five years. Justification is provided for capital expenditure in the areas of new products, increased production volume, and the replacement and improvement of test equipment.

(k) Product design

Test development engineering provides the product design department with test specifications, circuit diagrams and circuit descriptions for new products. Change notes for software and firmware are provided for the elimination of design faults. The design department provides test development engineering with testability data, design change requests and information on design problems associated with products. In the case of new products in their prototype stage, first time off reports and test specifications need to be provided.

1.4.2 Test stages during product manufacture

It is vitally important that product testing is fully integrated with its manufacture. The reason for this is that the cost of detecting faults increases exponentially as the manufacturing process progresses, for example

cost of finding fault at incoming goods testing	£1
cost of finding fault at in circuit testing	£10
cost of finding fault at function or system test	£100
cost of finding fault as a field repair	£1000

Figure 1.1 shows a typical scheme for integrating test operations with a products manufacturing cycle. Incoming components are tested by either supplier or purchaser before assembly. An assembled board is subjected to a comprehensive series of tests before being integrated into a complete system. The completed system is thoroughly tested before being shipped to the customer. The full details of all of the test operations are described alongside the associated manufacturing processes.

1.4.3 Quality assurance

Traditionally, quality assurance has been effected by performing a series of quality assurance tests. This practice is referred to as inspecting in quality. This philosophy only worked on the symptoms of problems. In effect a lot of effort was put into the detection of poor quality goods and little effort was put into determining the underlying problems. Today's quality assurance techniques concentrate on the prevention of problems. Thus faults can be designed out of a system, which makes it possible to achieve the goal of 'get it right first time'. This is implemented by designing in quality assurance techniques in order to monitor and then to control processes to the required standards. Thus the change in quality strategy can be summarized as going from inspecting in quality to designing in quality so as to get it right first time.

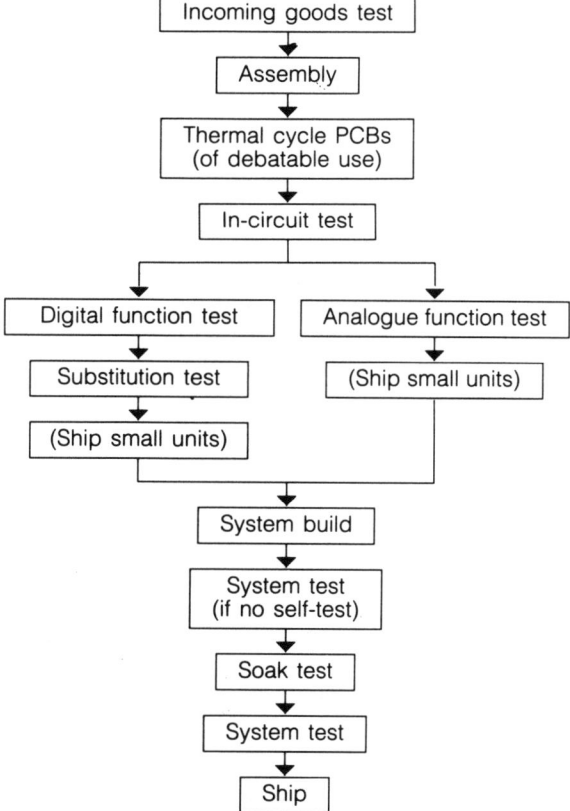

Figure 1.1 A typical product test cycle.

In order to implement good quality assurance it is necessary to develop a suitable strategy. This could take the written form of 'the maintenance and improvement of the quality of a product or service by the use of process control'. It is important to note that quality does not only apply to products; it must also apply to services such as customer support.

In order to be effective, it is important to be able to prove a company's quality assurance techniques to its customers. This is achieved by using approved standards to measure effectiveness. Examples of such standards are the BS 6301 standard for electrical safety and the BS 5750 or ISO 9000 series standards for services. In addition to statutory standards there may also be customer standards

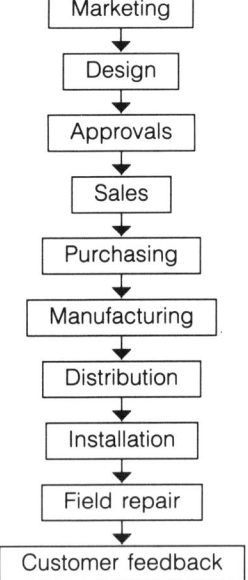

Figure 1.2 Company organization for quality.

such as the CCITT standard for European telecommunications and the BTR standard for British Telecom.

Quality assurance needs to be involved with a product from its conception through to its installation at a customer's site and the subsequent customer support. Figure 1.2 shows a typical product cycle in terms of a company's departments from the quality point of view. Functionally, quality assurance will be divided into engineering, components and operations subdivisions to oversee key operations. Nominated representatives are situated in areas which do not warrant a full quality assurance department but need some quality input. Nominated representatives would typically be situated in the sales, distribution, installation, field repair and customer feedback divisions.

Engineering quality assurance is concerned with the marketing, design and approvals departments. It is concerned with the quality of operation of the departments under its jurisdiction and ensuring that products conform to standards. This includes ensuring that good design practices are used, that products are well specified and planned, and that statutory and customer's requirements are adhered to.

Component quality assurance is concerned with the purchasing department. It is responsible for establishing quality agreements with suppliers. This includes obtaining supplier's assurances of components being defect free on arrival, and a maximum defect rate. Assurances may also be required that components are supplied tested to the buyer's specification.

Operations quality assurance is concerned with the manufacturing department. It is responsible for the identification and rectification of quality problems which occur within the manufacturing environment.

2

Electronic components

An electronic circuit consists of a number of electronic components and the necessary interconnections between components to produce the desired functionality. Electronic circuit interconnection methods have an additional role in that they have to provide mechanical support for the components.

Electronic components, when viewed from both an electronic engineer's and a manufacturing engineer's point of view, have three attributes, the actual component types, the components' packaging and the components' quality. A background knowledge of interconnection technology, component types, component packaging styles and component quality assurance procedures gives a good foundation for applying manufacturing technologies to the electronics industries.

2.1 COMPONENT INTERCONNECTION METHODS

Many methods have been devised for the interconnection of electronic circuits varying from the relatively crude chassis wiring to complex hybrids. However, the commonest vehicle for forming interconnections is the printed circuit board. Actually the term 'printed circuit board' has been universally accepted even though the description is not particularly accurate. A board only becomes a circuit when the components are connected in place; also, a printed circuit board is unlikely actually to have been printed.

A printed circuit board usually serves three distinct functions: to provide mechanical support for components; to provide the necessary electrical connections between components; and it often bears a legend which identifies the components which it carries. Printed circuit boards have until recently been almost compulsory for electronic circuits even though there may be more cost-effective methods of achieving the same effect. Some of the more sophisticated interconnection technologies are discussed in Chapter 8.

Many electronic manufacturing companies no longer manufacture their own printed circuit boards for production. This is because it is usually cheaper to purchase boards from a specialist bare board manufacturer. Printed circuit board manufacturers produce production batches of boards from customers' artwork to order. An electronics manufacturing company may, however, have a small bare board processing facility for the production of prototype printed circuit boards.

A typical printed circuit board is constructed out of one or more sheets of insulating material which carry the necessary interconnections. These connections take the form of copper tracks which are bonded to the surface of the insulating sheets. The copper tracks terminate in islands of copper, usually referred to as pads or lands, to which the electronic components are connected. The connections between components and the copper lands are usually achieved using solder – a lead–tin alloy with a low melting point. Chapter 5 gives a detailed description of the different types of printed circuit board and their associated manufacturing processes.

2.2 ELECTRONIC COMPONENTS

Electronic components can be broadly classified into mechanical devices, passive solid state devices and active solid state devices. This classification is based on the component's electrical characteristics.

Mechanical devices encompass a wide range of components which perform a simple make–break switching function. This includes everything from the small printed circuit board mounted DIP switches through to heavy-duty mains switches. Electromechanical devices such as relays, circuit breakers and even complex computer disc drive mechanisms can also be included under mechanical devices. In terms of manufacturing, mechanical devices are special cases which cannot in general be assembled using automatic equipment. Devices such as variable resistors (potentiometers) and variable capacitors can pose similar problems to manufacturing. Because of the diverse nature of mechanical devices no further detailed descriptions will be given. The manufacturing aspects of mechanical devices are covered under hand assembly in Chapter 6.

Passive components, which include resistors and capacitors, are the simplest electronic devices and have in general been available in one form or another for a long time. As a consequence of this they are available in a wide range of shapes and sizes which can be problematic for automatic assembly operations.

Active components, which include transistors and integrated circuits, are devices which have an electronic switching capability; they can allow or prevent an electric current or signal flowing in a particular direction. The majority of today's active components are semiconductor devices. Modern semiconductor devices, and in particular complex integrated circuits, are more standardized with respect to their packaging. Several of the units used to define the values of electronic components are extremely large with respect to commonly occurring values or a very large range of values are in common usage. In these cases the number of leading or trailing zeros in a component's value can be reduced by applying power of ten multipliers in the form of a prefix to the unit symbol (for example 1000 is abbreviated to k). There are a range of prefixes in common usage, which are mostly of Greek derivation and represent powers of 1000; these are shown in Table 2.1.

Table 2.1 Power of ten unit multiplier prefixes

Name	Symbol	Multiplying factor	
pico	p	0.000 000 000 001	(10^{-12})
nano	n	0.000 000 001	(10^{-9})
micro	μ	0.000 001	(10^{-6})
milli	m	0.001	(10^{-3})
kilo	k	1 000	(10^{3})
mega	M	1 000 000	(10^{6})
giga	G	1 000 000 000	(10^{9})
tera	T	1 000 000 000 000	(10^{12})

The major types of electronic components in common usage are described in the following sub-sections.

2.2.1 Resistors

Resistors are devices which resist the flow of electric current. The unit of resistance is the ohm, usually symbolized by the Greek letter Ω (omega). An electric current of 1 A flowing through a 1 Ω resistor will result in a voltage drop of 1 V across the resistor. The circuit symbol for a resistor can be either of the symbols indicated by R1 and R2 in Figure

R1

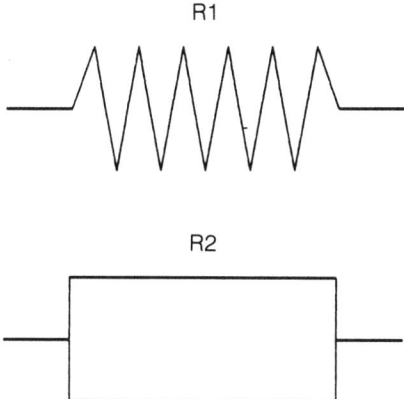

R2

Figure 2.1 Resistor circuit symbols.

2.1; the symbol indicated by R2 is rapidly becoming the standard. The major uses of resistors in electronic circuits are voltage dropping devices, potential dividers, current limiters and pull-up resistors. Voltage dropping resistors utilize the fact that an electric current flowing through a resistor causes a voltage drop. This effect is utilized to reduce a voltage to a desired level. Potential dividers enable smaller voltages to be tapped from larger voltages using resistors as shown in Figure 2.2. Current-limiting resistors are used to protect components from overloading by limiting the available electric current. Pull-up resistors are used in conjunction with logic integrated circuits to provide a logic-on state.

Standard printed circuit board mounting resistors are available in value ranges from 0.22 Ω to 10 MΩ. A shorthand notation for resistance values is often used which removes the usage of the symbol Ω and the decimal point. This system replaces the decimal point in the resistance value with a power of ten multiplier prefix, using R as the symbol for unity. A 0.22 Ω resistance is written as R22, a 1 Ω resistance is written as 1R and a 2200 Ω resistance is written as 2K2 etc. The characteristics of a physical resistor are defined by four primary parameters: resistance value, tolerance, maximum working voltage and power rating.

The tolerance is a percentage figure which gives the maximum deviation of resistance value from the marked nominal value. The maximum working voltage defines the safe maximum voltage which can be applied across a resistor without running the risk of the resistor breaking down. The power rating defines the maximum heat which

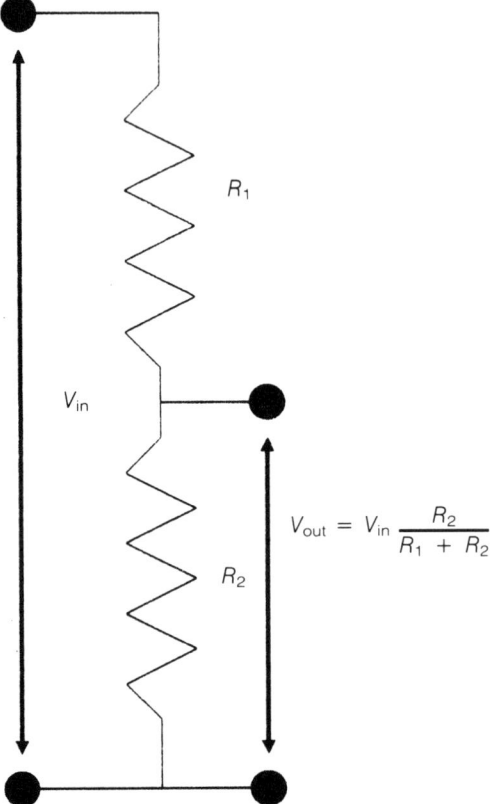

Figure 2.2 A potential divider circuit.

can be dissipated by the resistor before it starts to overheat. A resistor of resistance R (ohms) with an electric current I (amperes) flowing through it generates heat given by I^2R (watts).

The physical construction of a resistor is that of a ceramic cylinder which has two metal caps, usually one at each end from which connecting leads are attached. The resistance is created by means of a carbon film, a metal film or a length of resistance wire connected between the end caps. Carbon resistors are constructed using a thin film of carbon which has been deposited on the ceramic in a helical band between the end caps, the resistance value being defined by the length and thickness of the carbon film. Metal film resistors are constructed in a similar manner. Wire-wound resistors have the necessary length of resistance wire, which has a known resistance per

Table 2.2 Resistor colour codes

Colour	Band 1 (digit 1)	Band 2 (digit 2)	Band 3 (factor)	Band 4 (tolerance)
Silver			0.01	10%
Gold			0.1	5%
Black	0	0	1	
Brown	1	1	10	1%
Red	2	2	100	2%
Orange	3	3	1 000 (1K)	
Yellow	4	4	10 000 (10K)	
Green	5	5	100 000 (100K)	0.5%
Blue	6	6	1 000 000 (1M)	0.25%
Violet	7	7	10 000 000 (10M)	0.1%
Grey	8	8		
White	9	9		

unit length, wound on the ceramic between the end caps to achieve the desired resistance value.

The resistor values in ohms are coded on the individual devices either numerically or by a sequence of coloured bands. The most commonly used method, particularly for smaller devices, is the four-band coding system which is summarized in Table 2.2. The resistance value is calculated by ten times the band one value plus the band two value all multiplied by the factor defined by band three. Band four gives the tolerance of the resistor. An example of the four-band coding system is that a 2K7 resistor with a tolerance of 5% would be banded red, purple, red, gold. Resistors are commercially available in standard ranges of values. These are the E12 and E24 series which consist respectively of 12 and 24 combinations of the first two colour bands. The E12 series is a subset of the E24 series and the values supported are as follows:

1. for the E12 series, 10, 12, 15, 18, 22, 27, 33, 39, 47, 56, 68 and 82 – the actual values range from 1 Ω to 1 MΩ;
2. for the E24 series, 10, 11, 12, 13, 15, 16, 18, 20, 22, 24, 27, 30, 33, 36, 39, 43, 47, 51, 56, 62, 68, 75, 82 and 91 – the actual values range from 1 Ω to 1 MΩ.

There are also resistance ranges less than 1 Ω and greater than 1 MΩ which use the E12 colour codes. These are not necessarily considered part of the E12 range. A resistance value which is not supported in the E ranges can be generated by combining two or more E range resistors in series or parallel. Small values of resistors can be

Table 2.3 Commercial resistor characteristics

Material	Power (W)	Voltage (V)	Values	Tolerance
Carbon film	0.125	150	1R–1M	5%
Carbon film	0.333	250	1R–10M	5%
Metal film	0.6	250	1R–10M	1%
Carbon film	1	750	10R–10M	5%
Wire wound	3		R22–4K7	5%
Wire wound	7		R47–4K7	5%
Wire wound	10		R47–4K7	5%

made by winding a suitable length of resistance wire, for example constantan consisting of 55–60% copper and 45–40% nickel at $4.2 \ \Omega \ m^{-1}$, onto an insulator which provides mechanical support. Table 2.3 shows typical electrical characteristics for some commercially available resistors.

2.2.2 Capacitors

Capacitors are devices which store electric charge. The unit of capacitance is the farad (named after Faraday) which is huge in comparison with commonly occurring capacitances. Commercially available capacitors usually have capacitances which are tiny fractions of a farad and are usually described in terms of microfarads, nanofarads and picofarads. Common uses of capacitors include smoothing power supplies, DC blocking, filtering and timing circuits. Power supply smoothing capacitors are usually devices with a relatively large capacitance which are connected across the power supply. The capacitor's storage capability smooths out any fluctuations in voltage. DC blocking capacitors are used to remove any direct current bias in AC circuits such as audio amplifiers. Capacitors are important components in filter circuits which are used to remove unwanted AC frequencies such as carrier signals in radio applications. Capacitors also have an important function in the application of timing circuits. These can take the form of period timers and oscillators.

A capacitor consists of an insulating material, which can be air, sandwiched between a pair of conducting metal plates. These conductors must be in close proximity to each other but not in actual electrical contact. Commercially available capacitors usually take their type name from the material between the plates – the dielectric material. Some of the dielectric materials in common usage are shown

Table 2.4 Common capacitor dielectric materials

Dielectric material	Dielectric constant	Breakdown voltage (V)
Polyethylene	2.3	500–1000
Polypropylene	2.2–2.3	450–650
Polyester	3.0–3.5	1500–2000
Polystyrene	2.5–2.6	500–1000
Polycarbonate	2.97	400–450
PTFE	2.1	500
Polysulphone	2.82	420
Mica	5.42	500
Ceramics	30–6000	50–250

in Table 2.4. The capacitance of a capacitor is proportional to AK/d where A is the surface area of the conductor plate, K is the dielectric constant of the dielectric material and d is the separation distance between the plates. The surface area of a capacitor's plates, and hence its capacitance, can be increased by the use of several connected layers of smaller capacitors, usually in the form of a roll or a stack.

Capacitors can be either polarized or non-polarized. Polarized capacitors, such as electrolytic and tantalum capacitors, must be inserted into a circuit the correct way around in order to prevent damage to the device. The circuit symbols for capacitors are shown in Figure 2.3, where C1 represents a non-polarized capacitor and C2 represents a polarized capacitor. The electrical characteristics of a

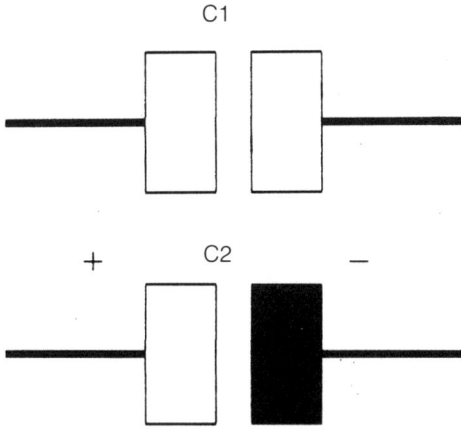

Figure 2.3 Capacitor circuit symbols.

capacitor are described using the four parameters of dielectric material, capacitance value, maximum working voltage and tolerance.

The dielectric material is an important aspect of a capacitor as it affects most of the other characteristics. Certain circuits may require a particular dielectric material, even though the other characteristics may be available with another material, owing to its performance and stability characteristics.

Capacitance values for commercially available devices usually follow the same numbering scheme as for the E12 series resistors. Unlike resistors there is no standard method of marking values on the actual devices. A colour coding system similar to that of resistors was in force for some of the older polyester devices. This has since been replaced by a numbering system. One big problem with capacitor marking is that a separate system is often in force for each dielectric type. A capacitor marked with the number 22 would be 22 pF for a ceramic capacitor and 22 nF for a polyester capacitor.

The maximum working voltage of a capacitor is the maximum DC voltage which can be applied across the capacitor without running the risk of the dielectric material breaking down. Typical working voltages vary from about 5 V to over 1000 V. The working voltage is usually marked as a number on the actual device.

The tolerance of a capacitor is a percentage figure defining the maximum variation in capacitance value from the marked nominal value. Tolerances usually fall in the range from 1% to 20% and are identified on actual devices by a number or a code letter.

Some of the commercially available capacitor types and their characteristics are shown in Table 2.5.

Table 2.5 Capacitor types

Dielectric	Voltage (V)	Values	Tolerance
Ceramic	100	1.8 pF–22 nF	2–10%
Monolithic ceramic	100	10 pF–47 μF	5–20%
Silvered mica	350	5 pF–4.7 nF	1%
Polystyrene	500	100 pF–22 nF	5%
Polyester	400	1 nF–1 μF	5–10%
Tantalum bead	35	1 μF–100 μF	20%
Electrolytic	10–450	0.47 μF–4.7 mF	20%
Can electrolytic	25–100	1 mF–47 mF	20%
Memory backup	5.5	1 F	20%+

2.2.3 Wound components

Wound components, as their name implies, are a category of devices which are fabricated by winding multiple turns of wire onto a core material. Copper wire is usually employed for winding, a range of wire thicknesses being used dependent on the current-carrying characteristics required. Usually the thicker the wire the better, although this can impose mechanical constraints. The core materials are usually iron-based materials such as ferrite. There are two main varieties of wound components, inductors and transformers. The circuit symbols for an inductor and a transformer are shown in Figure 2.4.

Inductors are devices which generate interacting magnetic fields when an electric current flows through them. The unit of inductance is the henry, which is a very large unit with respect to commonly occurring values. The value in henries of an inductor is equal to the square of the number of wound turns multiplied by the specific inductance of the core around which it is wound. Inductors are used in filter and timing circuits, usually in conjunction with capacitors.

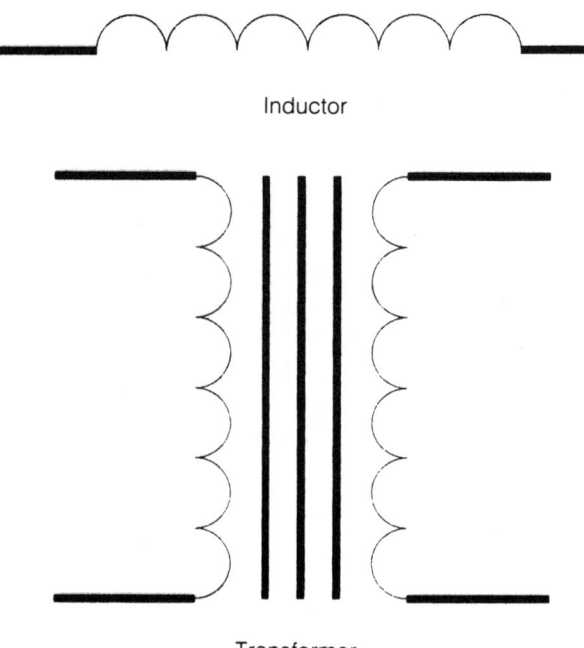

Inductor

Transformer

Figure 2.4 Wound component circuit symbols.

Inductors are also widely used in radio transmitter and receiver circuits, and in loudspeaker crossover units. Inductors are commercially available for certain applications; however, many inductors are custom made from standard-sized cores.

Transformers consist of two or more separate coils wound onto the same core material. The magnetic properties of the core material define the efficiency of the transformer. The core material, except in the case of high frequency transformers, is almost always laminated, the reason for this being that the specific inductance of a laminated core is much higher than that of a solid core.

Transformers are used to change the voltage of AC signals and to isolate a device from its power source. They are used both in power supplies and in radio frequency applications. Transformers are readily available commercially but are sometimes custom wound for specific applications. The ratio of the input voltage to the output voltage of a transformer is equal to the ratio of the number of turns in the primary coil to the number of turns in the secondary coil. The ratio of the input current to the output current is equal to the inverse of the ratio of turns in the coils.

A transformer is defined by two parameters, the voltage ratio (or the output voltage in the case of mains transformers) and its maximum power capability in VA (volts×amperes=watts).

2.2.4 Diodes

The word diode describes a device which has two electrical connections, usually referred to as the anode and the cathode. However, the term diode has been adopted to describe devices which conduct electricity in one direction only; they rectify. Conduction occurs if the anode has a more positive voltage applied than the cathode; this is referred to as forward bias. The major categories of commercially available diodes are rectifier diodes, Zener diodes and light-emitting diodes, the circuit symbols for which are shown in Figure 2.5.

(a) Rectifier diodes

Rectifier diodes are available in three major construction types: silicon, germanium and Schottky. The three types have slightly different electrical characteristics; in particular, diodes only conduct in forward bias mode when the voltage exceeds a certain threshold. This threshold is 0.6 V for silicon diodes, 0.2 V for germanium diodes and 0.41 V for

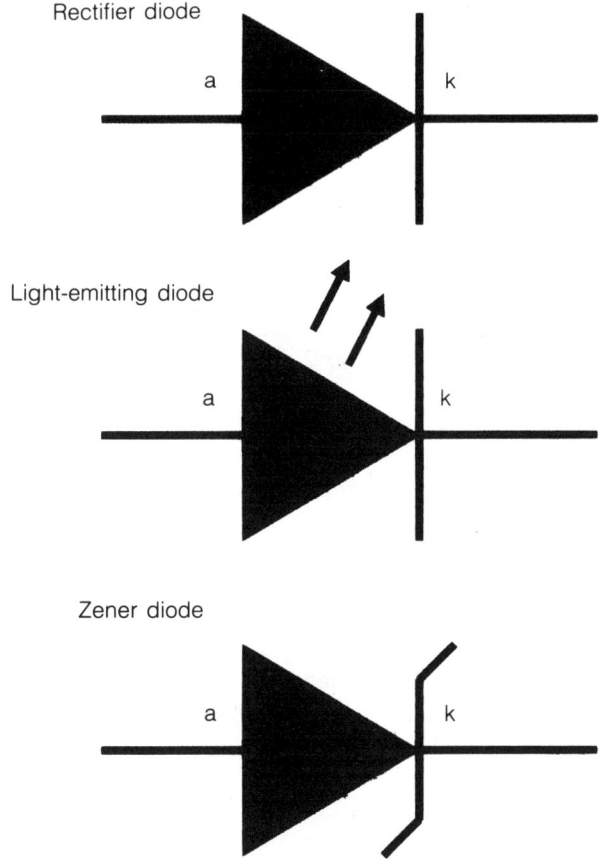

Figure 2.5 Diode circuit symbols.

Schottky diodes. Hence, although silicon diodes are in common usage, germanium and Schottky diodes are used for some radio applications where the signal is less than the 0.6 V silicon threshold. There are two further parameters which are used to describe commercially available diodes, the peak inverse voltage and the maximum forward current. The peak inverse voltage (PIV) is the maximum reverse voltage the device can withstand before running the risk of a catastrophic avalanche breakdown occurring. The maximum forward current (maximum I_F) is the maximum current flow which the device can withstand without running the risk of overheating. Major uses of rectifier diodes are AC to DC rectification and as detectors for radio

Table 2.6 Diode types

Device	Material	PIV	Maximum I_F	Usage
OA200	Silicon	50	8 mA	General purpose
AA119	Germanium	45	35 mA	AM radio detector
BAR28	Schottky	70	N/A	AM radio detector
1N4001	Silicon	50	1 A	Rectifier
1N5408	Silicon	1000	3 A	Rectifier

receivers. Some commercially available rectifier diodes and their characteristics are shown in Table 2.6.

(b) Zener diodes

Zener diodes are similar to rectifier diodes except that they are designed to conduct in reverse bias mode when the reverse voltage exceeds a predefined threshold. Zener diodes are so called as the reverse breakdown mechanism is the 'Zener effect' (in fact the Zener effect only applies to devices with small reverse breakdown voltages – higher breakdown voltages occur as a result of an avalanche breakdown mechanism). Commercially available Zener diodes are defined by the four parameters of maximum power dissipation, breakdown voltage and tolerance. Their major usages include voltage regulation and overvoltage protection circuits. Some commercially available Zener diodes and their characteristics are shown in Table 2.7. The available breakdown voltages of commercially available Zener diodes use the same numbering scheme as the E24 resistor values.

Table 2.7 Zener diode types

Code	Power	Voltage	Tolerance
BZX61C	1.3 W	2.7–30 V	5%
BZY88C	500 mW	4.7–75 V	5%

(c) Light-emitting diodes

Light-emitting diodes (LEDs) are diode devices which emit light when an electric current flows in forward bias mode. They are usually constructed from semiconductor materials such as gallium arsenide and are available in the colours infrared, red, orange, yellow and green. Light-emitting diodes are low power devices, with typical maximum values being 10–30 mA for forward current, 100 mW for power dissipation and a maximum reverse bias voltage of 5 V. Hence light-emitting diodes are easily destroyed electrically and several standard protection circuits have been developed in order to prevent their destruction. These include the use of a series resistor to limit the current and power which can flow through the device to a safe maximum. In the case of AC circuits, a rectifier diode should be connected either in series or in parallel with the light-emitting diode in order to prevent the maximum reverse bias voltage being exceeded.

2.2.5 Transistors

Transistors are basically electronic switching devices of which there are two major types, the bipolar junction transistor (BJT) and the field effect transistor (FET). Each type is available in two different polarities or channels. A more detailed description of the different types, construction and fabrication of transistors will be given in Chapter 4.

(a) Bipolar junction transistors

Bipolar junction transistors are the oldest and most common form of discrete transistor. They are capable of operating at very high frequencies which is of particular importance for VHF and UHF applications such as radio and television transmitters and receivers. Bipolar transistors are available in two types which are identified by their construction as NPN or PNP transistors. Most of today's transistors are fabricated from silicon although a few germanium devices are still available for specific applications.

A transistor has three terminal connections: the base, the collector and the emitter. The base connection is where the switching current is applied to the device and is so called because early devices were fabricated using the base layer as foundation. The collector is so called because it collects electric charge carriers, and the emitter emits charge carriers into the device. The circuit symbols for bipolar junction transistors are shown in Figure 2.6. The silicon NPN device is now the commonest variety of bipolar junction transistor. It is usually connected in one of the three configurations common base, common collector and common emitter as shown in Figure 2.7. The common emitter configuration is the most usual as it forms the basis of the transistor amplifier.

NPN

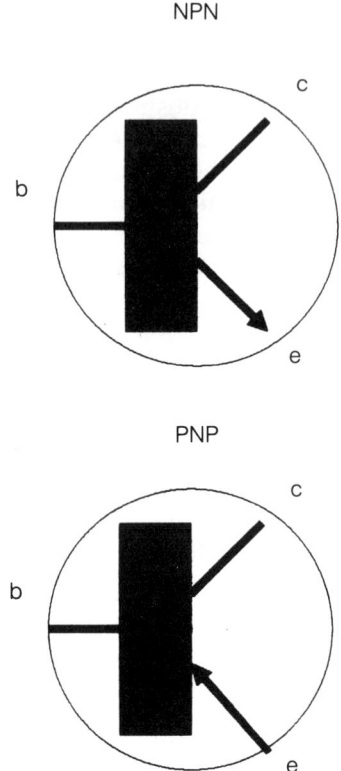

PNP

Figure 2.6 BJT circuit symbols.

A commercially available transistor has three operating characteristics, the maximum collector current I_c, the gain hfe and the maximum operating frequency. The gain value hfe is defined as the collector current divided by the base current. Some commercially available transistors and their characteristics are shown in Table 2.8.

The uses of bipolar junction transistors are manifold, including amplifiers, power supplies and logic circuits. Recent trends towards miniaturization have caused a shift from discrete transistors towards integrated circuits containing many transistors.

(b) Field effect transistors

Field effect transistors are available in two types, the junction field effect transistor (JFET) and the metal oxide semiconductor field effect

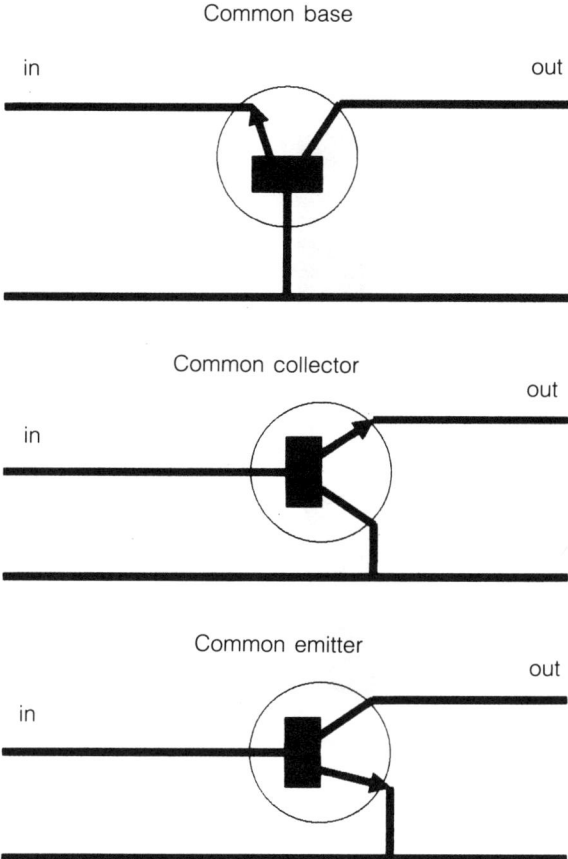

Figure 2.7 Transistor configurations.

Table 2.8 Bipolar transistor types

Code	Type	I_c	hfe	F	Usage
AC126	Ge PNP	100 mA	140	2.3 MHz	Audio preamplifier
BC108C	Si NPN	100 mA	520	300 MHz	General purpose
BC140	Si NPN	1 A	140	50 MHz	Audio amplifiers
2N2905	Si PNP	600 mA	200	200 MHz	High speed switch
2N3055	Si NPN	15 A	45	800 kHz	General purpose power
BFR90A	Si NPN	25 mA	90	5 GHz	VHF–UHF amplifiers

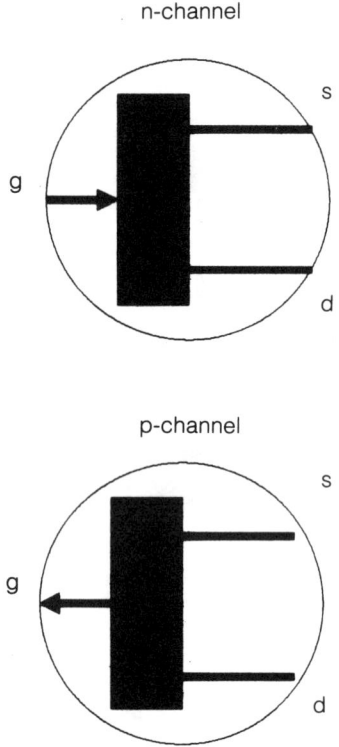

n-channel

p-channel

Figure 2.8 JFET circuit symbols.

transistor (MOSFET). The MOSFET is further divided into enhancement mode and depletion mode devices. The JFET and both types of MOSFET are available in p-channel and n-channel varieties. The different types and channels of field effect transistors will be described in more detail in Chapter 4.

Field effect transistors are not very common in discrete form but they are very widely used in integrated circuit form. Because of their electrical nature p-channel JFETs have poor high frequency performance and are less common than n-channel devices. MOSFETs are rarely seen in discrete form and they are very easily damaged by static electricity. Hence n-channel JFETs are the commonest discrete variety of field effect transistor.

A field effect transistor has three terminal connections, the drain, the gate and the source. The gate voltage controls the current flow between the drain and the source. The circuit symbols for JFETs are shown in Figure 2.8. MOSFETs have a fourth terminal connection to

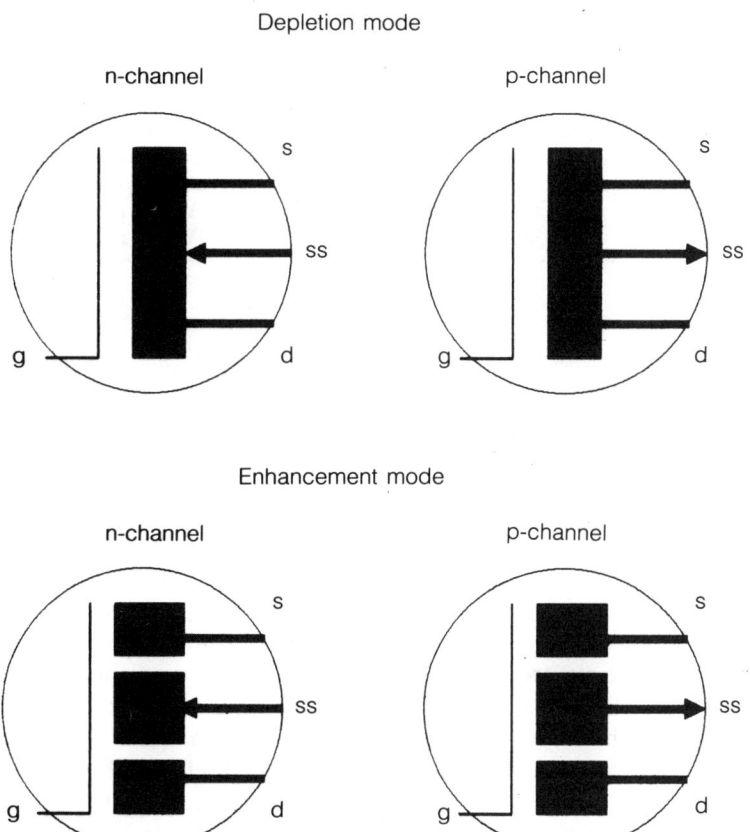

Figure 2.9 MOSFET circuit symbols.

their substrate material. This is often connected to earth in the case of n-channel devices and to the power supply in the case of p-channel devices. The circuit symbols for both types of MOSFET are shown in Figure 2.9.

A recent variant of the field effect transistor is the high power VFET – so called because it is constructed in a V shape. These have become very popular for use in high quality audio amplifiers. JFETs are mainly used in linear amplifiers and as voltage-controlled resistors. MOSFETs are mainly used in radio frequency amplifiers and in digital circuits, the p-channel enhancement and the n-channel depletion mode devices being preferred.

Other than the actual type, the main parameter used to describe commercially available field effect transistors is that of maximum

Table 2.9 Field effect transistor types

Code	Type	V_{max} (V)	Usage
2N3819	nJFET	30	DC amplifiers
2N5460	pJFET	40	Low level amplifiers
3SK88	nMOSFET	20	RF amplifiers
2SJ48	pVMOS	−120	Audio power amplifiers
2SK133	nVMOS	120	Audio power amplifiers

working voltage. Some commercially available FETs and their character-istics are shown in Table 2.9.

2.2.6 Integrated circuits

The term integrated circuit (IC) is used to describe a wide variety of devices ranging from simple logic gates through to complex state-of-the-art microprocessors. Integrated circuits basically consist of a circuit, typically made up from a number of transistors and their interconnec-tions, fabricated from a single semiconductor chip or die. Integrated circuits can be functionally divided into analogue devices, digital devices, computer devices and customized devices. The fabrication of integrated circuits is described in Chapter 4 and the category of customized devices is described in Chapter 8.

(a) Analogue integrated circuits

Analogue integrated circuits include a wide range of applications, many of which are highly specific. Some examples are the simple operational amplifiers and timers, and the more complex FM stereo decoders and single-chip FM radios.

The operational amplifier is one of the commonest varieties of analogue integrated circuit which has now largely replaced the use of discrete transistors for amplifier applications. There has been a trend towards fabricating the more commonly used analogue circuits into single-chip form. An example of this is the FM radio receiver, which is a fairly complex circuit when fabricated from discrete components. An FM radio receiver can now be constructed from an FM radio chip, an audio amplifier chip and a few discrete passive components.

(b) Digital integrated circuits

Digital integrated circuits are devices which are functionally based on logic gates (for example AND and OR gates). They are commercially available in families of devices which take their name from the fabrication method used to manufacture the devices. Each family has its own operational characteristics such as power supply requirements. In general, devices from different families are not readily compatible in the same circuit. The more common types of logic integrated circuits are typically represented in each family of devices. The most commonly available digital integrated circuit families are TTL, Schottky TTL, CMOS and the new high speed CMOS.

The TTL family, which is short for transistor transistor logic, has been in common usage for many applications including support logic for computer applications. The TTL devices are particularly important for high speed applications as, until recently, they have been the fastest operating logic family. TTL logic gates are constructed from NPN bipolar junction transistors; PNP bipolar junction transistors cannot be manufactured reliably in chip form. Commercially available TTL devices are identified by means of a 7400 series part number. Some examples of the range of commercially available TTL integrated circuits are shown in Table 2.10.

The CMOS family devices, short for complementary metal oxide semiconductor, have a very low power consumption which makes them very popular for many applications where very high speeds are not required. CMOS devices are constructed from complementary pairs of p-channel and n-channel enhancement mode MOSFETs. Care needs to be exercised when handling CMOS devices as they are easily damaged by static electric discharges. Commercially available CMOS devices are identified by means of a 4000 series part code. Some examples of the range of commercially available CMOS devices are

Table 2.10 TTL 7400 series devices

Code	Device	Inputs	Type
7401	Quad	2	NAND gate
7402	Quad	2	NOR gate
7408	Quad	2	AND gate
7410	Triple	3	NAND gate
7420	Dual	4	NAND gate
7430	Single	8	NAND gate
7432	Quad	2	OR gate
74133	Single	13	NAND gate

Table 2.11 CMOS 4000 series devices

Code	Device	Inputs	Type
4001	Quad	2	NOR gate
4011	Quad	2	NAND gate
4012	Dual	4	NAND gate
4070	Quad	2	XOR gate
4071	Quad	2	OR gate
4081	Quad	2	AND gate

shown in Table 2.11. Note that although most CMOS devices have a TTL equivalent, there is no commonality in part code numbering.

The Schottky TTL family of devices consists of low power versions of the standard TTL family of devices. The commercially available Schottky TTL devices use a 74LS00 series of part codes. Schottky TTL devices have the same range and logic functions and are pin compatible with the corresponding 7400 series devices.

The high speed CMOS family of devices has recently been introduced; they use CMOS technology but do not have the operating speed restrictions. High speed CMOS devices outperform all the older families of devices which are now being phased out. They are commercially available in two ranges in order to maintain compatibility with the TTL and CMOS devices which they are to replace. A 74HC00 series of part codes provides pin-compatible replacements for the 7400 and 74LS00 series TTL devices. A 74HC4000 series of devices provides pin-compatible replacements for the 4000 series CMOS devices. Table 2.12 shows a comparison between the operating characteristics of the different families of commercially available digital integrated circuits.

Table 2.12 A comparison between logic families

Family	Voltage (V)	Current (μA)	Power (mW)	Delay (ns)	Clock (MHz)
74	5	40	10	22	35
74LS	5	20	2	15	40
4000	3–15	1.6	0.6	250	5
74HC	5	0.5	0.001	15	40
74AC	5	0.1	0.001	5	100

(c) Computer integrated circuits

Computer integrated circuits are devices which form the active components of a computer system. They are often used in conjunction with digital integrated circuits which provide a 'glue logic' function. Computer integrated circuits can be functionally divided into microprocessors, memory devices and peripheral control devices.

Microprocessors form the nucleus of many computer systems and are amongst the most complex integrated circuit devices. They encompass a range of devices from the early 4-bit microprocessors to the modern state-of-the-art 32-bit microprocessors. An early microprocessor such as the 6502 or the 8080 works on 8-bit data and can directly address up to 64 kbytes of memory. The timing source for such devices comes from either a 1 MHz or a 2 MHz clock. These microprocessors had 40 external connection terminals. At the other end of the spectrum, an 80386 microprocessor works on 32-bit data and can directly address up to 4 Gbytes of memory. An 80386 can operate at clock speed of 33 MHz and contains 275 000 transistors. It is based on a variation of the high speed CMOS technology and has 132 external terminal connections.

Related to microprocessors are devices called coprocessors. These are integrated circuits which perform operations such as floating point arithmetic for a microprocessor, allowing it to perform other operations in parallel. The coprocessor can be seen as a device which enhances the microprocessor's operating speed and instruction set. An example of a numeric coprocessor is the 80387 which works in conjunction with the 80386 microprocessor. The recently announced 80486 microprocessor combines the functionality of both the 80386 and the 80387.

Memory devices are integrated circuits which store information for use by microprocessors and other such devices. Memory devices have three basic forms, static RAM, dynamic RAM and PROM. A static RAM, or random access memory, device is typically a two-dimensional array of storage bits. The term static means that once data is written to the device it remains there until either it is overwritten or the power supply is removed. Static RAMs are readily available with capacities of 256 kbits. These devices are organized as 32 768 8-bit words and have 28 external terminal connections.

Dynamic RAMs are used to achieve a higher memory capacity than static RAMs with fewer terminal connections. Dynamic RAMs are so called because data which is written to the device only remains available for a period of about 2 ms unless it is refreshed. The reason for this is that data is stored as an electric charge which decays in a finite time. Hence dynamic RAMs need to be refreshed at regular intervals. This is achieved by use of a small amount of external circuitry which addresses the data sequentially and independently of the device which is using the memory. Dynamic RAMs are readily available with capacities of 1 Mbit with 18 external terminal connections.

PROMs, or programmable read-only memories, are devices which store data on a permanent or semipermanent basis. Depending on the type of device, data can be written once or many times. The writing and erasure of data often requires the use of specific programming and erasure devices. A typical and widely used form of read-only memory is the erasable programmable read-only memory (EPROM). EPROMs are programmed by applying a programming voltage to an input of the device in conjunction with the data to be written. The erasure of EPROMs is achieved by exposure to ultraviolet light for a period of 20 min. Commercially available EPROMs have capacities of 512 kbits. This is organized as 65 536 8-bit words in a device with 28 external terminal connections.

Peripheral control devices are integrated circuits which are designed to interface external devices such as keyboards and disc drives directly to microprocessor systems. Typical examples of peripheral control devices are USARTs, keyboard controllers and CRT controllers.

A USART, or universal synchronous asynchronous receiver transmitter, is a device which interfaces microprocessors to serial communications channels. A microprocessor typically reads or writes 8-bit data to a USART which performs the necessary parallel-to-serial conversions, encoding and checking to effect data transfer with another USART at the other end of a serial data link.

A keyboard controller interfaces microprocessors with alphanumeric keyboards. When a key is depressed on a keyboard the controller performs the necessary debouncing and decoding operations in order to present the microprocessor with a unique identification code, such as an ASCII code, for the key.

A CRT controller enables a microprocessor to display alphanumeric and graphical information on a visual display unit. The CRT controller may have the capabilities of scrolling, cursor manipulation and light pen input.

2.3 COMPONENT PACKAGING

The term component packaging actually refers to two quite separate things which can be separated by using the terms component encapsulation and high level packaging. A component's encapsulation is the outer covering which gives an electronic device mechanical, electrical and environmental support. The mechanical and environmental support protects a device from physical damage, thermal stress and contamination. The electrical support provides a means of connecting a device into a circuit by means of leads or contacts. High level packaging is the method by which components are stored and transported and, where appropriate, input into automatic assembly machines. This can be a simple box in the case of bulk packaging or methods of storing individual components at the other extreme. High level packaging is dependent on the type of component encapsulation used, as each individual component's geometry will impose constraints. Thus high level packaging will be discussed alongside component encapsulation.

Leaded components' encapsulations fall into three major categories, axial, radial, and transistor and integrated circuit packages. Integrated circuit packaging, which includes dual-in-line (DIL or DIP) packages, includes a wide variety of encapsulation styles. The introduction of surface-mounted components has extended this range.

When considering high level packaging the increasing use of automatic assembly systems has placed constraints on the form in which components must be fed into a machine. This is of considerable importance for axial, radial, dual-in-line, and surface-mount component packaging.

2.3.1 Axial component packaging

The axial component encapsulation consists of a cylindrical body with a connecting lead protruding from each end. This form of encapsulation necessitates the preforming of component leads before they can be inserted into a PCB. Resistors, some types of capacitors, and diodes are commonly encapsulated in axial component form. The cathode end of a diode is usually indicated by a band marking on one end of the device. Although these components exhibit quite a wide range of body sizes, the total length between lead tips is kept to a standard 65 mm.

The high level packaging of axial components can be bulk packaging, body-taped bandoliers and lead-taped bandoliers.

Bulk packaging is simply a box or polythene bag containing loose axial components. A body-taped bandolier consists of a number of regularly spaced parallel axial components which are joined together by means of an adhesive tape attached to the component bodies as shown in Figure 2.10. A lead-taped bandolier consists of two parallel strips of cardboard or plastic tape which are attached to each end of a number of regularly spaced axial components' leads as shown in Figure 2.11.

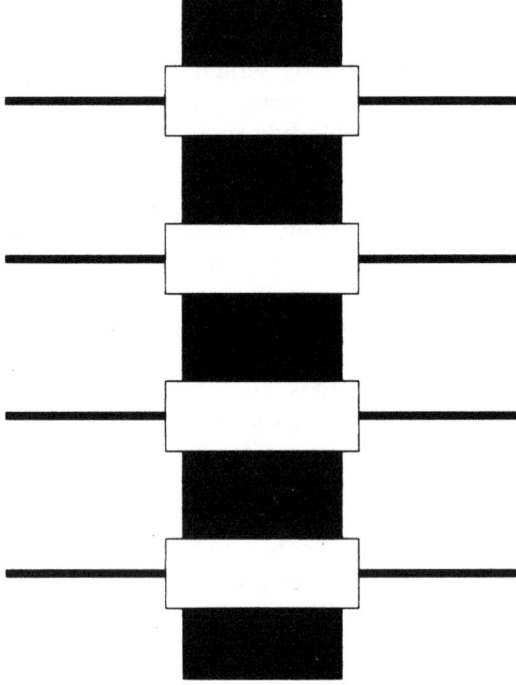

Figure 2.10 Body-taped bandolier.

Axial components have until recently been the commonest component type for automatic assembly, the reason for this being that the majority of axial components have similar-sized leads and were the nearest thing to a standard in the early days of automatic assembly. This was formalized when the Electronic Industry Association (EIA) developed the RS296 standard. This defines the lead-taped bandolier packaging specifications for axial components which have component body dimensions within a specified range. Modern axial components are almost universally available in a lead-taped bandolier form which conforms to the RS296 standard. The lead-taped bandoliers are typically 65 mm wide with a 5 or 10 mm component pitch. Bandoliers are typically supplied in reels containing up to several thousand components. The demands of automatic axial component insertion machines have effectively forced the suppliers to change almost universally from bulk form to bandolier form.

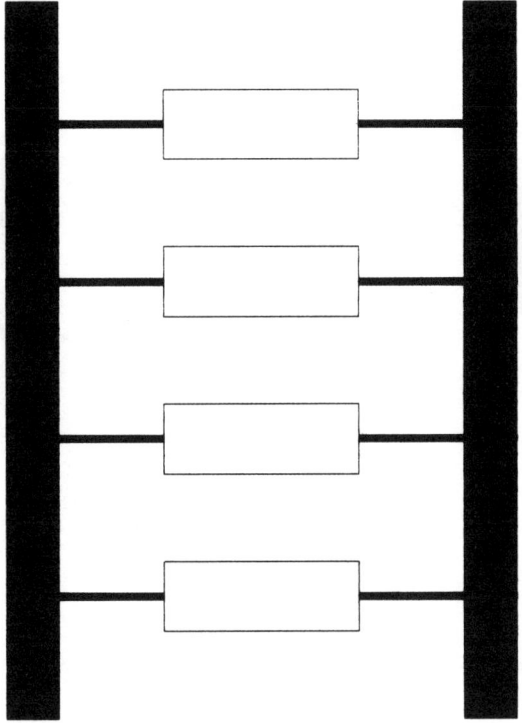

Figure 2.11 Lead-taped bandolier.

2.3.2 Radial components

The radial component encapsulation consists of a component body, which can take a wide range of actual forms, with connecting leads protruding in a parallel fashion from one side. Thus radial component leads do not necessarily have to be preformed before being inserted into a PCB. Radial components can be considered to be of two varieties depending on whether they have two, or more than two, terminal leads. Radial components with more than two leads are discussed under transistor packaging in the next section.

Two-leaded radial components are the simplest form and are principally capacitors and light-emitting diodes. The cathode of an LED is often marked by a flat on the casing or a shorter lead than the anode. The category of radial components can also include axial components which have had their leads formed for vertical mounting. Figure 2.12

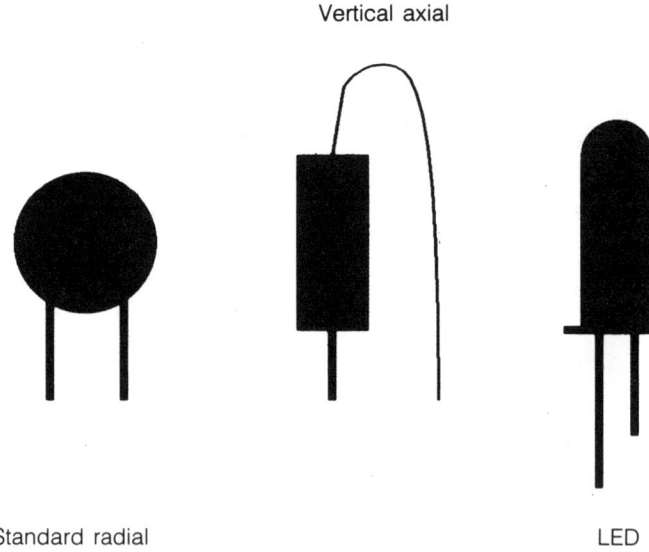

Vertical axial

Standard radial   LED

Figure 2.12 Radial component types.

shows a typical radial component and the vertically mounted axial component form.

Other than bulk form, the main method of high level packaging used in conjunction with radial components is the lead taping method as shown in Figure 2.13. Taped bonding is designed to facilitate the loading of radial components into automatic assembly machines. Component tape sizes were finally standardized in the early 1970s as a result of a standardization program. A common component lead spacing of 5 mm was also agreed. The standard radial component tapes also feature sprocket holes between components in order to facilitate automatic feeding mechanisms.

Figure 2.13 Lead-taped radial components.

2.3.3 Transistor packaging

A modern transistor is a very small device. The typical dimensions are 6 μm×30 μm. The base region may be as thin as 0.5 μm (the wavelength of green light is about 0.5 μm) and needs to have a terminal connection made to it. A consequence of this small size is that a transistor's encapsulation needs to be significantly larger than the device itself. This is particularly true in the case of high power transistors which need to dissipate a lot of heat.

In terms of encapsulation a transistor, which has three or sometimes four terminal connections, is usually encapsulated in a radial form. The actual body shape, however, can vary considerably between devices. Transistors can be encapsulated in either metal or plastic. Metal-encapsulated transistors often have an electrical connection between the casing and the collector electrode. In some encapsulations the metal case is the only collector connection.

Transistor cases are identified by a TO series casing description. The terminal leads can be identified by the geometry of the casing when viewed from the underside. The TO series of transistor casings are typified by the metal TO3 and TO5 cases and the plastic TO92 case as shown in Figure 2.14. The TO3 casing is an example where the collector, or in the case of an FET the source, connection is obtained from the metal casing.

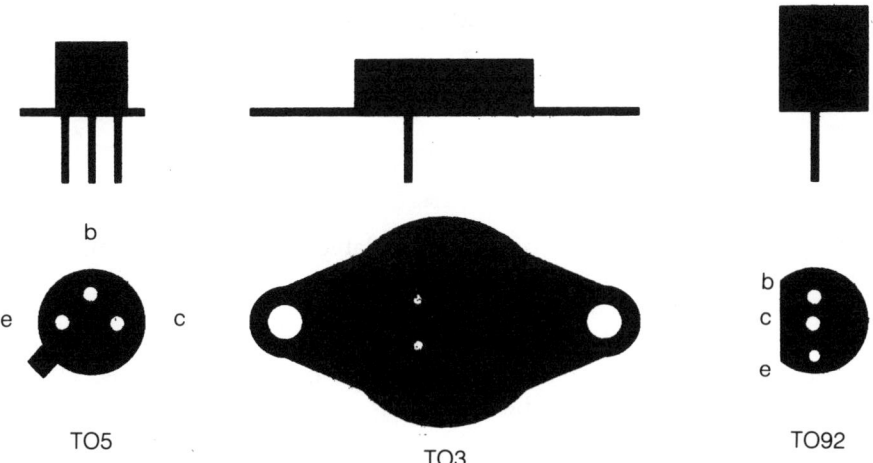

Figure 2.14 Common transistor encapsulations.

2.3.4 Surface mount component packaging

When obtained in surface-mountable form, components such as resistors, capacitors, diodes and transistors are very similar in appearance. The diversification which leads to the axial and radial component forms does not apply to surface-mounted components as the assembly of devices does not directly depend on the relative position of the components' terminal connections. The implementation of surface mount technology has often resulted in a radical redesign of components.

Surface-mountable resistors are typified by the chip resistor. This consists of a ceramic substrate onto which a resistance material has been applied by thick film techniques. Terminal connections are achieved by means of metal end caps. The construction of a chip resistor is shown in Figure 2.15. Chip resistors are actually available in a range of sizes; however, the 1206 body style which is 3.2 mm long by 1.6 mm wide by 0.6 mm high is in common usage.

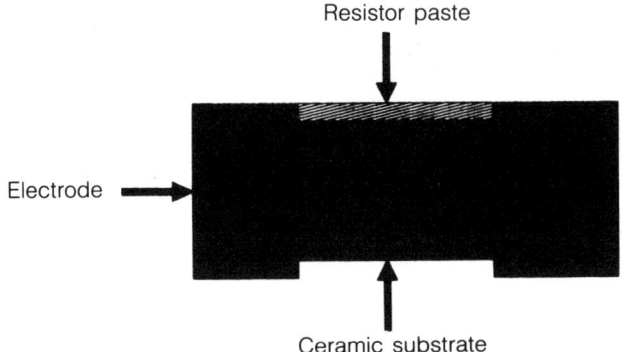

Figure 2.15 Chip resistor structure.

Surface-mountable capacitors are available in a chip form, for example the multilayer ceramic chip capacitor. This device is fabricated from layers of metal electrodes separated by a ceramic dielectric material as shown in cross-section in Figure 2.16. Table 2.13 shows the five industry standard sizes associated with multilayer ceramic chip capacitors (Coombs, 1988) (the codes are based on the component dimensions in inches).

Surface-mountable transistors are commonly available in the small outline transistor (SOT) packaging form. Transistors with power

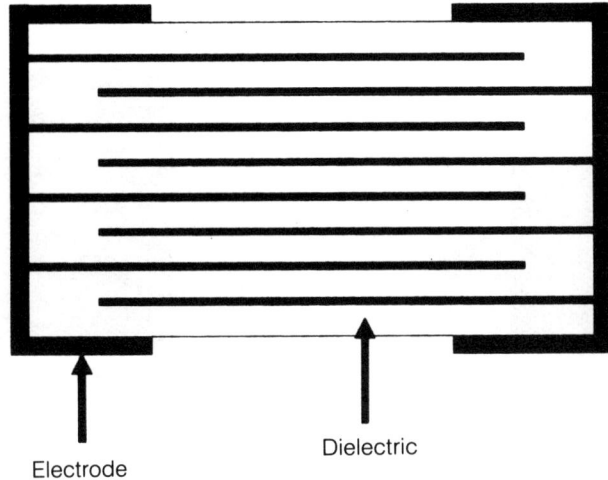

Figure 2.16 Ceramic chip capacitor structure.

Table 2.13 Standard chip capacitor sizes

Code	Length (mm)	Width (mm)	Height (mm)
0402	1.0	0.5	0.5
0603	1.5	0.8	0.8
0805	2.0	1.2	1.2
1206	3.2	1.6	1.5
1210	3.2	2.5	1.7
1812	4.6	3.2	1.7
1825	4.6	6.4	1.7

dissipations of less than 200 mW are typically packages in the SOT-23 style. Larger devices are packaged in the SOT-89 style which features a heat sink connection which can be soldered directly onto a printed circuit board in order to improve thermal conductivity. The SOT-23 and SOT-89 encapsulations are shown in Figure 2.17.

2.3.5 Integrated circuit packaging

The category of integrated circuit packaging covers a wide range of different types of encapsulations for semiconductor devices in both leaded and surface-mountable form. Integrated circuit sockets can also

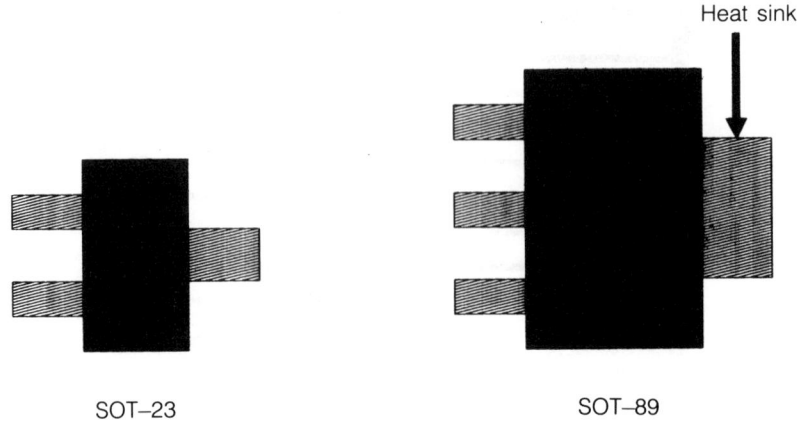

SOT–23   SOT–89

Figure 2.17 Surface mount transistor encapsulation.

be considered under this category as they are very similar to integrated circuits from the assembly point of view. When discussing the more complex packaging styles the distinction between leaded components and surface-mounted components becomes somewhat vague. The reason for this is that certain integrated circuit encapsulations have terminal connections of a surface form which are designed to be inserted into leaded integrated circuit sockets.

The ever-increasing complexity of semiconductor devices has its parallel in terms of the number of external terminal connections required for a device. A rule of thumb, which is described in more detail in Chapter 8, suggests that for every tenfold increase in device complexity, the number of external connections increases by a factor of four. This has necessitated the development of integrated circuit packaging with high pin counts. The major forms of integrated circuit packaging are dual-in-line, surface-mounted dual-in-line, quad packs, plastic leaded chip carriers and pin grid arrays.

(a) Dual-in-line packaging

The commonest form of integrated circuit encapsulation is that of the dual-in-line package, usually abbreviated to DIL or DIP. The DIL package takes the form of a component body with two rows of equally spaced parallel terminal connections as shown in Figure 2.18. The DIL package's lead spacing is based on a 0.1 in pitch, the leads within each row having a centre spacing of 0.1 in, and devices with up to 18 pins

Figure 2.18 A 24-pin DIL package.

have a row spacing of 0.4 in. Dual-in-line packages are commonly available with pin counts between 6 and 40, although 64-pin devices are available. The general relationship between DIL package pin count and the types of devices encapsulated is as follows. Six-pin DIL packages are used for simple devices such as optoisolators. Eight-pin packages are used for simple analogue devices, for example operational amplifiers and timers. Packages with 14 and 16 pins are the most commonly used for analogue and digital integrated circuits. Packages with 18, 20, 24 and 28 pins are used for the larger capacity computer memory devices. The simpler microprocessors and many of the peripheral control integrated circuits use 40-pin packages.

The correct orientation of a dual-in-line packaged device is marked by means of a cut-out slot at one end of the component's body or a dot marking the position of pin 1. Pins are numbered, when viewed from above with the slot at the top, from the top left as pin 1 down to the bottom left then from the bottom right to the top right which is the final pin.

Dual-in-line sockets are available for all types of dual-in-line integrated circuits. They are available in both a standard and a zero insertion force (ZIF) form. The standard form is typically soldered to a printed circuit board in the place of an integrated circuit, the integrated circuit being pushed into the socket at a later stage. Zero insertion force sockets are used in applications where integrated circuits are to be frequently inserted and removed from a socket. A typical example of this is an EPROM programmer where the use of a standard socket could easily lead to a device's leads becoming damaged. Zero insertion force sockets operate by means of a lever which when placed in a vertical position allows an IC to be dropped into the socket without having to apply a force. Once an IC is in place the lever is lowered to a horizontal position which clamps the leads of the IC and forms a good electrical and mechanical connection.

Dual-in-line packages have a 'natural' upper limit on their pin count of about 64, the reason for this being that for high pin count DIL packages the internal connection lengths to end pins are considerably longer than connections to central pins. This results in differing electrical characteristics such as capacitance which adversely affects the performance of high speed devices.

The standard method of high level packaging dual-in-line components is the stick form. A stick takes the form of a hollow tube which is shaped to accommodate dual-in-line packages in a fixed orientation. Stick packages are typically about a metre in length and are designed to be placed directly into automatic assembly machines which use gravity feed to extract the individual devices. Stick packages have a removable plug at each end to prevent devices from falling out of the ends of the sticks during transportation. The sticks are constructed from plastic; this may need to be an antistatic variety when used for high level packaging of CMOS devices.

(b) Surface-mounted dual-in-line packaging

The surface-mountable form of the dual-in-line package uses the same semiconductor die as the leaded version but is physically smaller in size. The terminal lead centre spacing of a surface-mountable DIL packaged is half that of its leaded equivalent at 0.05 in. A variety of body widths are available depending on the country of manufacture. The terminal leads of a surface-mountable DIL package are available in three configurations, L lead, J lead and I lead, as shown in Figure 2.19. The L lead configuration is well established and is by far the most common variety. It has the advantage of allowing easy visual inspection of solder joints. It has the disadvantages of effectively increasing the package size and the L leads are easily damaged during handling. The J lead configuration is much more robust but has the disadvantage of being difficult to form, which increases component

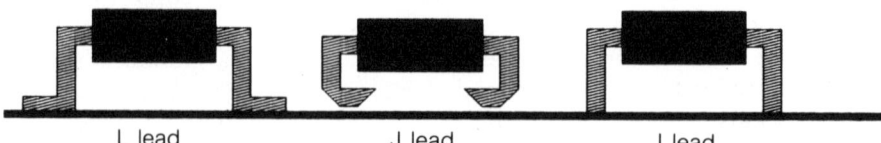

L lead   J lead   I lead

Figure 2.19 Surface mount lead configurations.

costs. The I lead is considered a good compromise between L and J lead configurations but has yet gained little recognition.

Surface-mountable dual-in-line packages are high level packages in stick form as for their leaded equivalents.

(c) Quad packs

Quad packs are a surface-mountable form of integrated circuit packaging for devices which require in excess of 84 terminal connections. Quad packs have a square profile with L lead terminal connections on all four sides as shown in Figure 2.20. Lead centre pitches are available in the range from 0.5 mm to 1.2 mm. The very fine pitch devices have very delicate leads which are very easily damaged during handling.

(d) Plastic leaded chip carriers

The plastic leaded chip carrier, or PLCC, is a variation on the theme of the quad pack but utilizes the J lead configuration. PLCCs feature a cut-off corner which provides orientation information. They are typically available with pin counts of 20, 28, 32, 44, 52, 68, 84 and 124, with a between-centre pitch of 0.05 in. Typical dimensions for a PLCC are between 20 and 40 mm square. PLCCs can either be treated as surface mounted devices for assembly purposes or be inserted into a

Figure 2.20 A quad pack.

PLCC socket. The PLCC socket is a leaded package which has the form of a pin grid array as described in the next subsection.

A variation on the theme of the PLCC is the leadless ceramic chip carrier, or LCCC. These are devices which have the form of a PLCC but with edge conductors in place of J leads. They can be directly surface mounted or socket mounted as for PLCCs.

(e) Pin grid arrays

Pin grid arrays, or PGAs, offer a greater pin count capability than PLCCs. A pin grid array consists of a two-dimensional array of pins on the underside of a square package. The centre region of a PGA does not have a pin population as that is the region of the semiconductor die itself. The centre region is usually occupied by a metal lid. A typical 132-pin PGA, as used to package the 80386 microprocessor, is shown in Figure 2.21. The upper limit for the pin count achievable using a PGA is predicted to be about 400.

Because of the very large number of pins it is very important to ensure that none of the pins is deformed before or during the insertion

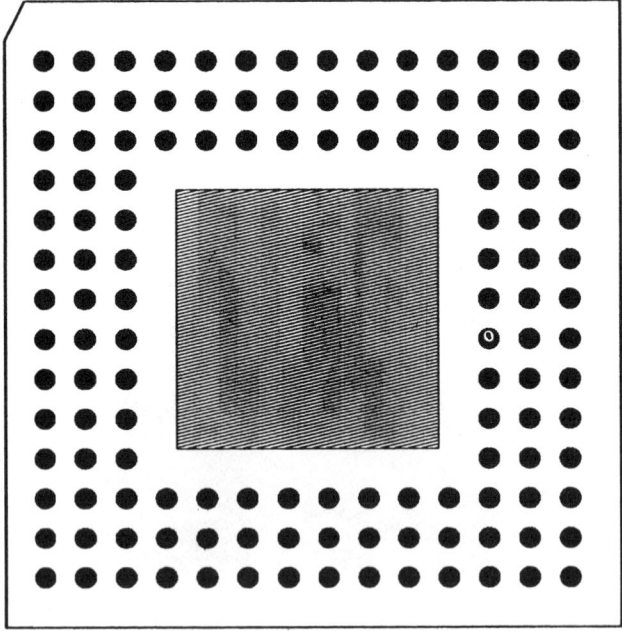

Figure 2.21 A pin grid array.

process. Once soldered in place it is almost impossible to correct a fault. Pin grid arrays are often mounted in socket form in order to minimize the possibilities of a device being destroyed as the devices are in general very expensive. Sockets for pin grid arrays are available in a low insertion force variety and in a zero insertion force variety as for dual-in-line components.

2.4 CABLING

When considering the performance of electronic devices which need to transmit data over large distances, an important consideration is that of the actual cabling used to provide the data channel. This is particularly important in the telecommunications industry and for large area networks of computers where the high speed, high integrity transmission of data is essential.

The traditional method of providing communications links is the use of wire-based cabling systems. Wire-based cabling is subject to signal losses and interference depending on the electrical characteristics of the cable and the environment through which it passes. There is an upper limit to the amount of data which can be transmitted down a wire-based cable in a given time. This is determined by the cable's bandwidth – a measure of the highest frequency signal which can be transmitted without being severely attenuated.

Many of the limitations of wire-based cabling can be eliminated by the use of fibre optic cabling. A fibre optic cable consists of a filament of a plastic, glass or silica material which has a higher refractive index at its core than at its periphery. A light beam can then be passed down the filament with very little loss as it undergoes total internal reflection whenever it encounters the walls of the fibre. Fibre optics have the following advantages over wire-based cables. They are immune to electromagnetic interference; in fact, there are some environments which generate so much interference that wire-based cables cannot be used and fibre optics is the only recommended method. Fibre optics also do not generate any electromagnetic interference, unlike the wire-based alternatives. The use of fibre optic cables eliminates the creation of a conductive path back to the transmitter or receiver which renders them immune from lightning strikes to the cable. Fibre optic cables are highly wear resistant and are much more difficult to tap into than wire-based cables. This has obvious advantages from the maintenance and security points of view. The major advantage which the use of fibre optic cabling has over wire-based cabling is that of the data carrying capability. Typically the product of the transmission distance and the maximum data transmission rate can be 100 times greater, particularly for longer transmission distances.

Fibre optic cables are readily available in lengths of 100 m; longer lengths are used for long-distance telecommunications work. Connections between cables are made by cutting the cable with a sharp knife and then polishing the cut end. A standard range of connectors are available which includes printed circuit board mountable transmitter and receiver units.

2.5 COMPONENT QUALITY ASSURANCE

Component quality assurance is an essential activity in order to prevent the assembly of defective components into products. As previously stated in Chapter 1, the earlier a fault is discovered during a product's manufacture the cheaper the correction and hence the product's manufacturing cost.

The traditional method of checking the quality of components was by means of exhaustive incoming goods testing. In its worst case, incoming goods testing involves the testing of each individual component as it is delivered. This is a very expensive operation and requires an entire department complete with a full range of test equipment for the component types to be tested. In the case of complex components such as microprocessors it is impossible to perform comprehensive testing as it would take a very long time. Some components such as protection devices cannot be tested as they operate by self-destructing in order to protect other devices. The number of incoming goods tests can be reduced by using techniques such as batch sampling. This may be applicable to simple components, such as resistors, which are automatically tested before automatic assembly.

The incoming goods testing of passive components takes the form of checking the component's value against the nominal value and the specified tolerance. Analogue integrated circuits are tested by checking their AC parameters. Digital integrated circuits are tested for their functionality. All prefabricated power supplies need to be individually tested for a period of about 15 min as a faulty power supply can cause an expensive destruction of components. In the case of capacitive keyboards dummy 'fingers' are used for testing purposes as human fingers do not test the keyboards sufficiently.

Recent trends in the electronics manufacturing industry are going towards the use of preferred suppliers. The principle behind this is that the purchasing company's incoming goods testing can be amalgamated with the supplier's outgoing goods testing. In order for this to be effective it is necessary for the two organizations to work closely together and that both companies benefit from the collaboration.

From the purchasing company's point of view the use of preferred suppliers virtually eliminates the need for incoming goods testing. This has the effect of reducing their manufacturing costs and hence improving profitability. The removal of the incoming goods testing stage also considerably reduces the amount of work in progress and storage requirements.

A purchasing company needs to cooperate with a supplier in order to ensure that their outgoing goods testing procedures meet the purchaser's requirements. A purchaser can assist a vendor company by providing information on commonly occurring faults, thus allowing them to eliminate manufacturing problems and to increase their overall quality.

The feedback of fault information to a preferred supplier can be very comprehensive. Component faults will usually show up during batch sampling or during production. Some organizations have a small facility which has the purpose of obtaining as much information as possible from faulty devices in order to feed this back to the suppliers. This information can help to identify problem areas in their manufacturing processes. This diagnosis can take the form of actually removing the encapsulation from an integrated circuit and identifying the exact area on the semiconductor die in which the problem occurs. This information can then be used to identify the precise stage during the component's manufacturing process which is at fault, and the nature of the manufacturing problem. The process of collaboration between supplier and purchaser as part of a total quality management scheme is an important step in the direction of getting it right first time.

3

Electronic design

The design process is a very important aspect of the electronics industry. In order to be able to manufacture products at a high quality and profit margin it is essential that the product is well designed. In today's manufacturing environment factors such as testability and quality have become important additions to a product's design process.

The design aspects of the electronics industry have certain common features such as the overall aims and objectives for the design of products and design constraints imposed by the marketplace. A product must have a well-defined market before resources are committed to its design and development. It is also important to ensure that a product can be manufactured at a competitive price.

Once a product has been specified it is necessary to produce an electronic circuit for it. This process can be either manual or computer assisted. In the case of integrated circuits, it is necessary to perform a design process for new and customer-specified devices.

The majority of electronic circuits are ultimately assembled on printed circuit boards. This necessitates the design of a printed circuit board layout, which minimizes manufacturing difficulties, from the circuit description of a product.

This chapter addresses the design aspects of the electronics industry in five categories. These are quality and reliability assessment philosophies, the product design process, circuit design, integrated circuit design and printed circuit board layout.

3.1 QUALITY AND RELIABILITY ASSESSMENT

The design processes of the electronics industry have undergone radical changes. Not only has the rapid pace of technology had to have been assimilated, but the philosophies of designed-in quality have also had to have been addressed.

During the design and implementation of new systems, occasional oversights and errors can occur owing to a number of contributing factors. It is essential that any such errors are detected and corrected as early as possible. The earlier a fault is corrected, the less cost it incurs. The use of frequent design reviews during a product's design and implementation phases is a well-established method of error detection and elimination. There are a number of different methods in use which can be used to assess the quality and reliability of a product. These methods include the low level review methods which examine the role of individual components and their effect on a product's quality, and the high level methods of quality management. The methods which will be examined are as follows: load–strength interference; failure mode effect and criticality analysis; fault tree analysis; and Taguchi methods.

3.1.1 Load–strength interference

Load–strength interference examines the safety margins of a device under the conditions in which it is to operate. In a complex system the factors of load and strength are of a probabilistic nature which means that an absolute safety factor cannot readily be derived. The load factor is defined to be the factors such as operating voltage, operating current and operating temperatures. The strength factor is defined to be the ability of a component to cope with a load, for example heat dissipation and breakdown voltages. The mean safety factor is defined as the difference between the mean strength and the mean load. Thus for a particular device and a particular operating parameter, the load and strength parameters of its component parts will follow a normal distribution curve. If these two curves overlap, the safety factor is inadequate and the device liable to fail.

An example of this would be in the case of an integrated circuit which has a defined operating voltage range. Each component transistor will have its own local heat dissipation for a given input voltage. The range of operating voltages which cause individual component transistors to fail must lie above the operating voltage range. Should the input voltage (load) cause the heating in a component transistor to exceed its capability (strength) the device will overheat.

The overlap of load and strength parameters is more likely if the standard deviations of either or both values are high. One practical, although expensive, method which can be used in the case of a high standard deviation in strength values is to overload components deliberately so as to eliminate the low strength components destructively. A related process is that of soak testing where devices are stressed such that low strength devices undergo an infant mortality.

3.1.2 Failure mode effect and criticality analysis

Failure mode effect and criticality analysis (FMECA) is an exhaustive process where each individual component of a system has its likely failure modes catalogued. The failure modes are recorded along with a probability of occurrence and the effect of the failure mode on the overall system. This is by definition a major operation; however, it does identify weaknesses from the design point of view and identifies maintenance problems. Diagnostic procedures can readily be determined by using FMECA techniques.

An example of this would be a resistor which is likely to go open circuit with a failure rate of 4×10^{-9} per hour. The effect of this is a failure of a power supply's voltage regulation which has a critical effect on the overall system.

3.1.3 Fault tree analysis

Fault tree analysis is a top-down approach unlike the bottom-up approach used by the FMECA method. Fault tree analysis operates by examining the failure modes of a system. Once identified, each failure mode is examined so as to determine the subsystems and components responsible for the fault in a top-down manner. This method is commonly used in safety analysis procedures. Like FMECA, fault tree analysis can be a very lengthy process, particularly in the case of large systems where the complex interactions of components can make the approach difficult. In these cases the approach can be reserved for the worst-case faults.

Fault tree analysis can be represented in the form of a logic diagram using conventional AND and OR gate symbols. The AND gate structure indicates that a failure only occurs if all the input conditions fail. An OR gate is used when several different failures can produce the same outcome in terms of system failure.

3.1.4 Taguchi methods

Taguchi methods are quality control methods developed by the Japanese engineer Genichi Taguchi which have had a major impact worldwide. The aspects of Taguchi methods which are of particular importance are the loss function and the parametric design techniques (Ross, 1988).

(a) The loss function

The Taguchi loss function introduces the concept that a product or service's quality has an associated loss to society. This loss to society can take the form of costs incurred by usage of a product, for example replacement costs and repairing any damage which a product's failure causes. It can also include factors such as inconvenience, pollution or time wastage. High quality products are thus defined as products which impart little overall loss on society.

A typical manufacturing parameter for a product is that of a nominal value with an associated tolerance. Traditionally, a product is of a sufficient quality if all its parameters lie within the tolerance. In fact manufacturing costs can be reduced by allowing parameters to fall towards one extreme of a tolerance. Manufacturing to the lower end of a tolerance can result in savings of materials. Taguchi states that any deviation from the nominal value of a parameter introduces a loss to society in that the product does not perform up to expectation.

An example of this is a torch bulb which operates at a nominal voltage of 2.4 V. Batteries are manufactured to within a tolerance of ± 0.1 V, i.e. a working range of 2.3 V–2.5 V. Batteries with an output of 2.3 V will produce a dim light from the bulb. On the other extreme, batteries with an output of 2.5 V will overload the bulb and reduce its working life. Hence from a customer's point of view any battery which operates at anything but the nominal 2.4 V introduces a loss factor, either dim light or shortened bulb life. Manufacturers can, on the other hand, make savings by using the tolerance specification.

The loss function for a particular component is evaluated in a quadratic form: loss$=K(y-m)^2$, where K is a constant defined by the cost of replacement etc., m is the nominal parameter value and y is the actual component value. Thus every component which does not have a nominal parameter value has a loss associated with it.

The adoption of the Taguchi loss function philosophy effectively redefines the nature of a tolerance and hence the definition of a product's quality. A high quality product has all its toleranced parameters close to their nominal values. A corollary of this is that a manufacturer who makes a saving by working to a tolerance which is less than the loss incurred to society by the product's usage is worse than a thief. A thief incurs no net loss to society as the cost to the victim is offset by the gain to the thief.

(b) Parametric design

Parametric design philosophies are perhaps the most important aspects of Taguchi methods. The traditional method for dealing with factors which affect a product's performance is by diagnosis and correction. Hence if an operating parameter such as ambient temperature causes reliability problems in a product, the approach has been to specify an operating temperature range and to install expensive air conditioning. The Taguchi method of parametric design approaches the problem from the other direction. If a variable causes a product to fail it is better to reduce the product's dependence on the variable rather than to eliminate the variable.

Taguchi views the design process for a product in three phases: system design, parameter design and tolerance design.

System design is the introduction of new ideas and technologies into the design of new products. Many of these introductions, particularly in the case of the electronics industry, are technology driven. The introduction of new technology only tends to give a short-term advantage as technological advances are readily copied by competitors. Parametric design is the reduction or elimination of external factors which affect a product's performance. The application of parametric design can make a significant saving in the cost of a product. Tolerance design is the improvement of a product's quality by the tightening of the tolerances on its component parts. Although the use of high tolerance parts will improve the overall quality, this use of higher tolerance parts can considerably increase costs. Parametric design can overcome this by reducing the tolerance dependence.

An example of the use of parametric design is an electronic product which has an output dependent on the values of two of its components. The output will have a nominal value and a tolerance within which it must remain. At the design stage nominal values will be given to the two components which dictate the output. The output tolerance will then enforce constraints on the tolerances of these components. This may enforce a very tight tolerance on one of the components which may make it very expensive. A parametric design would examine the relationships between the component values and the resultant output in order to find the optimal component values. These optimal values are those which allow the greatest component tolerances whilst still maintaining the required output tolerance. This allows the use of lower tolerance, and hence lower cost, components.

3.2 THE PRODUCT DESIGN PROCESS

Whenever a new product is to be introduced it is necessary to perform a comprehensive design phase. Although the design of the actual product is important, the design phase has the two additional functions of ensuring that the product is viable and that it can be manufactured to the desired quality.

The product viability aspect needs to assess the product's potential marketplace in terms of whether there is a market for the product and what retail price can be applied. There is no purpose in producing a product which has no market or cannot be manufactured cheaply enough for the market to which it is intended. If a product is found not to be commercially viable it is important to ascertain the fact as soon as possible in order to minimize wasted expenditure.

A product's manufacturing quality aspects establish whether the necessary compromises between functionality, cost, testability etc. can be satisfactorily achieved. It is important to be able to identify and eliminate design and manufacturing faults as soon as possible in order to reduce costs.

Designs are usually a compromise between a number of factors, in particular between cost and performance. The production cost is highly dependent on the number of products to be produced. Complex printed circuit boards are very expensive to produce in small quantities. The bare printed circuit board manufacturers charge high rates for small quantities. On large batches the price can be reduced considerably. Therefore products to be produced in large numbers can have a much higher performance due to the reduced cost constraints.

The design process for a new product can be considered as having four phases; feasibility, prototype, preproduction and production. Each phase ends in a design review which assesses whether the product should proceed into the next phase.

3.2.1 The feasibility stage

A new product's feasibility stage has the function of determining whether or not the product is economically viable. This is the cheapest stage for a non-viable product to be terminated as detailed design and manufacturing resources will not have been utilized. The feasibility stage utilizes the inputs of market survey information and estimated manufacturing costs to determine whether a new product is saleable and at the right price.

The market survey is an important aspect of the feasibility stage as it gives information as to whether a product will sell. The first stage of a market survey is to determine whether the proposed product will be in direct competition with a competitor's product which is already on sale. Given the short lifetimes of electronic products, a product can only compete with an existing product if it can offer an improvement such as improved or more reliable functionality or can be sold at a lower price. An exception to this would be the case of products which have a very high consumer demand and it is possible to capture a share of a large market.

The next stage of a market survey is to determine its marketplace. This would return information as to how many items are likely to sell and the maximum sale price which the market can sustain. The market survey may return requests for changes in the product's specification in order to improve marketability. An estimation of manufacuring costs is required in order to establish a minimum sale price for a product to return a profit. This estimate must make allowances for costs incurred in the product's design, testing and evaluation as well as the parts and labour costs associated with its manufacture.

The feasibility stage feeds information into a new product's design review which makes the decision as to whether or not to allow the product to proceed to the next stage. The factors of marketability, maximum sustainable market price and minimum sale price needed to show a profit are considered along with a prediction of the product's life when making the decision.

3.2.2 The prototype stage

The prototype stage is where the product specification, as approved in the feasibility stage, is used to make a first attempt at a working model. This stage's main function is to determine whether the design specification can actually be realized within the cost constraints imposed by the market.

The first part of the prototype stage is where development engineers interpret the requirements of the design specification into an actual electronic circuit. This design activity is described in more detail in section 3.3. There are several areas where decisions and compromises need to be made at this stage. Given a particular functionality, the important aspects of cost, ease of manufacture and testability can often result in conflicting requirements.

Decisions need to be made as to whether to produce circuit components in gate array form. A gate array is a customized integrated circuit which replaces circuits normally constructed from discrete components. Gate arrays are described in more detail in Chapter 8. The use of gate arrays can considerably reduce manufacturing costs but the higher cost of these devices may make their usage uneconomical for products with smaller production numbers.

The requirements of a product's testability often conflict with the requirements for ease of manufacture. To be fully testable a circuit needs to have a large number of test points and removable links. These features by definition increase the size and complexity of the printed circuit board. In addition, a large number of test points increases the time required to test each board and hence adds to the manufacturing costs. A compromise therefore has to be reached between the comprehensiveness of the testing and the manufacturing costs. This compromise is usually measured as a percentage of faults which can be detected.

The prototype stage is followed by a design review which determines whether the product is ready to go forward into the preproduction stage, the main requirement being that the product can be manufactured at a reasonable cost. Additional factors such as the availability of components also need to be taken into account. If a product falls short of the requirements to go forward into the next stage it may either undergo a further design stage or be abandoned.

3.2.3 The preproduction stage

The preproduction stage, sometimes referred to as the A model stage, is where a prototype product is prepared for production. The requirements for a product to be ready for production are that the documentation and the component parts are all that is required to manufacture the product. The product also needs to be fully testable to within the maximum fault tolerance.

It is essential at this stage that full documentation of the product is available. This prevents a product from becoming unsupportable in the event of the original designers leaving the company. The documentation includes the functional specification of the products, circuit diagrams, parts lists and test specifications.

At the preproduction stage the first proper printed circuit board is produced and a full parts list is generated. Any mechanical constraints, such as the orientation of components for soldering, need to have been incorporated into the printed circuit board design.

A preproduction team has the function of establishing whether a product is ready for production. The team is given all the documentation, a printed circuit board and a set of parts. It then attempts to manufacture the product from the information given and with no external assistance. This activity is usually not possible initially owing to errors in either the product design or the documentation. Any problems encountered are fed back to the product's designers where they can be corrected. The process is repeated until the preproduction team can manufacture the product successfully.

In the cases where the printed circuit board forms part of a larger system, the first attempts at system integration can be made at the preproduction stage. Incompatibilities between subsystems can be identified and fed back to the system's designers for correction.

The preproduction verification of a product needs to run in parallel with the testability verification. The printed circuit board needs to be fully testable to the required standard. Any problems with the testing of a printed circuit board need to be overcome before progressing from this stage. Test activities can be performed on the product's prototype model while waiting for the first preproduction model to be successfully manufactured by the preproduction team.

A design review follows the preproduction stage which examines all the reported problems and reviews the development amendments. The availability of all components needs to be determined at this stage. In the event of a component being unavailable an alternative needs to be found in order to proceed to the next stage. It is important to eliminate all potential design and manufacturing problems and to ensure that the printed circuit board is fully testable to the required standard. The reason for this is that production versions of the printed circuit board need to be available in sufficiently large numbers for the production stage to function. A single printed circuit board can cost several hundred pounds and hence the scrapping of printed circuit boards after this stage can be very expensive.

3.2.4 The production stage

The purpose of the production stage, which is sometimes referred to as the B model stage, is to prove that a product's documentation is capable of supporting its production. This activity is usually performed by a first-time build subdivision of an organization's production facility. The reason for this is that it is inadvisable to run an unproven design through the full production facility as any problems encountered could cause an expensive stoppage in the production of other products. Using the already available printed circuit boards and documentation, the first-time build facility will attempt to manufacture and test the product. This should work first time as any problems should have been eliminated in previous stages. The production stage is the last chance to eliminate any faults in a product before it goes into full production. Fault fixing at customer sites is a very expensive and undesirable activity.

A product undergoes a final review following the production stage. This review must ensure that all known and potential problems have been eliminated. Once the final review has been passed the product goes into full production.

Once a design has been finalized there are still things which can go wrong. One of the commonest problems is that the customer's specification changes. There are also problems associated with the availability of and changes in components. In the worst case a component can become obsolete, which requires that alternatives be found. Another potential source of problems is that of component specification. Often components, particularly integrated circuits, can be obtained in a variety of different packaging styles, for example plastic and ceramic casing. Differences in packaging can cause differences in specification, particularly with respect to working temperatures and humidities. If production uses a plastic encapsulation in place of a ceramic encapsulation the product might not work.

In some cases faults can occur as a result of a combination of effects which cannot be predicted in advance. These can also be caused by communication errors between departments.

3.3 CIRCUIT DESIGN

Circuit design is the process where a design specification for an electronic circuit is realized into a number of electronic components and their interconnection. The design specification will specify a circuit's functionality in terms of inputs, outputs and operational parameters. Inputs can take a large number of forms from the pressing of buttons through to the reception of radio signals. Outputs are the circuit's responses to inputs. Operational characteristics can take the form of speed of operation, power consumption (for example, whether the device is portable and needs to be battery powered) and environmental compatibility. The latter is particularly important if the device is intended to be used in a hostile environment, for example extremes of temperature or in areas subject to electromagnetic interference.

There are three types of circuit design which require different approaches. These are analogue circuit design, digital circuit design and computer-aided circuit design. In general the design of electronic circuits, in particular analogue circuits and the more complex computer circuits, requires a detailed knowledge of electronics. Hence detailed descriptions of the actual circuit design processes are beyond the scope of this book.

3.3.1 Analogue circuit design

Analogue circuit design is the oldest of the design methods and can be the most complex as it uses many discrete components which must be made to match electrically. Analogue circuits can be functionally divided into a series of relatively standard subcircuits. For example, a transistor radio can be divided into a signal receiver, a signal decoder and an audio amplifier.

Many of the subcircuits which form the building blocks for analogue circuits have one or more well-established circuit diagrams associated with them. Each circuit diagram defines the circuit in terms of the individual discrete components required and defines which component values need to be modified in order to achieve the desired operational characteristics. An example of this is an oscillator circuit, of which there are many different but well-defined circuits which achieve this function. Each circuit has an optimal range of operating frequencies and a known accuracy. The actual frequency of operation can be specified by calculating the required values for critical components – usually capacitors. The actual oscillator circuit which is best suited to a particular application can be selected from the desired operational characteristics.

Although many analogue circuits can be assembled from well-defined building blocks, the connections between building blocks are not always straightforward. A good example of this is the electrical characteristic impedance which applies to all connections between electronic devices, including cables. If the impedances of connected circuits do not match, i.e. a high impedance feeds into a low impedance or vice versa, the result is that the signals will be severely attenuated and adversely affect the total circuit's performance. Thus care must be taken during circuit design in order to ensure that the components are compatible.

Modern trends towards fabricating commonly occurring circuits into integrated circuit form are increasing the tendency towards the building block philosophy. This has the added benefit of reducing the number of components which make up a circuit and hence improving reliability and reducing manufacturing costs.

3.3.2 Digital circuit design

Digital circuits are in many respects much easier to design than analogue circuits because the concept of using circuit building blocks is well established. The relatively recent adoption of digital circuits on a large scale has resulted in the use of discrete components being rare. Although digital circuits can be designed using discrete transistors, this is very rarely done owing to the abundance of low price digital integrated circuits.

Digital electronic circuits are based on the principles of Boolean logic. A number of logic gates are defined which have a number of inputs and outputs which can adopt exactly one of the two states of low and high (or one and zero, or off and on). Boolean logic is based on the AND, OR and NOT gates. An AND gate has a high output if all its inputs are high. An OR gate has a high output if any of its inputs is high. A NOT gate's output is the opposite of its input.

Digital integrated circuits are available which contain AND, OR and NOT gates as described in Chapter 2. In practice the commonest gates are the NAND gate, the NOR gate and the NOT gate. A NAND gate (Not AND) has a high output if any of its inputs are low. A NOR gate (Not OR) has a high output if all its inputs are low. The NOT gate is usually referred to as an inverter – the term is more descriptive of its operation.

The design of a digital circuit can often be simply the interconnection of the logic gates required to achieve the functionality. Provided that a single logic family of integrated circuits, e.g. CMOS, is adhered to, the electrical considerations are often reduced to power supply considerations, decoupling and fan out. Decoupling is the use of capacitors to prevent the current surges which can result from logic gates changing state from disrupting the power supply to other devices. Fan out is the maximum number of logic gate inputs which can be directly driven from a logic gate's output without overloading the device. In the case of complex digital circuits such as computer systems the principle is very similar. Much of the functionality of a computer is available in the form of a small number of integrated circuits. The interconnection between these functional units is performed by glue logic. Glue logic is constructed from simple digital integrated circuits such as logic gates. In the case of computer systems a detailed knowledge of digital electronics is required as the relative timing of signals is very critical.

3.3.3 Computer-aided circuit design

Computer-aided design techniques are becoming increasingly popular for the design of circuits. This is particularly true in the case of analogue circuits where considerable time savings can be achieved using computer-aided techniques.

The traditional method of designing circuits is by drawing discrete component symbols, subcircuit symbols and logic gate symbols, along with their interconnections, using pen and paper. This process has been computerized by replacing the pen and paper with a computer screen and a graphical input device such as a mouse.

Computer-aided circuit design systems use component databases which contain the descriptions of components, their circuit symbols and their electrical characteristics. A circuit is designed by selecting components from the database and then specifying a location for the component in the circuit which is built up on the display. Connections between components can be specified by indicating the points to be connected to the system. Once a circuit has been designed, the output from the system can be used to facilitate circuit layout procedures.

Computer-aided circuit design systems offer the added advantage of being able to perform simulations of circuits once they have been designed. These simulations take the form of specifying input signals to the circuit; the system then simulates how the actual electronic circuit would perform. This simulation is performed by using the electrical characteristics of the components, as stored in the component database, to determine how the ideal circuit would operate. This facility allows the basic functionality of a circuit to be checked and hence reduces the costs incurred in correcting a faulty circuit at the prototype stage. This simulation will not be perfect as effects such as stray inductances and capacitances associated with the component interconnections cannot easily be catered for.

The component database and the circuit's components and their interconnections as output by the computer-aided circuit design system can be used as input into a computer-aided circuit layout system. This is described in section 3.5.

3.4 INTEGRATED CIRCUIT DESIGN

The fundamental purpose of an integrated circuit's design process, as is true for the design of many products, is to take a customer's requirements as an input and to produce an output which can be used by manufacturers. From the design and manufacturing points of view, an integrated circuit is a three-dimensional structure consisting of a semiconductor substrate onto which layers of materials are built. These layers, and their geometries, which can be conducting, semiconducting or insulating, need to be specified in the design process. A cross-section of a typical integrated circuit transistor is shown in Figure 3.1. A more detailed description of the layer materials and geometries and the actual integrated circuit manufacturing processes is given in Chapter 4.

The design process for an integrated circuit involves the stages of customer specification, circuit design, functionality simulations, layer geometry generation, verification and mask pattern generation. The relationships between these design stages are shown in Figure 3.2.

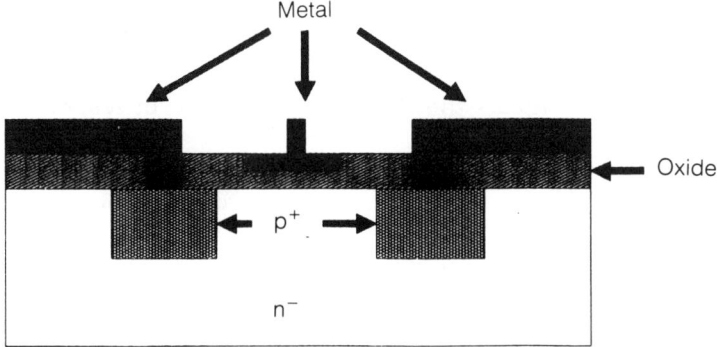

Figure 3.1 A transistor cross-section.

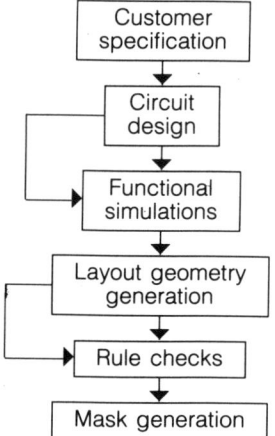

Figure 3.2 The integrated circuit design process.

3.4.1 Customer specification

The first stage of an integrated circuit's design process is the specification stage. This stage is where the customer's requirements are written in the form of a functional specification for the device being designed. The functional specification would typically take the form of input–output specifications, timing specifications and environmental requirements. It is important that the designer collaborates closely with the customer at this stage in order to ensure the desired functionality and to avoid expensive mistakes.

The input–output specifications define the functionality of the device in terms of input signals and the resultant output signals. The input specifications would define the number of different types of input signals which are to be applied to the device. The output specifications define what output signals the device will produce in response to all possible inputs.

The timing specifications define how quickly the device will respond to input signals. Timing specifications may dictate the method of fabrication of the device if high speeds are required.

Environmental requirements may also dictate the fabrication methods and in particular the packaging methods used for the manufacture of the device. Environmental factors include operating voltages, operating temperatures and radiation resistance. The operating voltage may dictate the fabrication method; for example, TTL requires a 5 V power

supply. Operating temperatures which are more extreme may necessitate the use of hermetically sealed ceramic packages. Devices which
are to operate in environments which have high radiation levels such
as satellites may require specialized materials such as the silicon on
sapphire (SOS) substrates.

In addition to the specification of completely new integrated circuits,
a customer specification stage is also required for the customization of
general-purpose devices – application-specific integrated circuits or
ASICs. These devices, which are described in more detail in Chapter 8,
allow a customer to specify the interconnection of standard circuits
which have been fabricated into integrated circuit form.

3.4.2 Circuit design

Following the customer specification stage it is necessary to implement
the specification by means of circuit design. The circuit design process,
which is analogous to the circuit design process described in section
3.3, involves the implementation of the customer's specification in
terms of high level gates. These gates would typically be the AND and
OR gate digital circuits and functional units such as memory cells. This
process can be done manually; however, for today's highly complex
VLSI devices the use of sophisticated computer-aided design systems is
almost essential.

3.4.3 Functionality simulations

In the case where circuits have been designed using a computer-aided
design system, simulations can be performed in order to check that the
circuit functions correctly. These simulations, which are analogous to
the analogue circuit simulations, are essential in the case of complex
devices in order to prevent expensive mistakes. The simulations take
the form of simulating the customer's input specifications and using
the computer to calculate the circuit's output responses. These can
then be checked against the customer's specifications and thus allow
the circuit's functionality to be checked.

Any functionality errors detected by the simulations can then be fed
back to the circuit designer for correction.

3.4.4 Layer geometry layout

Once a circuit has been designed and verified, it is necessary to convert the circuit gate descriptions into geometrical data for the device's manufacture. This layout process is analogous to the conversion of a circuit diagram into a printed circuit board layout. The geometrical data takes the form of a series of masks, one for each of the layers which make up the three-dimensional structure of the device in integrated circuit form, which are used in photolithographic processes during the devices' manufacture.

The manual method of producing layout geometries is to use sheets of transparent film, one sheet per layer, to define the mask patterns. These films are typically in the order of a metre square for the fabrication of devices which are about 5 mm square. The use of such a large magnification pattern allows the designer to produce the details for very small geometries at a more convenient scale. A common practice is to use different colours for defining each layer geometry, the reason for this being that when all the films are superimposed it is possible to discern the full three-dimensional structure of the device.

The layout process involves the placement of the layer geometry for each gate in the circuit design onto an area of the transparent film. Interconnections between gates are provided by metallization layers. The manual layout of devices can be an extremely complex operation.

When computer-aided design systems are used for integrated circuit design, the layer geometries for a range of logic gates, complete with internal connections, are stored in an internal library. These layer patterns can be called up and positioned by the designer as required. Computer-aided design systems are equipped with automatic routeing routines which facilitate the formation of metallization layers which provide the interconnections between gates. The systems can produce a hard copy output of a finished device in the form of a multicoloured chip plot.

Once a layer geometry layout has been produced certain checks are made in order to verify that no electrical or manufacturing rules have been broken. These checks are important as the resultant device may not be manufacturable or may not work otherwise. Another important check is to ensure that the gate layout agrees with the circuit design. Further functionality simulations may be performed at this stage in order to ensure that the device meets its specification.

Once the layout patterns for each layer of the device have been created a tape is produced, containing all the layer geometry information in digitized form. This tape is sent to a mask maker who produces the actual masks for the device's manufacture. Masks are very expensive to manufacture and hence the use of functionality simulations is essential if expensive mistakes are to be avoided. Any changes required to correct a fault require a new set of masks to be made.

3.5 CIRCUIT LAYOUT

The process of circuit layout is the interface between the electronic engineer and the manufacturing engineer. The electronic circuit, as produced in the circuit design stage, needs to be converted into a layout for a printed circuit board to be manufactured from. This process is by no means straightforward as the geometry of a circuit symbol can bear no relationship to the geometry of the physical device. A good example of this is an audio amplifier integrated circuit which has greatly differing physical and symbol geometries as shown in Figure 3.3. The layout specifications produced by the circuit layout process are used to fabricate the actual printed circuit boards. The fabrication processes are described in Chapter 5. The circuit layout process can be performed both manually and using computer-aided

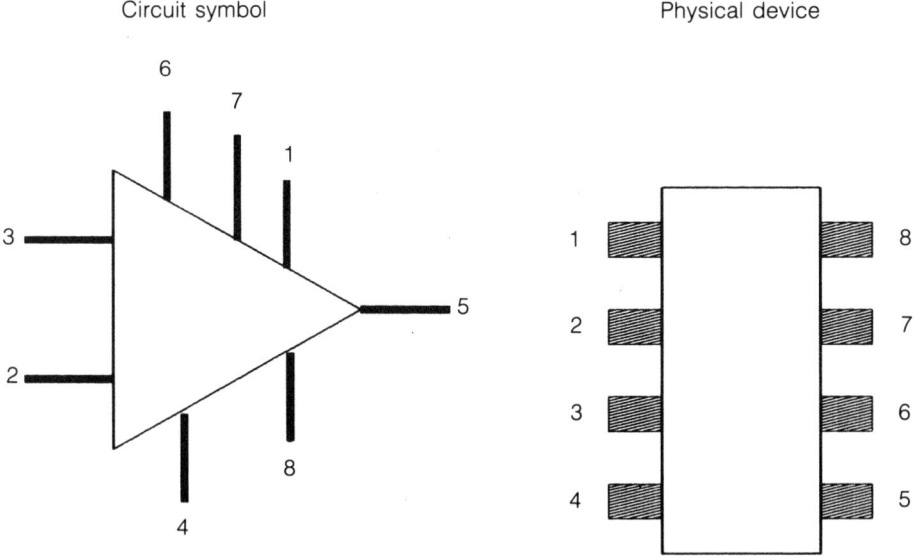

Figure 3.3 TBA820M amplifier pin configurations.

design techniques. The use of computers allows the integration of the circuit layout process with circuit design and with certain manufacturing processes. The layout process has a number of different aspects which include the following: the layout specification; layout constraints; artwork generation methods; and computer-aided design techniques.

3.5.1 Layout specification

The layout specification defines the input and output parameters required to achieve the objectives of circuit layout. The input to the layout process is a circuit diagram and a parts list for the device to be manufactured. The output from the layout process is a series of layout diagrams, usually referred to as artwork, which include a drill template, one or more track layout diagrams, solder resist patterns and a legend.

The drill template defines the locations of any holes which need to be drilled through the printed circuit board. This template will also contain information as to required hole diameters. When computer-aided design systems are used the drill template can be output in the form of a CNC tape which can be fed directly into CNC drilling machines. The actual locations of drill holes are dictated by the track layouts.

The track layout diagrams are the fundamental aspect of the layout process. They define all the interconnections between the devices which make up the circuit to be laid out. Track layouts take the form of photographic positive or negative images for use with the photolithographic processes used for printed circuit board fabrication. The number of track layout diagrams for a single application can be one, two or as many as fifteen, dependent on whether the target printed circuit board is single sided, double sided or multilayer. Where more than one track layout diagram is produced it is necessary to provide methods of registration such that the track layers can be correctly aligned in the manufacturing process.

Track layout actually consists of two processes, component layout and interconnection routeing. The component layout stage involves determining the placement of each physical component of a circuit onto an area of a printed circuit board. The interconnection process then determines the routeing of all interconnections between devices. It may be necessary to iterate between the two processes in order to achieve a satisfactory result.

The solder resist layer defines areas of a printed circuit board where soldering does not take place. A protective layer is applied to these areas in order to prevent solder from adhering and causing problems as described in Chapter 6.

The legend layer contains outlines of component and component identification numbers. This layer is screen printed onto a printed circuit board in order to facilitate the component assembly processes.

3.5.2 Layout constraints

There are a number of constrains which need to be taken into consideration when laying out a circuit diagram. These constraints, which can have either electrical or mechanical origins, must be taken into consideration if the resultant artwork is to lead to manufacturable printed circuit boards which work.

One of the most fundamental layout constraints is that of the geometric scale used to define track layouts. This includes constraints such as minimum track geometries and hole diameters. Track geometries define the widths of individual interconnecting tracks, the spacing between adjacent tracks and track routeing. The high component packing densities required for today's electronic devices demand the use of very fine tracks which are very closely spaced. Track widths and spacings of 0.3 mm are in common usage with a trend towards decreasing them to 0.254 mm. Ideally track spacings need to be reduced to 0.15 mm. From the manufacturing point of view very fine track spacings are highly problematic. Very fine tracks are prone to breakage and short circuiting with adjacent tracks. When selecting the track spacing defined at the layout stage it is necessary to take into account the associated manufacturing costs. The specification of very fine track spacing may prove to be very expensive as a result of a high reject rate during manufacture.

Track routeing is important both from the mechanical aspect of space availability and from electrical constraints. The general rule is that interconnecting tracks should be as short as possible. It is also important to ensure that there are no sharp corners in tracks as these can lead to both mechanical and electrical problems. When it is necessary to route a track through an acute angle it is better to make a series of obtuse angle turns as shown in Figure 3.4.

Hole diameters provide constraints in terms of minimum and maximum sizes. When a hole is to accommodate a component lead, a standard specification is that the hole must have a minimum diameter of the lead diameter plus 0.1 mm. The maximum diameter must be 2.5

Incorrect cornering   Correct cornering

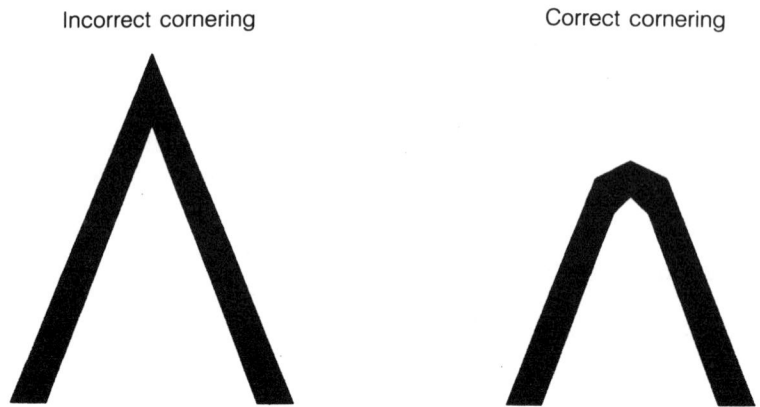

Figure 3.4 Correct and incorrect track cornering.

times the lead diameter. Holes which fall outside this specification cause problems with soldering. In the case of via holes, which connect tracking in double-sided and multilayer printed circuit boards, the holes should be as small as possible for space-saving reasons. However, there is a minimum hole diameter, which is dependent on the board thickness, below which it is not possible to form an electrical connection through the hole.

There are a number of constraints which are introduced to facilitate the manufacture of printed circuit boards. In particular it is standard practice to lay out a board such that all components have a standard orientation. Integrated circuits which have dual-in-line packages are usually placed in the same orientation on the board. Discrete components such as resistors and capacitors are usually placed such that they are oriented either parallel or perpendicular to each other and to integrated circuits. In the case of double-sided printed circuit boards it is standard practice to run the tracks on one side of the board orthogonally to the tracks on the other side. In particular, tracks on the component side often run predominantly orthogonal to the general component orientation. The tracks on the non-component side run predominantly parallel to the general component orientation.

In general, printed circuit board layouts conform to a standard grid spacing for component placing and track routeing. The introduction of non-standard surface mount components has, however, resulted in the previously standard grid spacings of 0.1, 0.5 and 0.025 in becoming inadequate.

3.5.3 Artwork generation methods

Artwork is the term used to describe the track layouts of a printed circuit board. As with many of the design processes artwork can be generated either manually or by computer-aided design methods, the latter being preferable in today's manufacturing environment.

In the early days printed circuit board layout was performed using a technique known as black taped artwork. This consisted of a 2:1 sized transparent film onto which black tape was stuck in order to create the tracks and pads. This system had several major disadvantages including a tendency for the tape strips to fall off, especially after being in storage. Black taped artwork could not easily be used to create double-sided printed circuit boards as they required two separate masks which were very difficult to register and align correctly.

Black taped artwork was superseded by red and blue taped artwork which was used until superseded in the late 1970s by computer-aided design. Red and blue taped artwork worked on the same principle as its predecessor except that it could cater for double-sided PCBs. Red tape was used to define the tracks on one side of a printed circuit board and blue tape was used for the other side. Both red and blue tapes were stuck onto the same piece of film. The two layers could be differentiated during the photolithographic process by using coloured light for the exposures. It was possible to run tracks of 2.5 mm pitch between two pads using taped artwork. All taped artwork is difficult to maintain as the tape has a tendency to drop off during storage and it is difficult to modify.

The manual method of achieving component placement and track routeing often utilized paper cutouts which had the shape of the actual components. These cutouts could be moved around a diagram of the printed circuit board outline until a desirable configuration was achieved. The routeing was performed by drawing lines between the terminal representations of the component paper cutouts.

From the late 1970s computer-aided design (CAD) systems became available for electronic circuit layout: these included systems such as Calma, Maxi, Cadet and Racal Redac Visula.

The Calma system, costing £25 000 in 1974–1976, enabled an engineer to produce digitizable masters of solder side tracks, and component and pad layout. The masters were entered into the system using a digitizer by retrained taped artwork personnel. The system then produced a 2:1 pen plot of the inputted artwork which then replaced the taped masters. A fresh pen plot was made for each design before any reprocessing occurred.

The Maxi system, based on a DEC PDP 11 minicomputer, had facilities for automatic placement and routeing. The system was capable of generating up to 16 layers including solder resist, silk screen marking and a drill template. Maxi cost £70 000 and was capable of producing about 150 designs per year.

In general these systems were totally incompatible with each other. For example, it was found that an operator conversant with the Maxi system could not be retrained to use the Calma system and vice versa.

The Cadet system used a Hewlett–Packard workstation connected to a PDP 11 minicomputer. It was capable of generating two layers. Many of the CAD systems assumed that all designs conformed to a 0.025 in grid system. Most systems made use of monochrome displays which caused much confusion when multilayers were being generated.

After 1985 component technology changed with the introduction of surface-mountable devices. As a result of this components no longer conformed to the 0.025 in grid system. It was possible to overcome this limitation; however, as a result of this some of the facilities such as automatic clearance checking between tracks ceased to function on many computer-aided design systems. Many systems assumed that components were only mounted on one side of the printed circuit board, and this also changed. In particular, the introduction of the very small and non-standard surface-mounted components violated many of the assumed layout standards.

More recent systems such as the Racal Redac Visula, based on the Apollo DN3000 32-bit workstation, incorporate software options which allow the integration of computer-aided design systems for circuit design and circuit layout.

3.5.4 Computer-aided design techniques

The use of computer-aided design systems for the various design processes associated with electronic circuits allows the automation of many time-consuming activities. The benefits obtainable from the use of such systems are component libraries, automatic component placing and routeing and systems integration.

(a) Component libraries

Component libraries are databases which are used to drive the circuit design and circuit layout computer-aided design systems. In fact there are two types of component libraries which can be separated by using the terms component library and parts library. A component library is a database which contains the definitions of all the commonly used electronic components which are used in electronic circuit designs. This library contains the component information required for printed circuit board layout. Each component of a library is identified by means of a part code. This part code can be an index number into the database, a manufacturer's part code for a particular component, or a company-specific part code as used in conjunction with material requirements planning and bills of quantity. Associated with each part code is a description of the physical component. This description would typically start with the overall dimensions of the device, assuming that it is rectangular, and the number of pads, or terminal connections, which the component has. The overall dimensioning information is followed by the positions of each of the component's pads with respect to a reference point such as the lower left-hand corner of the device. In order to complete the definition of each pad a pad code is required which specifies the shape and size of the actual terminal lead. Dimensional information will usually be specified in either absolute dimensions or as multiples of the grid spacing which is used to facilitate printed circuit board layout. In a typical application a separate component library can be used for related component types. For example, a separate library could be used for discrete components, TTL integrated circuits and CMOS integrated circuits. Parts libraries contain the actual specifications of components for use with a circuit design system. Like the component library, each component is identified by means of a part code. Each part code will have a second part code associated with it which identifies the component library and the entry in the component library corresponding to the part. These part codes may be the same. Following the part code, entries are required identifying the individual pins of the device. This will contain information as to pin equivalence and pin designation. Pin equivalence gives information as to which pins have the same function and can be interchanged. An example of this is a multi-input logic gate where it does not matter which of the input pins is used for a particular input signal. The pin designations will indicate the functionality of the pin. Examples of pin designations are inputs, outputs, power input, circuit ground, tristate, unknown or not connected.

An example of a commercially available component library is the Racal Redac Visula Plus which can hold over 6000 part definitions. The library can contain components of all technology types (for example TTL and CMOS). This can also include customized devices and hybrid circuits. The customized device libraries also include the facility for designing ASICs from manufacturer's gate libraries as described in Chapter 8. Library systems such as Visula can be used in conjunction with networked design systems, which allow a single part library to be accessed by all the designers who can access the network.

The graphical symbols used to represent electronic devices have international standards produced by the bodies IEEE, ANSI, IEC and BSI, to which all component library systems should now conform.

(b) Automatic placement and routeing

The automatic component placement and interconnection routeing facilities are very powerful and time-saving tools offered by computer-aided layout systems. These processes are iterative in nature and may be run several times on a particular application in order to achieve the best results. Both manual and automatic placement and routeing methods apply to both printed circuit board layout and integrated circuit layouts. The only difference between the two layout operations from the placement and routeing point of view is that of scale.

The first stage in a layout procedure is to define the size and shape of the target printed circuit board. This may be a standard size such as a eurocard or a specialized shape for a particular application. Following the board specification, it is necessary to define the actual components which are to be placed on the board. This can be done manually or can be taken from the output of a circuit design package. The latter will provide information as to component identities and their inter-connections.

Automatic component placement requires that all fixed tracking areas such as connectors are defined on the board, and that at least one component is assigned a fixed position on the board. The remaining components are designated as unfixed and there must be at least one connection between an unfixed component and a fixed component. The automatic placement routine operates by examining the unfixed components and selecting one that has the most connections to a fixed component. The system will then proceed to position the selected unfixed component as close as possible to the fixed component. This then becomes a fixed component and the procedure is repeated until all the unfixed components have been assigned a position. All fixed components are considered as a group, i.e. a single component, when selecting the unfixed component with the most connections. The automatic placements of components may be restricted to a particular area of a printed circuit board by defining an area for placement before activating the autorouteing procedure.

Automatic routeing converts the interconnection information between components into a physical routeing for a copper track. This procedure can provide interconnections using multiple layers of tracking. The routeing process occurs after components have been assigned a position on the board by either manual or automatic component placement methods. Before any routeing takes place it is necessary to define areas of a printed circuit board through which no tracking must pass. This includes areas such as holes in a board and the position of large components.

The first stage of a routeing operation is to provide the power and ground connections to all components which require them. Power and ground connections also need to be connected to the power supply which will either be on an edge connector or to a power or earth plane in the case of multilayer boards. Automatic routeing systems will need to be provided with information as to any rules for tracking. These can take the form of specifications of the predominant direction for tracking on a particular side of a board. This is done by defining a majority axial direction and then specifying that all tracks must run either parallel or normal to this direction. When a direction is specified tracks are allowed to make small deviations from the dominant direction in order to avoid obstructions such as component pads.

The system achieves a routeing by working from one end of the connection to the other, avoiding any other tracks and obstacles. The routeing may make use of via holes wherever necessary. In general once an automatic routeing has been performed it will be necessary to do some manual editing in order to remove excessively long tracks. In extreme cases it may be necessary to change the component placing and to rerun the routeing procedure.

Modern computer-based autorouteing facilities such as the IBM PC compatible 80386-based Racal Redac CADSTAR 386 autorouter have additional features for catering for particular applications. These include a memory router, automatic corner mitring and a track fattener. The memory router is designed for the efficient interconnection of banks of memory using a regular pattern of 45° corners. The automatic corner mitring facility adds mitres to 90° corners which improves the manufacturability and reliability of the printed circuit board. The track fattening facility allows the routeing to be performed with minimum width tracks which allows a high routeing density to be achieved. Following routeing, the tracks are fattened wherever possible to the normal track width.

Autorouters can be configured to minimize the number of via holes or even to eliminate via holes completely if required.

Computer-aided track routeing is a very time-consuming process which can easily miss methods of simplifying the problem unless they have been catered for in the program. Computer routeing does have a number of advantages over the manual approach in that it will not make connection errors (unless it has been programmed incorrectly). A human can easily make mistakes, especially when making modifications. A good example of this is when two tracks are to be interchanged and when one of them has a T junction connection part way along it. It is all too easy just to change the termination connections of the track and to forget to adjust the junction. The combination of automatic and manual routeing still offers the best results. This is sometimes referred to as human-aided computer design.

(c) Systems integration

Systems integration is the interfacing of computer-aided design and manufacturing systems towards a complete computer-integrated engineering solution. The circuit design and circuit layout computer-aided design packages are effectively integrated as they can use common part libraries. The output from a design system can then provide most of the information required for circuit layout.

Once the circuit layout operation has been performed, the information required for many of the manufacturing processes is available in machine-readable form. The drill template specification from the layout system is now commonly used to generate a tape which can be used to program a CNC drilling machine. This greatly speeds up the interface between a new design and a drilling machine as it is no longer necessary to program a drilling machine manually.

A further level of integration can be achieved by using the component identity and positioning information, which was used to derive the circuit layout, to program an automatic component insertion machine. The use of factory-wide computer networks allows information such as component databases to be available to all departments which require the information. In the case of component databases these would include the purchasing, design, quality assurance, test engineering and manufacturing departments.

4

Semiconductor device manufacture

Semiconductor devices, and in particular integrated circuits, are the basic building blocks of modern electronic circuits.

Integrated circuits, like the circuits which they form a part of, need to be designed, manufactured and tested. In fact there are a number of similarities between the design and manufacture of integrated circuits and the design and manufacture of printed circuit boards.

This chapter is concerned with the materials and processes required to turn the mask information generated in an integrated circuit's design stage, as described in Chapter 3, into a physical device. The important aspects of integrated circuit manufacture are the semiconductor materials used for device fabrication, clean room requirements, semiconductor wafer fabrication, integrated circuit manufacturing processes and the packaging and testing of devices.

In simple terms, an integrated circuit consists of a flat semiconductor substrate onto which a number of layers of material have been added. Each layer consists of insulator, semiconductor or conductor materials, which can form part of, the isolation of or the interconnection between the constituent units of the device. The fabrication of integrated circuits involves a number of different processes for the formation of the material layers which constitute the device. There are a number of different processes, each of which can be used in the fabrication of one or more different layer types. The actual processes used, and their sequence of application, are dependent on the technological type of device to be fabricated. Therefore the discussion of the integrated circuit manufacturing processes will consist of discussions of the major processes used followed by typical examples of processing sequences. Two processing sequences will be used as examples: the fabrication of bipolar junction transistors and the fabrication of metal oxide semiconductor field effect transistors, in integrated circuit form.

4.1 SEMICONDUCTOR MATERIALS

Although most electronic semiconductor devices are manufactured from silicon, there are many other semiconductor materials which can be used to fabricate semiconductor devices. The main reasons why silicon is the most commonly used are that silicon is very abundant and that it is very easy to work with. Other semiconductor materials are in use for more specialized devices. In order to obtain an insight into what constitutes a semiconductor material it is necessary to enter into a brief discussion of atomic structure. In simple terms an atom consists of a positively charged nucleus which is surrounded by a number of negatively charged electrons. The laws of quantum mechanics dictate that each electron must have one of a number of discrete amounts of energy and that the electrons are organized into shells around the atomic nucleus. The number of electrons which can exist in a shell follow the sequence 2, 8, . . ., $2n^2$. Each shell n is made up of n sub-shells which contains numbers of electrons which follow the sequence 2, 6, . . ., $2(2n-1)$. The sequence in which these shells and sub-shells are filled is complex and beyond the scope of this book. The outermost shell has between one and eight electrons; the actual number dictates the element's chemical properties, and corresponds to the column position of the element in the periodic table. The elements which lie between columns two and three of the periodic table warrant a bit more explanation. These elements are called transition elements where sub-shells of inner shells are being filled. These elements can behave as if they have different numbers of outer shell electrons (i.e. iron can behave chemically as if it has two or three outer electrons). When atoms combine to form a solid, and in particular a crystal, some of or all the outermost electrons are used to bind the atoms together. These electrons are referred to as valence band electrons. Any surplus electrons are referred to as conduction band electrons. It is the conduction band electrons which carry electric currents through the material. It is possible for valence band electrons to jump into the conduction band if supplied with enough energy. This energy can be supplied in the form of heat or by applying a sufficiently large voltage across the material. In general, elements of groups I, II and III, with one, two and three outer shell electrons respectively, are metallic and are conductors of electricity. Elements of groups V, VI and VII, with five, six and seven outer shell electrons respectively, are non-metals and are insulators. Group VIII elements are inert gases. Group IV elements, with four outer shell electrons, including the elements carbon, silicon, germanium, tin and lead, are on the boundary between being conductors and insulators. A crystal of carbon, a diamond, is a good insulator; tin and lead are metallic. Silicon and germanium are intermediate between being conductors and insulators; they are semiconductors. In fact silicon and germanium are referred to as intrinsic semiconductors.

Although silicon and germanium are the only elemental intrinsic semiconductors, other intrinsic semiconductors can be obtained from a one-to-one combination of a group III element with a group V element, or a one-to-one combination of a group II element with a group VI element. Examples of group III and V intrinsic semiconductors are gallium arsenide (GaAs) and gallium antimonide (GaSb). Examples of the group II and VI intrinsic semiconductors are zinc sulphide (ZnS) and cadmium sulphide (CdS).

Intrinsic semiconductors are actually rarely used in the fabrication of electronic devices. However, the addition of small quantities of impurities, usually group III and V elements, into an intrinsic semiconductor's crystal structure produces doped semiconductors which are more conductive than intrinsic semiconductors and form the basis of most semiconductor electronic devices. There are two varieties of doped semiconductors which are referred to as n-type and p-type semiconductors.

The addition of a group V element, for example arsenic, to an intrinsic semiconductor crystal makes it electron rich, increases its conductivity and produces an n-type semiconductor. This is sometimes referred to as donor doping as the impurity donates electrons. The addition of a group III element, for example gallium, to an intrinsic semiconductor crystal makes it electron deficient, increases its conductivity and produces a p-type semiconductor. This is sometimes referred to as acceptor doping, as the crystal structure has holes where there are electrons missing, making it readily accept electrons.

A crystal consisting of an n-type semiconductor in contact with a p-type semiconductor material produces what is known as a p–n junction which only conducts electricity in one direction – a rectifier or diode junction.

The group III and V semiconductor material gallium arsenide is more difficult to dope than elemental semiconductors. Typically gallium arsenide is doped p type with the group II element zinc, and n type with the group VI element sulphur.

Some of the more common semiconductor materials and their usages are as follows:

germanium	diodes, transistors
silicon	diodes, transistors, integrated circuits

gallium arsenide   fast diodes and transistors, LEDs, lasers, micro-
                    wave generators
cadmium sulphide   electroluminescent materials, photo-electric cells
lead sulphide   infrared radiation detectors

4.2 CLEAN ROOM REQUIREMENTS

The trend towards ever-increasing component densities in electronic
devices has resulted in more and more devices, i.e. transistors, being
fabricated on the same-sized semiconductor die. A consequence of this
has been that the physical geometries of the component devices of
integrated circuits have become progressively smaller. Table 4.1 shows
the rate at which component dimensions have decreased from 1976
until 1989.

Table 4.1 IC component
dimension reduction

Year	Dimensions (μm)
1976	8
1981	5
1985	3
1987	1.5
1989	1

The very small geometries used for the manufacture of integrated
circuits have introduced the problem that particle contamination can
cause significant problems. It can be seen from Table 4.2, which shows
the dimensions of commonly occurring contamination particles, that
smoke particles and even bacteria are of a similar size to that of an
integrated circuit's component transistors. Thus a single contaminant
particle can result in components being incorrectly manufactured and
hence measures need to be taken in order to reduce the number of
such contamination sources.

Semiconductor manufacturers utilize a specially controlled environment called a clean room which reduces the number of contamination
particles to a suitable level for the semiconductor geometries to be
fabricated. There are two major sources of contamination, atmospheric
particles and particles carried physically by human operators or by
equipment.

The first line of defence against atmospheric particles is an air-

Table 4.2 Commonly occurring particle sizes

Particle type	Particle size (μm)
Wear particles	50–500
Fine sand	20–200
Human hair	30–100
Plant spores and pollen	10–100
Coal and cement dust	1–100
Bacteria	0.3–30
Ground talc	0.5–300
Red blood cells	7.5
Clay	<2
Oil and tobacco smoke	0.01–1
Carbon black	0.1–0.3
Combustion nuclei	0.01–0.1
Viruses	0.003–0.05

conditioning system. All air entering the clean room environment needs to be temperature and humidity controlled. Air-borne particles are removed by passing all incoming air through high efficiency particulate air (HEPA) filters. A HEPA filter must be 99.97% efficient at removing particles which are over 0.3 μm in size. In addition, the air supply may need to be passed through charcoal filters to remove any chemical contamination which may adversely affect the manufacturing processes. In order to ensure that all the air which enters a clean room has passed through the filtering stages, a clean room is pressurized by at least 25 Pa relative to the local air pressure. This pressurization ensures that any air leakage is in an outwards direction and hence prevents the introduction of any external air-borne contamination.

The biggest source of particle contamination which adversely affects a clean room's environment comes from people. People are intrinsically dirty from the particle generation point of view as they constantly shed particles from their skin, clothing and breathing. Although eating, drinking and particularly smoking are strictly prohibited in all clean rooms, a smoker will exhale tobacco smoke particles for up to an hour after smoking a cigarette.

In order to protect a clean room environment from its workforce, people are required to dress in specialized clothing. This clothing can in its simplest form consist of gowns, gloves and hair covers. Where the particle sizes must be kept very low, personnel may be required to wear bunny suits which completely cover the body. These come complete with goggles and surgical masks. In extreme cases personnel will be completely isolated from the clean room environment and have an external air supply so that they do not breathe the clean room's air.

On entering a clean room, personnel have to pass through an air lock type of system which separates the clean room's atmosphere from the external atmosphere. Personnel have to pass through air showers which direct jets of air to blow particles off the person's body and clothing. The floor is equipped with adhesive mats which remove dust particles from shoes.

When designing a clean room it is important to consider the air flow of the room. Turbulent air flow around furniture and people can result in local concentrations of particles which can be considerably higher than the permitted maximum. All particle-generating materials such as wood and paper products are strictly banned from clean room environments. Cosmetics in the form of makeup may also need to be controlled, or even completely banned. This can cause potential industrial relations problems with the workforce.

The cleanliness of a clean room is described by a standardized classification number which is usually a power of ten, for example a class 100 clean room. The classification number gives an upper limit on the number of particles which are 0.5 μm in size or greater per cubic foot (or 3.5 l) of air. Normal atmospheric air contains in excess of 100 000 particles per cubic foot. A class 1000 clean room must consistently maintain a particle count (of over 0.5 μm) less than 1000 per cubic foot. Class 1000 or class 100 clean room environments are generally adequate for the general clean room atmosphere; however, they are not adequate for the localized areas where the actual devices are manufactured. Modern VLSI circuits require a clean room environment of class 10 or better. A class 10 clean room requires that the air be changed 610 times per hour and filtered to submicron levels.

In order to achieve very low particle counts in the localities where device manufacturing processes are carried out, a work surface will be equipped with a laminar flow hood. This device acts as a secondary particle removal system which provides a continuous flow of non-turbulent and ultraclean air. The hood draws air from the clean room environment and passes it through a HEPA filtering stage. Once filtered, the air is forced through baffles which induce laminar air flow. The result of this is an ultraclean air flow from the hood which passes over the work surface before rejoining the rest of the clean room's atmosphere. This has the effect of isolating the work surface from the dirtier room air.

Another important requirement in addition to the clean room air is that the processing chemicals are themselves very pure and particle free. Clean room practices are increasingly dictating that processing chemicals need to be filtered before use.

In addition to particulate control it is also necessary to control carefully the temperature and humidity of a clean room environment. Typical values would be $21\pm0.5\,°C$ for temperature and $40\%\pm2\%$ relative humidity.

4.3 SILICON WAFER MANUFACTURE

The first manufacturing process associated with semiconductor devices in integrated circuit form is the fabrication of the semiconductor substrate material. This substrate consists of a single crystal of a semiconductor material and is also known as a wafer owing to its shape. The commonest variety of wafer is made from silicon. This either can be in its intrinsic form or may be doped p-type or n-type. There are other forms of wafer substrates which include the silicon on insulator substrates as typified by the silicon on sapphire substrates used for the fabrication of high performance devices.

The raw materials required for the initial stages in the manufacture of a silicon substrate are quartzite and carbon. Quartzite, which is a form of silicon dioxide (SiO_2), is commonly available in the form of sand. Carbon is usually obtained in the form of coal or coke. The raw materials are combined in an electric arc furnace where they are melted and various chemical reactions take place to produce liquid silicon which sinks to the bottom, and various gaseous waste products. The liquid silicon is drawn off and allowed to solidify into metallurgical grade silicon which is about 98% pure. This metallurgical silicon is not sufficiently pure for electronic purposes so further purification stages are required.

The metallurgical silicon is pulverized and reacted with hydrogen chloride in a fluid bed at a temperature of about 300 °C. Chemical reactions take place to produce a liquid silicon chloride and various impurities which themselves are mainly chlorides. This mixture is then fractionally distilled to produce pure silicon chloride. A vapour deposition process involving hydrogen is used to reduce the silicon chloride to electronic grade silicon in polycrystalline form. This is as near as possible to 100% pure silicon according to traditional chemical assay techniques.

In order to produce a substrate it is necessary to form single silicon crystals from the polycrystalline electronic grade silicon. This is achieved using the Czochralski method of crystal growth. The electronic grade silicon is melted in a quartz crucible where a single crystal of silicon is 'pulled' from the melt. This is achieved by placing a seed crystal, which is attached to a rod called a puller, in contact with the melt. The melt material then starts to solidify onto the seed crystal forming a larger crystal. The seed crystal is slowly pulled away from the molten silicon and rotated continuously. The result of this is that a large single crystal emerges from the molten silicon. This single crystal is called a boule and is up to 15 cm in diameter and over 1 m long. For certain applications the substrate needs to be doped to either p-type or n-type silicon. In these cases dopant material is added to the electronic grade silicon in the crucible before the boule is produced. In the cases where the silicon is doped it is important to control the dopant impurity concentrations carefully in order to reduce changes in dopant levels along the length of a boule. During the crystal growth stage it is important to minimize the amount of contamination in the silicon. The crucible itself, being quartz, tends to add small amounts of oxygen to the molten silicon. The crystal growth is often performed in a vacuum or an inert gas atmosphere, such as argon, in order to prevent further contamination from atmospheric gases such as oxygen.

Once produced, a silicon boule needs to be tested for crystal defects and for its electrical characteristics. Any parts of the boule which are found to be defective are removed. The remainder of the boule is turned into a cylinder on a lathe and indexing flats are ground into the cylinder for handling purposes. These flats also identify the orientation of the crystal lattice. The cylinders are sawed into wafers using a diamond saw. The wafers are etched to remove the surface layer and any crystal defects introduced by the sawing process. The final stage is to polish the wafers to a mirror finish and place them in packaging ready for delivery to device fabrication facilities.

Silicon wafers are typically manufactured by a small number of specialist companies. Companies which manufacture the silicon devices themselves usually purchase the blank wafers from the specialist companies and do not have their own wafer fabrication facilities. A typical silicon wafer may cost in the order of £30.

Wafer materials other than silicon require different manufacturing processes. High performance applications demand high substrate resistivities, and for very critical applications insulating substrates are preferred. This is particularly the case when semiconductor devices are subject to ionizing radiation such as cosmic rays in the case of satellite systems. Radiation can change the crystal structure of a substrate which can result in device failure. The use of an insulating substrate reduces this effect. An example of an insulating substrate is sapphire, which is a crystalline form of aluminium oxide (Al_2O_3). When an insulating substrate is used, a layer of silicon is formed on the substrate's surface using an epitaxial growth process. The effectiveness of this process is dependent on how closely the crystal structures of the insulating material and silicon match. The sapphire crystal structure does not match that of silicon very well, which leads to the silicon layer being highly stressed.

4.4 PHOTOLITHOGRAPHY

A modern integrated circuit contains millions of individual elements, typically a few microns across. No physical tool is adequate for fabrication on these small scales. In order to achieve the fine patterning required for microelectronic circuits it is necessary to utilize optical techniques in a process akin to photography. The geometries used for integrated circuit manufacture preclude the use of visible light as the component geometries are of a similar size to the visible light wavelengths. In order to achieve good imaging it is necessary to use radiation which has a wavelength at least an order of magnitude smaller than the items to be imaged. This can be achieved by using electromagnetic radiation in the form of ultraviolet light or X-rays. Electron beams are used to achieve higher resolutions for the smaller geometries.

Photolithography is the process of projecting an image onto a base material which has been coated with a photosensitive material in order to define the required patterns. This image is then developed to leave selected areas of the base material masked by the photosensitive material. This allows selective processing of the base material's surface.

The photolithographic process depends on the use of a photosensitive film which is called a photoresist, sometimes abbreviated to resist. The basic principle is that the resist, when exposed to a suitable radiation, becomes either more or less soluble to an etchant solution. Resist materials which become more soluble on exposure to radiation are referred to as positive resists. Negative resists are materials which become less soluble on exposure to radiation. The more soluble areas of the resist material can then be washed away, leaving selected areas of the underlying base material exposed. The remaining resist material must be able to protect the underlying base material from the process which is applied to the exposed areas.

In photolithographic processes used for the manufacture of integrated circuits, a film of photoresist is applied to the semiconductor substrate. Radiation is projected through a mask, as defined by a design process, which defines the shape of the desired pattern. The areas exposed to radiation are changed in solubility, whereas the areas in the mask's shadow are unaffected. This process parallels conventional photography, and is called exposure even if it uses electrons instead of light.

Following the exposure process, the substrate is washed with a solvent which preferentially removes the higher solubility resist. These areas are either the exposed or unexposed regions, depending on the actual type of resist used.

After development the substrate is exposed to an etchant which removes the portions of the substrate which are not covered by a layer of resist. The final process in each layer's photolithography is the removal of the remaining resist layer.

The principal components of photolithographic processes are mask manufacture, photoresist materials, exposure methods and etching processes. The etching process which removes the more soluble form of a photoresist material after exposure should not be confused with any etching processes which are applied to the base material. Etching processes are described in section 4.5.

4.4.1 Mask manufacture

Before a pattern can be lithographed onto a silicon substrate it is first of all necessary to produce the mask through which exposure occurs. The mask is in fact itself produced by a photolithography process. In this case the pattern is derived from design data in the form of an optical image or digital output from a computer-aided design system.

In the early days of microelectronics the mask pattern was cut, by hand, from a large coloured plastic sheet. This was photoreduced by a large camera system to produce a mask of the desired size.

In recent years the process has been automated by using a pattern generator. This device takes the design information in the form of a design tape which has been output from a computer-aided design system. The design is then analysed down into a series of picture elements of pixels. The master mask plate, from which the actual working chip masks will be produced, is scanned by the pattern generator. This uses a beam of light controlled by the pixel information to selectively expose the plate. In recent years the light beam has been increasingly replaced by an electron beam, which is capable of much finer resolutions.

The pattern generation process is a complex and time-consuming operation and hence the number of masks generated in this fashion should be kept to a minimum. The wafer masks required for the manufacture of a particular integrated circuit will typically require many copies of the same mask. The reason for this is that it is standard practice to fabricate several hundred identical devices from each wafer. It would be very time consuming and costly to repeat the mask-making operation several tens of hundreds of times to make a complete wafer mask. It is common practice to use pattern generation for a single device and then to reproduce the pattern repeatedly to form the two-dimensional array of devices for the complete wafer. A step-and-repeat camera is used to perform this operation. This produces a plate mask which contains the full array of individual chip masks.

4.4.2 Photoresist

The photoresists used in the manufacture of integrated circuits can be either negative resist, which remains on the exposed areas after etching, or positive resist, which remains on the unexposed areas after etching. An ideal photoresist material will have the following properties: it should undergo a large change in solubility on exposure to radiation; the boundaries between exposed and unexposed areas should form vertical walls after etching; the less soluble form of the resist should be readily removable after processing.

Negative resists can be made of a number of different materials; however, one of the first to gain widespread use was polyisoprene in the form of cyclized rubber. This substance becomes highly insoluble on exposure to ultraviolet light. Cyclized rubber resists are in many ways ideal photoresist materials as the change in solubility resulting from exposure is so large that the exposed areas are almost totally unaffected by the solvent. Negative resists have a crucial weakness in that they produce poor resolution for fine lines (resist walls are far from vertical) and have a practical resolution limit of 2–3 μm.

Positive resists are typically made from materials called diazo oxides which on exposure to ultraviolet light can be removed with a weak sodium hydroxide solution. Positive resists can produce good resolutions but the etching process needs to be carefully monitored as the etchant also slowly removes the unexposed resist areas.

4.4.3 Image exposure

There are three methods which are commonly used to exposure photoresist layers to radiation through the desired mask pattern. These are direct through mask, enlarged mask image and direct write. The radiation used to make the exposure can be light, usually ultraviolet, or electron beams. The image resolution possible with a particular form of radiation is dependent on the wavelengths used. Electron beams are used because electrons can behave like a very short wave radiation. Ultraviolet light has a wavelength in the order of 10^{-7} m whereas an electron beam can have a wavelength in the order of 10^{-12} m and is capable of achieving very fine resolutions.

The direct through mask method uses a chip mask or plate mask, which is the same size as the devices to be fabricated, through which exposure is made. The step-and-repeat operation, used to make a plate mask from a single chip mask, can also be used to expose a complete wafer from a single mask.

The enlarged mask image method utilizes a mask which is ten times the actual required size. The image is optically reduced by a factor of ten when projected onto the wafer.

The direct write method, which is the subject of investigation at present, bypasses the requirement of a mask. A design tape, as output from a computer-aided design system, is used to control the positioning of a light or electron beam directly onto the photoresist material. This eliminates the need to manufacture masks. The process, which is akin to the pattern generation process used to produce mask masters, has the disadvantage of being very time consuming. The major advantage of the method is that it eliminates any error sources associated with masks.

Before any resist exposure takes place it is important to ensure that the image will be correctly aligned with the existing features on a substrate. In the case of simple devices the actual device structure can be used to determine alignment. However, for more complex devices the actual geometry may not give much assistance, in which case special features are built into masks called alignment marks. These can take of a number of forms, for example a square inside a box.

4.5 LAYER FABRICATION PROCESSES

In simple terms an integrated circuit is manufactured by starting with a silicon substrate or wafer and building a number of layers, one at a time, onto the substrate. Each layer is built up in a three-stage process which involves a photolithographic process, a layer fabrication process and the removal of remaining resist material.

The photolithographic process can be a several-stage process in that a photoresist material may be used selectively to lay down or remove material which is to be used as a mask for another process. The layer fabrication process can be either additive or subtractive in that material may need to be added or removed or both. The major processes used for the fabrication of layers are oxidation, dopant diffusion, vapour deposition and etching.

4.5.1 Oxidation

The process of dopant diffusion, which will be discussed in the next section, is most effective when it is selective. This requires the use of a masking layer which blocks the diffusion process selectively from the substrate. Ideally the masking layer should adhere firmly to the substrate material without any cracks or holes. The substrate material should ideally be unaffected by the etchant used for the removal of the mask layer so that any over-etching does not affect the substrate.

Silicon dioxide has all of these properties, which is one of the reasons why many devices are fabricated from silicon. Silicon dioxide is also a very good insulator, which enables its use as an integral part of the electronic components which are fabricated on a substrate.

When heated in the presence of an oxidant such as oxygen or steam, silicon readily forms a uniform oxide layer. This process makes the creation of an oxide masking layer fairly straightforward.

The silicon oxidization process is performed in a furnace where the silicon substrate is exposed to an oxidizing agent. Silicon oxidizes much more readily in steam than in pure oxygen. Hence steam is used for forming thicker oxide layers. Steam can be produced by using boiling water; however, this method can lead to condensation, which can be problematic. Another method of generating steam is to use a hydrogen injection process. Hydrogen gas is burnt in oxygen to produce pure water vapour. Care must be taken in order to prevent explosive concentrations of hydrogen from accumulating.

4.5.2 Dopant diffusion

Dopant diffusion is the process used to create regions of p-type or n-type semiconductor on a substrate. The principle involved is to apply a dopant source to the substrate and to heat it in a furnace to allow the dopant material to diffuse into the substrate. The dopant source compound usually consists of an oxide of the dopant element. The most direct application method is to form a slurry of the oxide and to spray or spin coat the slurry onto the substrate's surface. Other methods include the evaporation of a powdered oxide, causing it to coat the substrate, and the formation of the oxide by chemical reaction in a furnace which then coats the substrate.

The substrate when coated with a dopant source is heated in a furnace which allows the dopant atoms to replace some of the silicon atoms in the substrate. The diffusion of dopant materials into silicon requires that the dopant atoms replace silicon atoms in the crystal structure. Hence a dopant atom cannot enter the crystal lattice until a silicon atom has been displaced. This displacement occurs as a result of the thermal energy in the crystal and is a relatively slow process. Boron is commonly used for n-type doping, p-type doping usually uses arsenic or antimony.

There is another form of diffusion process where dopant atoms occupy the spaces between silicon atoms in the crystal lattice. This diffusion usually occurs between metals and silicon and is much faster than dopant diffusion as no silicon atoms need to be displaced.

4.5.3 Vapour deposition

Vapour deposition is a process which can be used for the addition of layers such as silicon nitride and metallization which provides electrical contacts to a device. There are two principle vapour deposition methods in common usage, vacuum deposition and chemical vapour deposition (CVD).

(a) Vacuum deposition

The principle of vacuum deposition is that when a substance is melted in a vacuum it will immediately boil and deposit a layer of the substance on everything which is in range of the source. This works well for elemental metals such as aluminium. However, it does not work for alloys as the component metals will have different vapour pressures and tend to separate out. The resultant film which is deposited will be richer in the metal with the lower melting point. This effect can be overcome by enriching the melt with the higher melting point metal. This enrichment compensates for the lower vapour pressure and leaves a coating of the required mixture.

In vacuum deposition processes the vapours propagate out in a straight line from the source of material. This produces problems in coating the vertical portion of a step in a substrate. The step will be parallel to the vapour movement and hence will not be covered. This effect can be compensated for by causing the vapour to rotate, forming a conical, as opposed to parallel, jet of vapour. A similar effect can be obtained by rotating the substrate to be coated such that it meets the vapour at a range of incident angles.

One important factor to be taken into account in vapour deposition processes is the elimination of impurities. The standard method of melting materials is to use a directly heated crucible. The trouble with this method is that crucible materials can dissolve in the molten material and thus form impurities. This effect can be eliminated by using electron beam heating. This process directs a beam of electrons into the centre of a crucible, thus only melting the central area so that the crucible does not come into contact with the molten material. The electron beam needs to be generated away from the open end of the crucible so that the beam generation equipment is coated by vapour deposition. This seemingly contradictory requirement is achieved by generating the electron beam out of range of the vapour and directing it at the crucible by magnetic fields.

(b) Chemical vapour deposition

Chemical vapour deposition is a process which is used for depositing thin films of mainly non-metallic materials onto the surface of a substrate. The process operates by supplying reactive gases, often by means of a carrier gas which does not become involved in the chemical reaction, to a substrate's surface under conditions which encourage chemical reactions to take place. Ideally the chemical reactions only take place on the substrate's surface and nowhere else. In the case of integrated circuit fabrication, chemical vapour deposition is commonly used to form layers of silicon dioxide, silicon nitride and additional silicon.

The chemical vapour deposition process requires one or more gases to react on a substrate's surface to form a thin surface film of uniform thickness and composition. The reactive molecules must first reach the surface of the substrate by means of diffusion. The reactants must then be absorbed by the substrate's surface and the desired chemical reactions take place. Any reaction by-products must leave the substrate's surface and diffuse away through the gas. There are numerous methods by which CVD can be achieved; most of them cause hot gases to pass over the substrates to be processed at a carefully controlled pressure and flow rate. Some of the common materials which are deposited by chemical vapour deposition and their associated processes are as follows.

Silicon dioxide, as described in section 4.5.1, is an important material in semiconductor fabrication. The direct oxidation method is the most effective way of producing a silicon dioxide layer if the substrate's surface is silicon. In cases where a silicon dioxide layer needs to be grown over materials other than silicon, such as a metal or silicon nitride, it is necessary to use another technique, such as chemical vapour deposition. The chemical vapour deposition of silicon dioxide is performed by reacting a silicon-containing compound and an oxidant in vapour form on the substrate's surface. Silicon-containing compounds in use include silicon chlorides ($SiCl_4$ and SiH_2Cl_2), silicon bromide ($SiBr_4$) and tetraethoxysilane ($Si(OC_2H_5)_4$). Oxidants include oxygen (O_2), nitrogen oxides (NO and N_2O) and carbon dioxide with hydrogen. A more common process involves the reaction of silane and oxygen:

$$SiH_4 + O_2 \rightarrow SiO_2 + 2H_2$$

Silicon nitride (Si_3N_4) is another important layer material as it is often used as a mask for the direct oxidation of silicon. Silicon nitride is difficult to form by the direct nitridation of silicon. Hence a chemical vapour deposition process is used. The reaction is usually achieved by reacting a silicon-containing substance, as for the production of silicon dioxide, and ammonia. A commonly used reaction is that between silane and ammonia:

$$3SiH_4 + 4NH_3 \rightarrow Si_3N_4 + 12H_2$$

Polycrystalline silicon, when doped to a low resistivity, is commonly used as a conductor. It can also be used to fabricate on-chip resistors. The vapour deposition process for depositing polycrystalline silicon involves the direct reduction of silane by heat:

$$SiH_4 \rightarrow Si + 2H_2$$

A variation on the theme of chemical vapour deposition is that of vapour phase epitaxy. The main difference between the processes is that epaxial growth adds material which extends the substrate's crystal structure rather than just depositing a surface layer. The commonest material which is added by epitaxial growth is silicon. As the crystal structure of the substrate is to be extended it is important that the deposition process be very carefully controlled. This is achieved by using high temperatures and by slowing the reactions down by diluting the reagent gases with hydrogen. It is essential that the substrate's surface be very clean before epitaxial growth in order to reduce the number of crystal defects in the deposited layer. Common methods include the thermal reduction of silane as for the chemical vapour deposition of polycrystalline silicon.

Many vapour deposition processes have potentially serious safety implications. Many of the substances used, such as silane and many chlorine-containing substances, are highly toxic. Gases such as hydrogen and silane are highly flammable and can easily build up to explosive concentrations. Ammonia and chlorine-containing compounds are also highly corrosive. Silane is a particularly unpleasant substance as, in addition to being toxic and flammable, it spontaneously combusts in the presence of oxygen. It is therefore important to ensure that the equipment used for vapour deposition does not have any gas leaks and that it is equipped with suitable extraction and disposal systems.

4.5.4 Etching

Etching processes are concerned with the removal of material from the surface of a substrate. The etching is usually performed selectively – the areas which are not to be etched are covered by a masking material. The masking material can be either a photoresist material after exposure and the removal of the more soluble material, or a layer such as silicon oxide. Some of the substances which need to be removed by the etching process are as follows: semiconductor materials such as silicon; insulating materials such as silicon oxide or nitride, aluminium metal; and the final removal of photoresist after the substrate has been processed. There are two types of etching methods in common use, namely wet etching and plasma etching.

Wet etching is a chemical process which is commonly performed using acids. One of the biggest problems associated with chemical etching is that of controlling the reaction such that the correct amount of material is removed. Under-etching results in insufficient material being removed. Over-etching is where the etchant undercuts the resist

Under-etched

Ideally etched

Over-etched

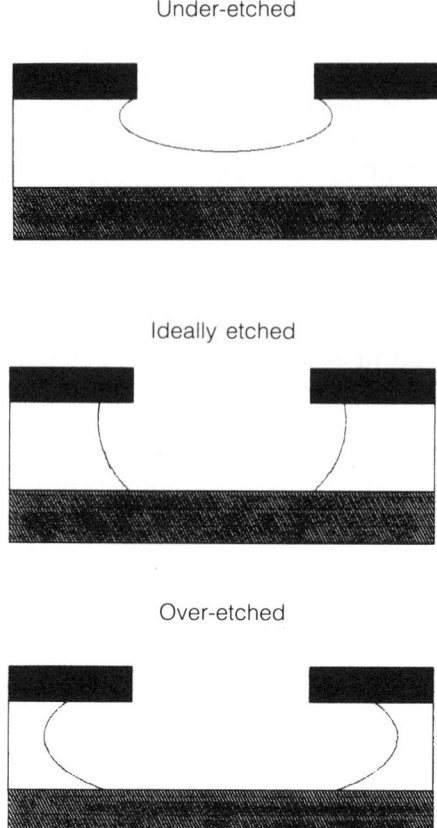

Figure 4.1 Etching profiles.

layer, removing too much material. Figure 4.1 shows the substrate profiles associated with under-etching, correct etching, and over-etching. In order to achieve the desired results it is necessary to control the process carefully. This involves monitoring the etchant solution strengths and the etching times. The use of liquid etchants can introduce random factors such as the presence of bubbles, which can cause areas to be unaffected by the etchant, and irregular flow patterns which result in non-uniform etching. Plasma etching involves the application of an ionized gas. The high energy gas molecules react with the surface of the substrate, removing material by evaporation. Plasma etchant materials are usually fluorine- or chlorine-containing compounds.

The etching process for the removal of silicon dioxide is performed chemically using a solution of hydrofluoric acid. Hydrofluoric acid does not react with silicon but readily reacts with the oxide layer. It is also easy to determine when the etching process is complete by observing the wetting properties of silicon and its oxide. Silicon is hydrophobic and repels water; silicon dioxide is hydrophilic and attracts water. A completely etched substrate when dipped in water will instantly shed the water on removal. It is important to note that hydrofluoric acid is a particularly unpleasant substance in that unlike other acids it does not cause painful acid burns. Instead it penetrates the body and causes severe tissue and bone damage without pain. Therefore extreme caution must always be exercised when handling hydrofluoric acid.

Silicon is etched using a mixture of nitric acid and hydrofluoric acid. The nitric acid oxidizes the silicon to silicon dioxide which is then dissolved by the hydrofluoric acid.

Silicon nitride can be etched using hydrofluoric acid. However, as silicon nitride is usually used as a mask for the selective production of a silicon dioxide layer, hydrofluoric acid is of little use as it removes both the oxide and the nitride layers. A preferred etchant for silicon nitride is boiling phosphoric acid. Care must be exercised when using this method as the boiling phosphoric acid readily removes photoresist materials. This problem can be overcome by applying a secondary mask layer of silicon dioxide which acts as an etch resist for the nitride layer.

Metal layers such as aluminium are easily etched with acids. A common etchant solution for aluminium is a mixture of phosphoric, nitric and acetic acids. Hydrochloric acid can also be used.

Resist removal or stripping is performed using strong oxidizing agents. These can be in the form of a chemical, for example chromic acid, or an oxygen-based plasma etching process.

Other semiconductor materials such as gallium arsenide are quite problematic when it comes to finding a suitable etchant. The main problem with etching gallium arsenide crystals is that the material consists of alternate layers of gallium and arsenic atoms. Gallium and arsenic have completely different chemical properties and hence etchants often need to consist of two different substances. Some etchants for gallium arsenide include bromine in methanol, dilute sulphuric or phosphoric acid, and sodium hydroxide.

4.6 BIPOLAR JUNCTION TRANSISTOR FABRICATION

Bipolar junction transistors are constructed from a sandwich of n-type and p-type semiconductor material and can be in either an NPN or a PNP configuration. An NPN transistor consists of a thin layer of p-type semiconductor sandwiched between two layers of n-type semiconductor; a PNP transistor is a thin layer of n-type semiconductor sandwiched between two layers of p-type semiconductor. Terminal connections are made to all three semiconductor layers. Figure 4.2 shows the relationship between the circuit symbols and structures of bipolar junction transistors. The thin middle layer is referred to as the base whch is so called because this layer used to form the base on which early transistor devices were constructed. In a typical transistor the base region is only about 0.5 μm thick. The wavelength of green light is about 0.5 μm. The outer two layers are the emitter, which emits charge carriers into the device, and the collector, which collects charge carriers (about 98%).

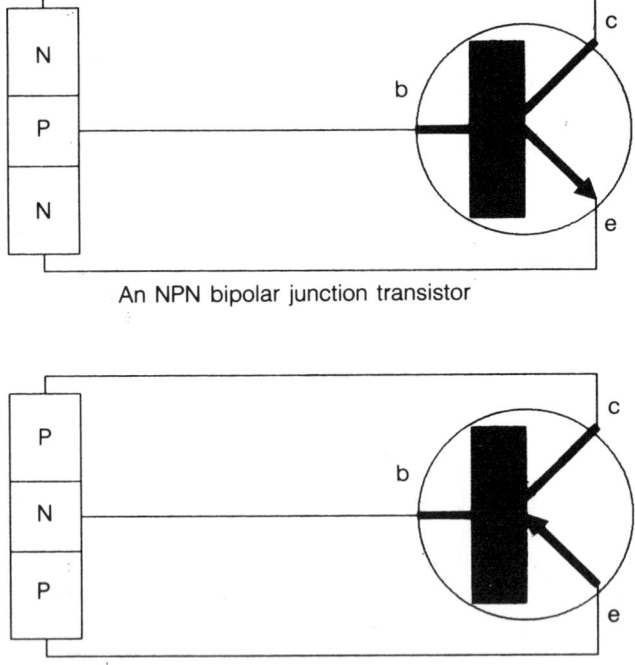

An NPN bipolar junction transistor

A PNP bipolar junction transistor

Figure 4.2 Bipolar junction transistor structures.

In order to construct a bipolar transistor in integrated circuit form it is necessary to make the transistor structure compatible with integrated circuit geometries. This can be achieved by fabricating the transistor structure in a layered form and providing surface terminal connections to the lower layers. These connections are provided by fabricating the device as shown in Figure 4.3p. It can be noted that although the transistor definition specifies a very thin base region the actual fabricated base region is physically larger than the emitter region. In fact the actual transistor junctions occur in the regions where the base region is thinnest.

If an integrated circuit was fabricated by just building the collector, base and emitter regions of its component transistors it would not function as all the transistors' collector regions would be short circuited together. In order to eliminate this problem each device is surrounded by regions of material which perform a device isolation function. Device isolation is achieved by surrounding each transistor with p–n junctions which prevent the flow of electric current between devices through the substrate.

The fabrication processes required to fabricate NPN bipolar junction transistors in integrated circuit form are shown diagrammatically in Figure 4.3. The various photolithographic stages are not shown in order to avoid repetition. When the process involves the selective application of a silicon dioxide layer, this is in fact a multiprocess operation. The first stage of selective oxidization involves the use of a photolithographic process which leaves a resist layer on the areas which are to be oxidized. A chemical vapour deposition process is used to apply a layer of silicon nitride onto the exposed substrate areas. The silicon nitride layer is to be used as a mask for selective oxidization. The photoresist material is etched away after nitride application. At this stage the oxide layer is created using an oxidization process. After oxidation, the silicon nitride mask is removed by etching in boiling phosphoric acid.

The fabrication process for bipolar junction transistors starts with a wafer of p-type silicon. The substrate is p-type as it forms part of the device isolation. A silicon dioxide mask layer is applied (Figure 4.3a) which leaves exposed substrate areas which form part of the device isolation. A dopant diffusion process is used to implant n-type silicon into the exposed surface area (Figure 4.3b). This implanted region consists of highly doped n-type silicon (n^+) which forms a more effective p–n junction with the p-type substrate then the more lightly doped collector region. After dopant diffusion the silicon dioxide mask is removed (Figure 4.3c).

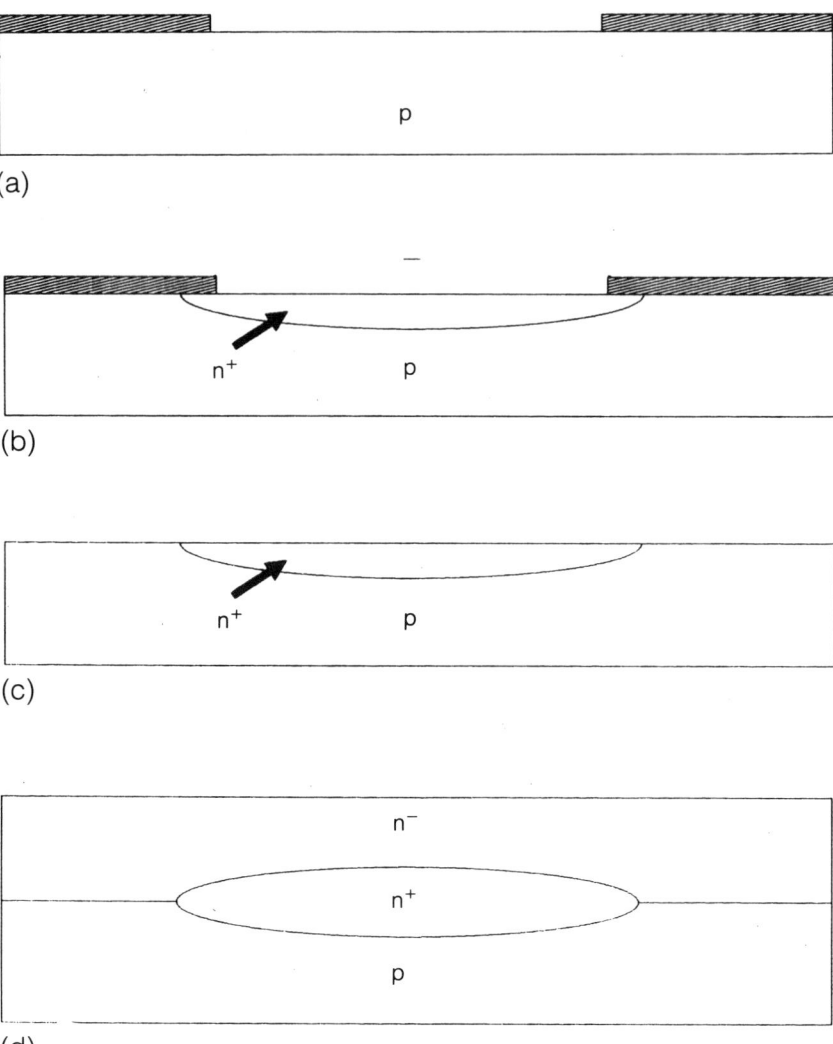

(a)

(b)

(c)

(d)

Figure 4.3 Bipolar junction transistor fabrication process: (a) silicon dioxide mask oxidation; (b) n-type dopant diffusion; (c) etch strip oxide layer; (d) epitaxial growth of n-silicon; (e) silicon dioxide mask oxidation; (f) p-type dopant diffusion; (g) etch strip oxide layer; (h) silicon dioxide mask oxidation; (i) p-type dopant diffusion; (j) etch strip oxide layer; (k) silicon dioxide mask oxidation; (l) n-type dopant diffusion; (m) etch strip oxide layer; (n) silicon dioxide mask oxidation; (o) vacuum deposit metallization layer; (p) etch metal layer.

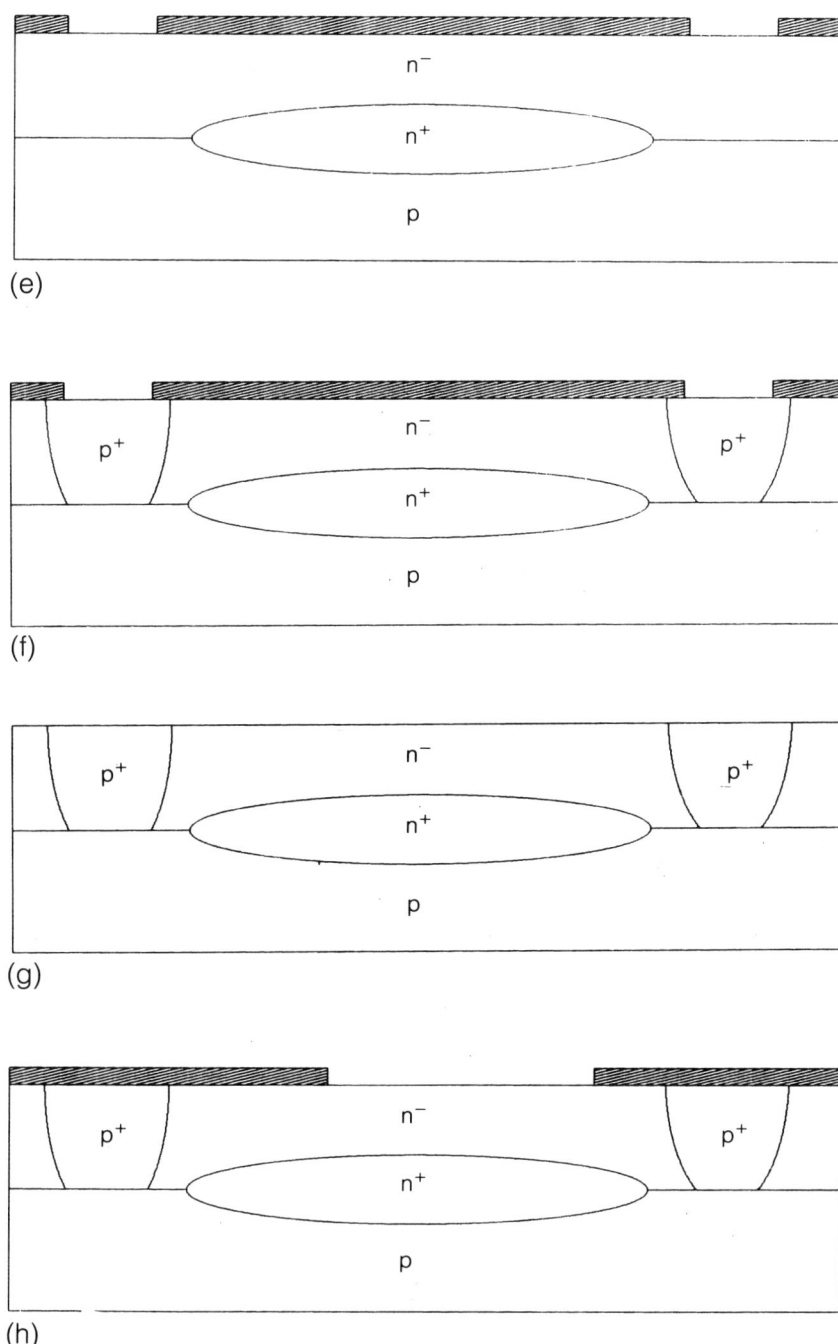

(e)

(f)

(g)

(h)

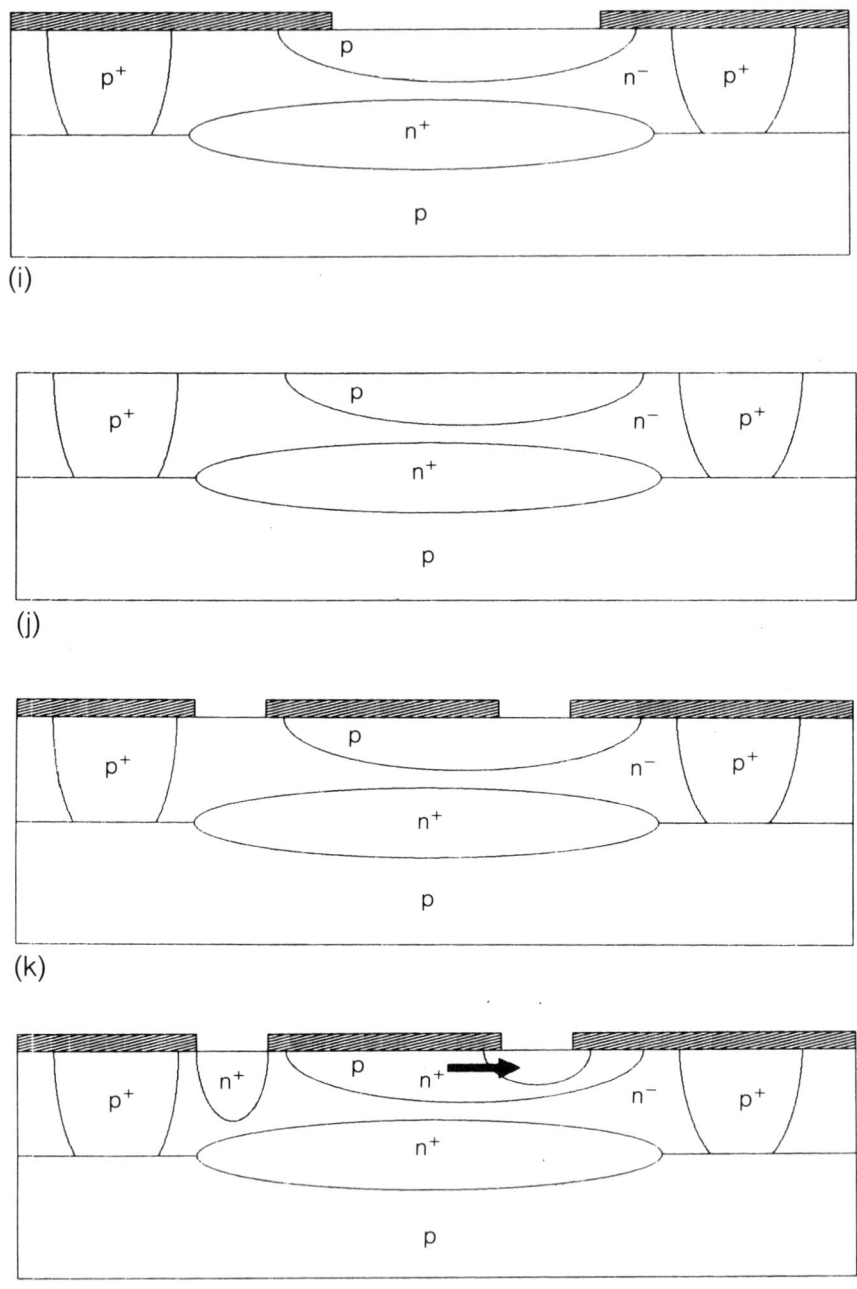

(i)

(j)

(k)

(l)

Figure 4.3 (continued)

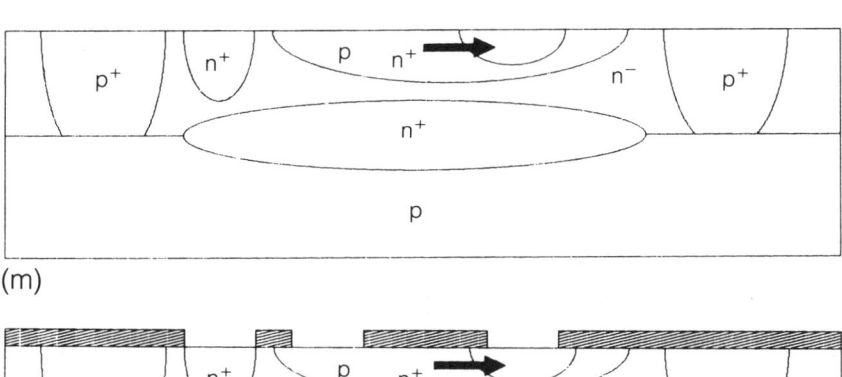

(m)

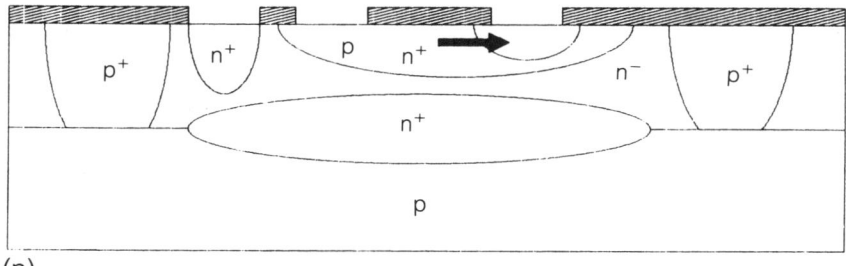

(n)

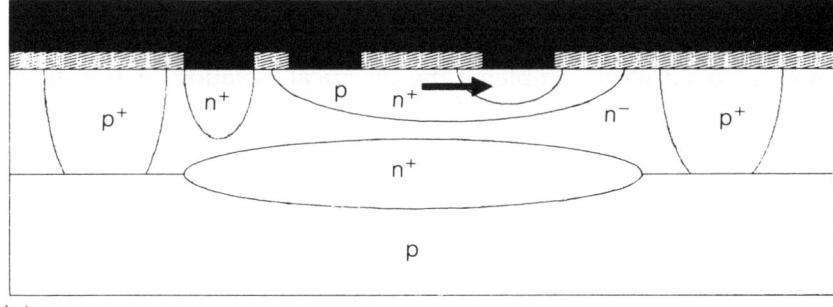

(o)

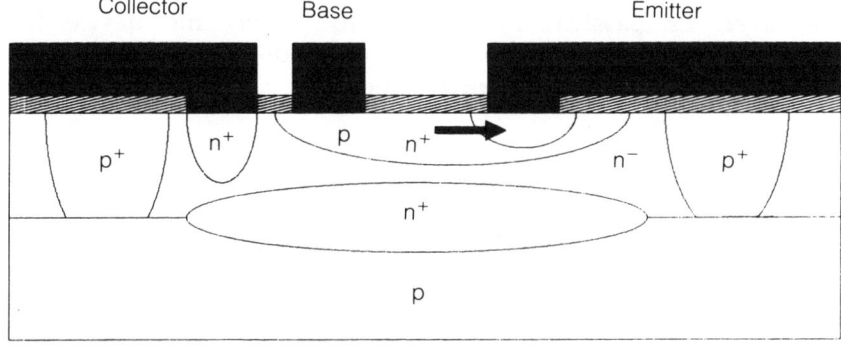

(p)

A vapour phase epitaxy process is used to grow a layer of lightly doped n-type silicon onto the substrate (Figure 4.3d). This layer forms the collector region of the transistor. The final part of the device isolation is formed by the application of a silicon dioxide mask (Figure 4.3e) and the dopant diffusion of heavily doped p-type silicon (Figure 4.3f). This p-type region forms the p–n junctions between adjacent transistors' collector regions and must pass all the way through the n-type layer to the underlying p-type substrate. The silicon dioxide mask is etch stripped after diffusion (Figure 4.3g).

The next stage of the fabrication process is to create the base region. This is performed by applying a silicon dioxide mask (Figure 4.3h) and then using a dopant diffusion process to implant p-type silicon (Figure 4.3i) which forms the base region. The silicon dioxide mask is etch stripped after diffusion (Figure 4.3j).

The emitter region and a collector contact plug are fabricated by applying a silicon dioxide mask (Figure 4.3k) and using a dopant diffusion process to implant heavily doped n-type silicon (Figure 4.3l). These regions are heavily doped in order to reduce the regions' resistivities. The silicon dioxide layer is etch stripped (Figure 4.3m) and a further silicon dioxide layer is applied which defines the terminal connection points of the device (Figure 4.3n). The silicon dioxide mask is not removed as it completes the electrical isolation of the device, leaving only the contact areas exposed. The final stage of the fabrication is to apply a layer of metal (Figure 4.3o), which is usually aluminium, by vacuum deposition. This layer is selectively etched (Figure 4.3p), using a photolithographic process, to produce the device's terminal connections and the interconnections between devices. The metallization may be applied in multiple layers, each separated by an insulating silicon dioxide layer, for more complex interconnections. The finished device is finally coated with a layer of silicon dioxide by means of a chemical vapour deposition process. This final layer, or passivation, is used to protect the device from mechanical and chemical damage during handling and from the long term effects of the operating environment.

4.7 FIELD EFFECT TRANSISTOR FABRICATION

There are three types of field effect transistor, the junction field effect transistor and the enhancement and depletion mode metal oxide semiconductor field effect transistors. Each type of field effect transistor can be either a p-channel or an n-channel device. There are three major differences between field effect transistors and bipolar junction transistors.

1. The current flow in field effect transistors is purely by majority charge carriers; this makes them unipolar (as opposed to bipolar).
2. Current control in field effect transistors is achieved by means of an electric field. Hence in theory no current flows through the gate electrode. This means that field effect transistors have a very high input impedance, normally in excess of 10 MΩ.
3. Field effect transistors are simpler to fabricate in integrated circuit form than bipolar junction transistors and take up less space.

Junction field effect transistors most commonly occur in the n-channel form; they are constructed from a conducting bar of n-type semiconductor which has a connection at each end. These connections are called the source and the drain. Two heavily doped p-type semiconductor regions are diffused into the bar on opposite sides, which form the gate connection. The structures of junction field effect transistors in relation to their circuit symbols are shown in Figure 4.4.

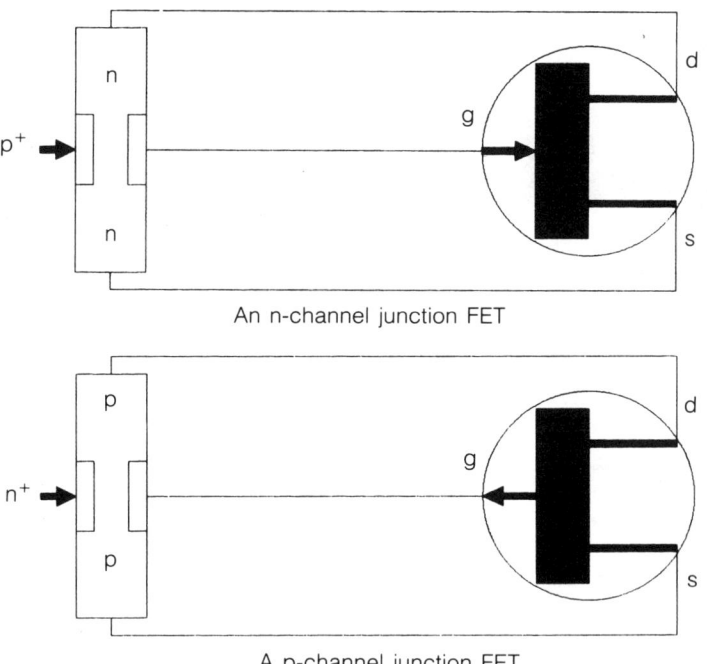

An n-channel junction FET

A p-channel junction FET

Figure 4.4 Junction FET structures.

P-channel junction field effect transistors are available but because of the nature of their construction they are very poor for high frequency applications (because low mobility holes are the charge carriers) and are seldom used.

Metal oxide semiconductor field effect transistors (MOSFETs) are suited to being fabricated in integrated circuit form owing to their simplicity. The two varieties of MOSFET are called enhancement mode and depletion mode because of their method of operation.

A p-channel enhancement mode MOSFET is fabricated from a lightly doped, and actually nearly intrinsic, n-type semiconductor substrate into which two separate p-type semiconductor channels are diffused which form the source and drain connections. A metal gate electrode is placed over the substrate between the channels, separated by a very thin layer of silicon dioxide of about 0.15 μm thickness. Figure 4.5 shows the construction of enhancement mode MOSFETs in relation to their circuit symbols. When the source is more positive than the drain and no voltage is present on the gate electrode, no current flows as a result of the reverse-biased p–n junction at the drain. This electrical separation of the source and drain regions is illustrated in the device's circuit symbol by the breaks in the channel. When a voltage is applied to the gate it induces a p-type region in the substrate between

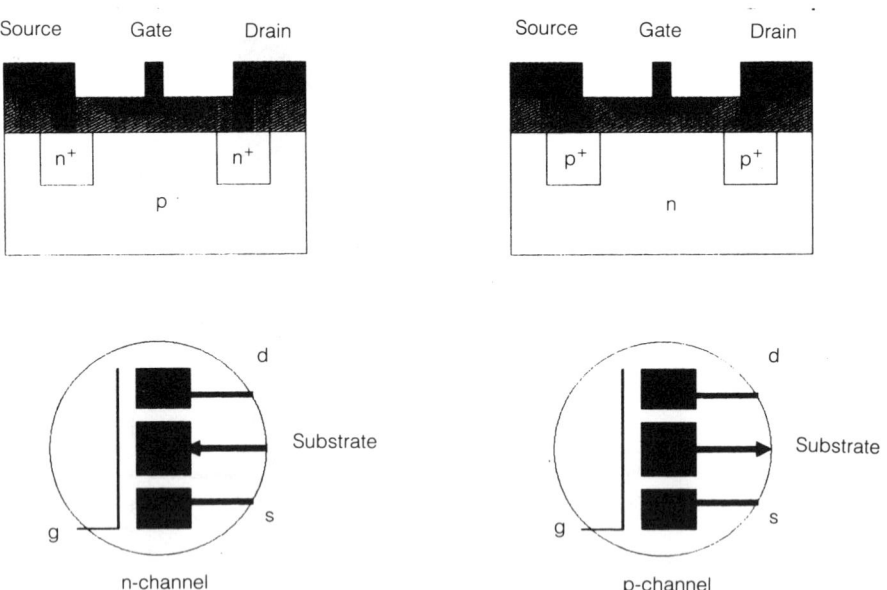

Figure 4.5 Enhancement mode MOSFET structures.

the source and drain regions, thus allowing a current to flow. The device is called enhancement mode as a gate voltage enhances the drain current.

A p-channel depletion mode MOSFET is constructed in a similar manner to the enhancement mode MOSFET except that a channel of p-type semiconductor is diffused between the source and drain regions. Figure 4.6 shows the construction of depletion mode MOSFETs in relation to their circuit symbol. In the absence of a gate voltage, current can freely flow from the source to the drain via the connecting channel. When a voltage is applied to the gate electrode it reduces the current flow by depleting the connecting channel of charge carriers; hence the name depletion mode.

All MOSFETs are highly sensitive to damage from static electricity as a static charge easily can break through the thin gate–substrate insulation, destroying the device. To provide some protection from static electricity most MOSFET logic circuits have an input protection circuit to minimize the risk of destruction from static electricity.

In terms of the integrated circuit form of field effect transistors, the type which is most commonly used is the enhancement mode MOSFET. A common family of field effect transistor integrated circuits is the CMOS family which is constructed from complementary pairs of

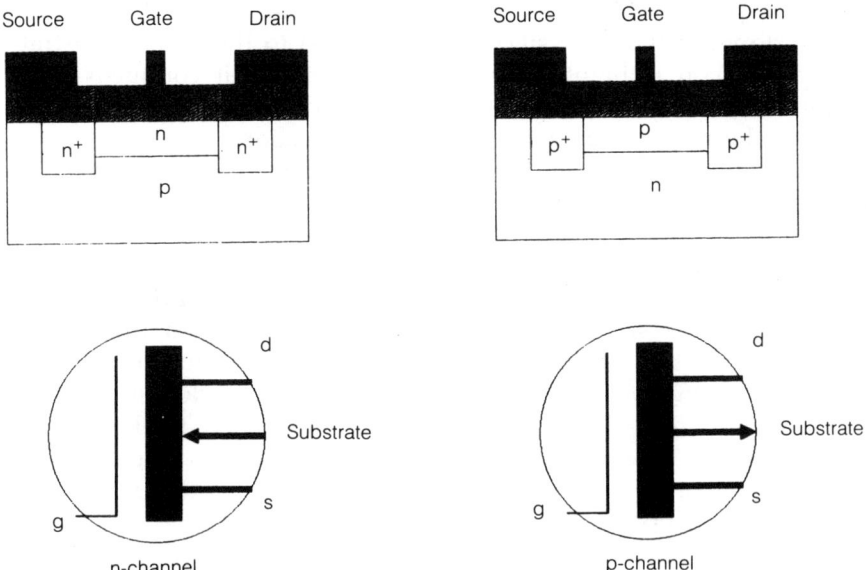

Figure 4.6 Depletion mode MOSFET structures.

p-channel and n-channel enhancement mode MOSFETs.

The fabrication of CMOS integrated circuits can be shown by describing the fabrication of a p-channel MOSFET and an n-channel MOSFET on the same substrate as shown in Figure 4.7. MOSFETs are simpler to fabricate in integrated circuit form than bipolar junction transistors as the process does not require as many of the complex selective silicon dioxide application processes.

The fabrication of CMOS devices starts with a p-type silicon wafer. The p-type wafer substrate forms the body of the n-channel transistors. A silicon dioxide mask layer is applied (Figure 4.7a), which defines the areas which are to form the p-channel devices. The body of the p-channel transistors is created by dopant diffusing n-type silicon into the substrate (Figure 4.7b). The oxide layer is etch stripped (Figure 4.6c) after diffusion.

The next operation is to form the isolation between devices, which in the case of MOSFETs takes the form of simple insulation. A silicon nitride layer is deposited by chemical vapour deposition (Figure 4.7d), which covers the areas into which the actual transistors are to be fabricated. The isolation is created by the selective oxidation (Figure 4.7e) of the substrate areas between devices. The silicon nitride layer is etched away (Figure 4.7f) after oxidation.

The gate electrode and its associated insulation are fabricated by an oxidation process (Figure 4.7g) and the chemical vapour deposition of highly doped n-type polysilicon (Figure 4.7h) to the whole substrate. The polysilicon is highly doped n-type to make it conductive. The silicon dioxide and polysilicon layers are selectively etched (Figure 4.7i) to leave the required gate electrode and insulation.

The source and drain regions of the n-channel transistors are fabricated by using a photolithographic process to cover the p-channel transistors with resist (Figure 4.7j). Highly doped n-type silicon is then dopant diffused into the exposed substrate areas to form the regions (Figure 4.7k). The source and drain regions of the p-channel transistors are created in a similar fashion. The resist is stripped from the p-channel transistors and a new resist layer is applied to the n-channel transistors using photolithography (Figure 4.7l). A dopant diffusion process with highly doped p-type silicon is applied to the exposed substrate areas to form the source and drain regions (Figure 4.7m). After the dopant diffusion, the resist material is stripped from the p-channel transistors (Figure 4.7n).

The final processing involves the application of the metallization layer using vacuum deposition and etching (Figures 4.7o and 4.7p). As for bipolar junction transistors, the metallization may be applied in

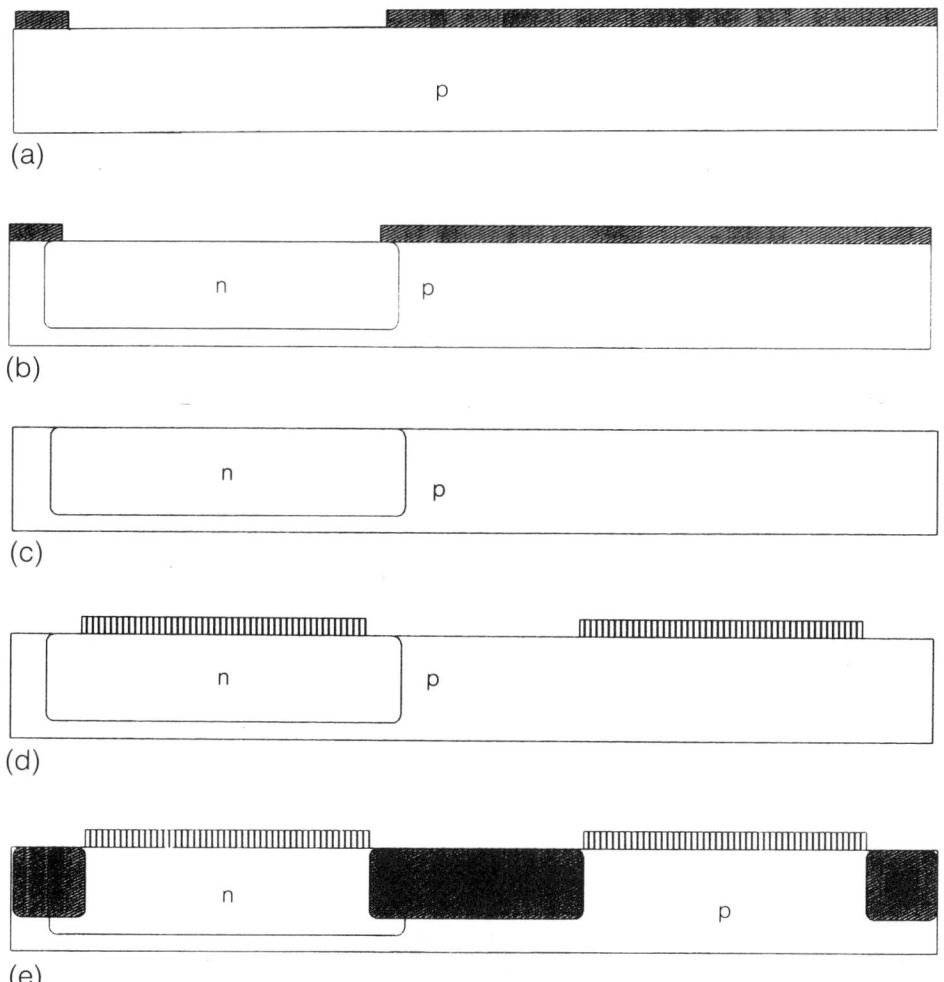

(a)

(b)

(c)

(d)

(e)

Figure 4.7 CMOS transistor fabrication process: (a) silicon dioxide mask oxidation; (b) n-type dopant diffusion; (c) etch strip oxide layer; (d) chemically vapour deposit nitride layer; (e) selective oxidation; (f) etch strip nitride layer; (g) gate oxidation; (h) n^+-polysilicon chemical vapour deposition; (i) selectively etch oxide layer; (j) apply photoresist layer; (k) n^+ dopant diffusion; (l) strip resist and apply photoresist layer; (m) p^+ dopant diffusion; (n) strip resist; (o) vacuum deposit metal layer; (p) etch metal layer.

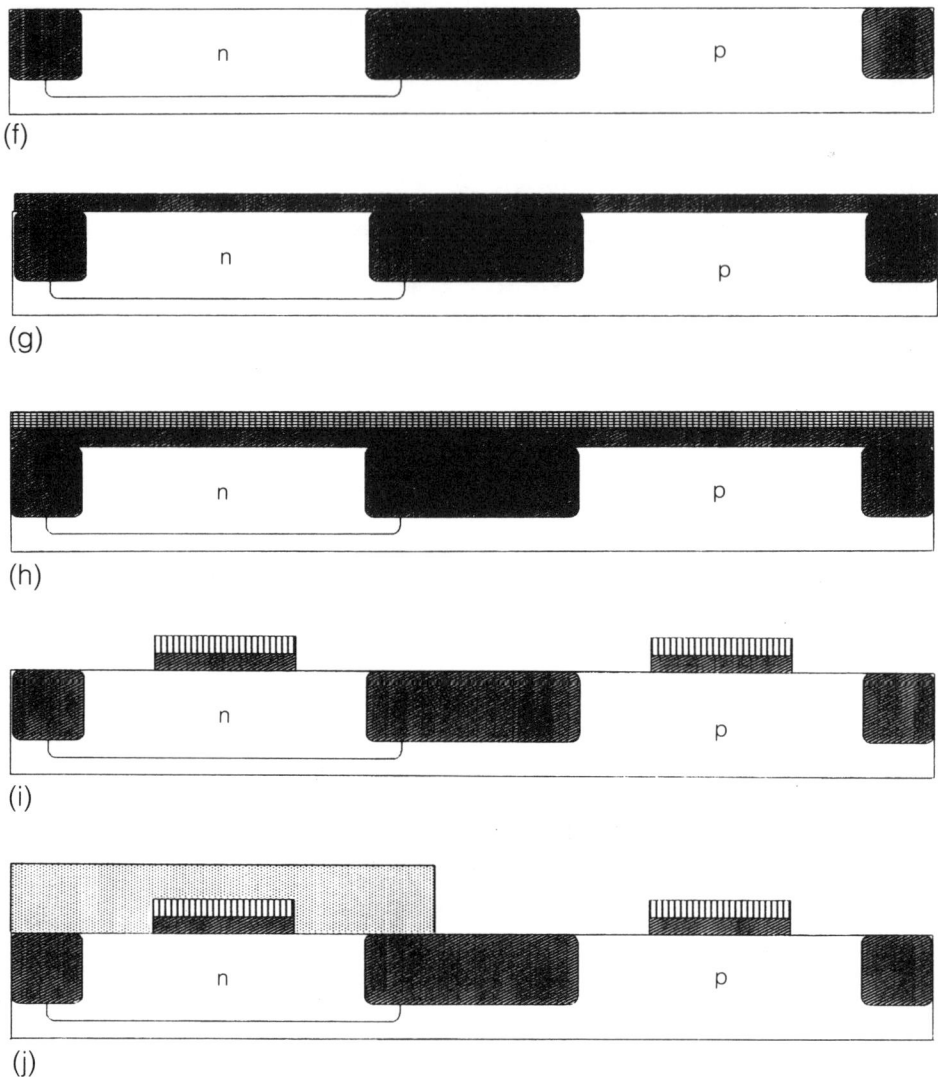

Figure 4.7 (continued)

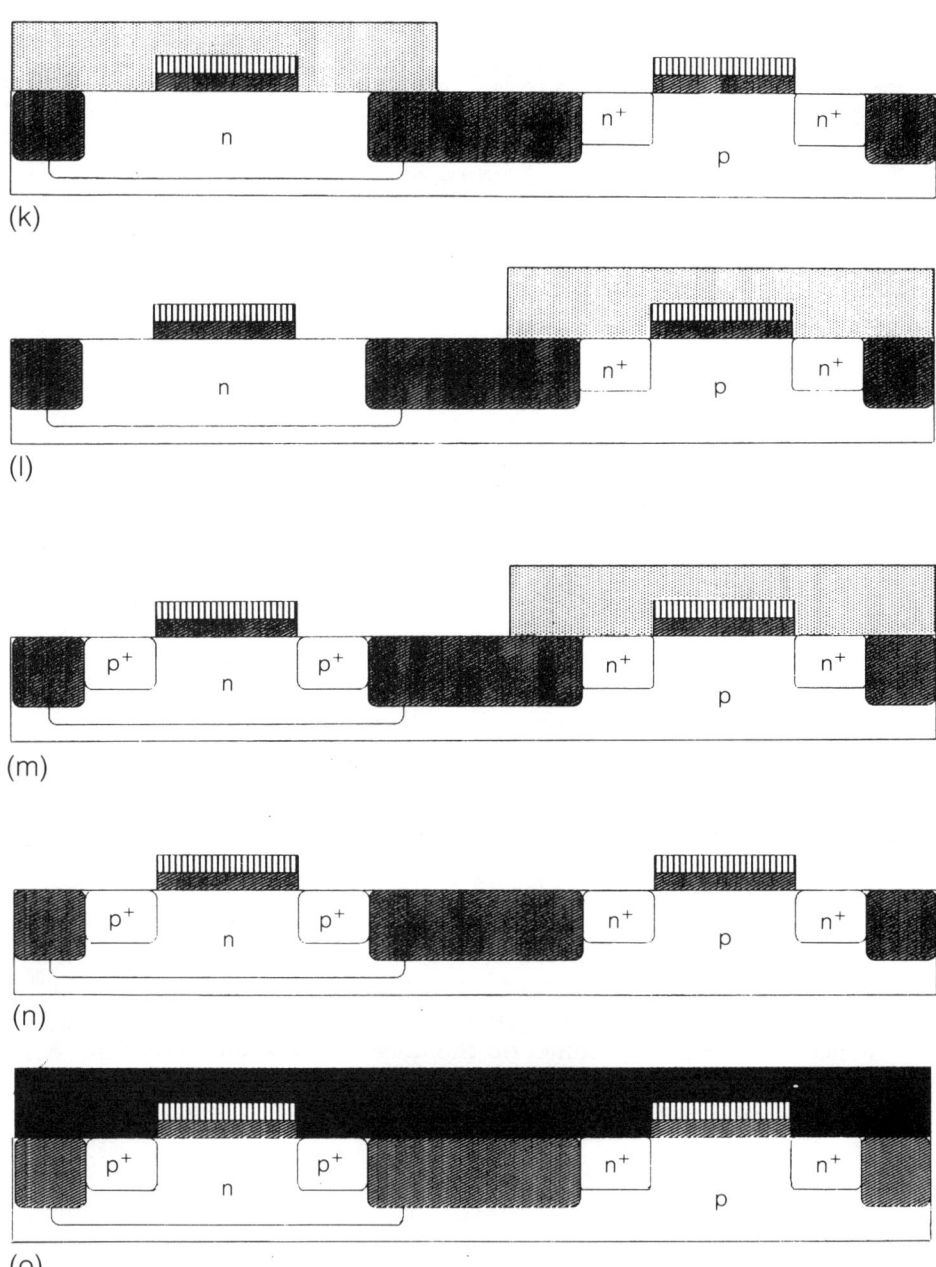

(k)

(l)

(m)

(n)

(o)

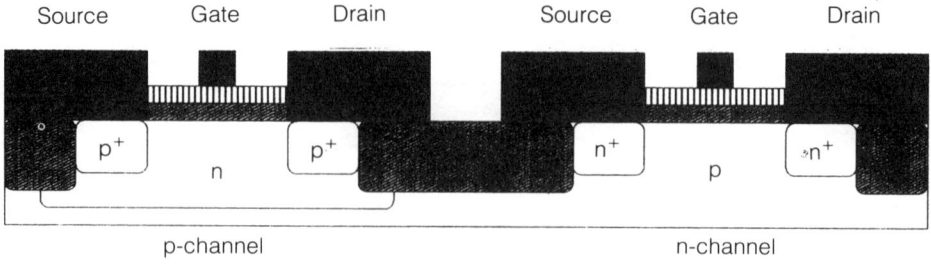

(p)

Figure 4.7 (continued)

multiple layers and the finished device is coated with a silicon dioxide passivation layer by chemical vapour deposition.

4.8 INTEGRATED CIRCUIT PACKAGING AND TESTING

After fabrication, each substrate contains a large number of individual devices which are in a rectangular array of elements called dice. Each die is typically in the order of 5 mm square. In order to produce saleable devices it is necessary to slice the substrate into individual dice and place each functional die in a package. This package must provide mechanical protection for the die and allow electrical connections to the outside world. The fabrication processes have very tight tolerances which can result in some of the dice on a substrate being non-functional. In order to minimize wastage by packaging non-functional devices, each wafer needs to be thoroughly tested immediately after processing.

The major stages from substrate fabrication to shipping are die separation, packaging and testing. The percentage of working devices on a substrate is described by a yield function which is dependent on many of the manufacturing processes.

4.8.1 Die testing and die separation

Because there is a significant number of dice on a given substrate it is necessary to perform a comprehensive testing process on the dice immediately after fabrication. Integrated circuit packages are quite expensive and this testing minimizes the number of faulty dice which are packaged.

The substrate testing is highly automated and computerized for speed of operation and accuracy. A set of needle-like probes are configured onto a fixture called a probe card which matches the connecting pads of the individual die. The probes are applied to each die on the substrate in turn and a test program is executed. If a device is found to be faulty a drop of ink is squirted onto the die to indicate that it is to be discarded. The test procedure will initially test for gross faults such as short or open circuits between pads. This reduces unnecessary testing of badly flawed devices. The computerized testing will then proceed to perform a functionality test and finally a test that the device performs to within specification. The computer system will also maintain a record of the number of functional devices per wafer, the yield.

After testing, the wafer has to be cut up into its component dice and the faulty dice discarded. A wafer is sawed up using a computer-controlled diamond saw. Wafers may also be diced by scribing and breaking like glass or ceramic tiles. Because of the small size of the dice the saw 'blade' consists of a thin flexible material which is diamond impregnated. The flexible material becomes a rigid saw when rotated at high speed. After sawing, the faulty dice, as marked with ink drops, are discarded.

The now separated dice which passed the probe test are visually tested for flaws which may cause the device to fail when in operation. Visual inspection will identify flaws such as breaks and nodules in metal tracks and other large-scale defects. Faulty dice, or dice which have unacceptable features, are discarded at this stage.

4.8.2 Packaging

Each individual die is only a few millimetres square and is very fragile. The connecting pads, which are large by microelectronic standards but tiny by normal standards, are far too small to be connected to by conventional wiring techniques. The dice are easily destroyed both by physical damage and by chemical damage from contamination and need to be protected. In addition a die may generate a significant amount of heat when under operation which needs to be carried away to prevent overheating.

It is the function of the packaging to provide all of these functions. There are a number of different styles of packaging which include the dual-in-line package (DIL or DIP) consisting of two rows of legs, the chip carrier which has no legs but has contacts all around the sides, and the pin array consisting of a two-dimensional array of pins on the underside. The various forms of integrated circuit packaging are described in Chapter 2.

When selecting the actual type of packaging to be used to encapsulate a particular die type there are a number of factors which need to be taken into consideration as follows.

1. Pin count: the number of pins on the package must be greater than or equal to the number of connections on the die.
2. Physical package size or footprint may be limited by space constraints. This is particularly true in the case of customized devices. Any such size constraints may influence the type of packaging used.
3. The method of mounting the integrated circuit on a printed circuit board: examples of printed circuit board mounting methods which may influence the packaging style are leaded component technology, surface mount technology and the use of integrated circuit sockets.
4. Reliability and hermeticity: the environment in which the device is to operate may dictate the packaging style. For example, ceramic packaging may need to be used in place of plastic packaging, which is less resistant to extreme conditions.
5. Resistance, inductance, capacitance and length of conductor runs: in the case of very high speed devices the electrical characteristics and lengths of the conductors between the die's contacts and the pins of the package can be critical. In particular, the large difference in conductor length between central and end pins of a DIL package can cause functional problems for some devices.
6. Heat dissipation: the package must be able to carry away the maximum heat that a device can generate.
7. Cost: packages can cost between a few pence and tens of pounds, depending on their construction. The cost of the package must not cause a device to be too expensive.
8. Handling: the packaging of a device must be compatible with the feed mechanisms used for the automatic assembly of target printed circuit boards.

9. Availability: particularly for devices which are to be produced in large numbers, the selected packaging must be readily available.

There are a number of trends associated with integrated circuit packaging styles which include steadily increasing pin counts, increasing die sizes, a preference for surface-mountable components, and improving packaging reliabilities.

The first stage of the actual packaging process is to bond the die physically to the package. This can be achieved by a number of different methods. The die can be metallized at the back and then soldered onto a metal pad on the package. Alternatively, the die can be bonded using a polymer adhesive. It is often required that the connection between die and package be conductive, which can dictate the bonding process. After a die has been bonded to its package an inspection of the bond may take place; this is especially important for high performance devices.

The next operation is the wire bonding stage where the die's contact pads are wired to the package's leads. The connection leads, which are usually aluminium, can be attached by either pressure bonding or ultrasonic bonding techniques. The wire bonds are non-destructively tested by being pulled by tiny hooks. The hooks pull at a predefined force which will cause defective wire bonds to fail. An optical inspection will be performed at this stage to check for faults such as a wire bond overhanging the pad to which it is connected.

Once the bonding operations are complete, the package needs to be closed and sealed. It is important to exclude moisture, dust and contaminants at this stage. Plastic packages may need to be moulded around the die and leads. Ceramic packages have either two halves which need to be fused together, or a metal cover which needs to be soldered in place. Other packages have a metal cover which needs to be soldered in place.

Dependent on the type of package used, some final operations may be required. These operations include the tin plating, cropping and forming of leads.

Some of the more innovative and non-standard packaging methods are described in Chapter 8.

4.8.3 Testing

After the packaging operation is complete, the integrated circuits are subjected to a final test procedure. This test will identify devices which have been damaged in the assembly operation. In addition, the devices' performance characteristics can be measured.

High reliability devices will be subjected to burn-in and screening operations prior to final testing. Some of these tests are as follows.

In order to eliminate devices which are liable to fail by 'infant mortality' they may be subject to high temperature storage. This test typically involves storing devices at 125 °C for a period of 24 h. A test stage after storage eliminates devices which have failed.

Temperature cycling can be applied to devices, particularly if they are to be used in environments subject to large temperature changes. Each device is subjected to a temperature cycle of between +125 and −55 °C for ten cycles.

When devices may be subjected to operation under large accelerations or vibrations a centrifuging test can be applied. Devices are subjected to high accelerations in a centrifuge.

The hermeticity of the device's packaging can be tested by means of a fine leak test and a gross leak test. A fine leak test involves exposing devices to a high pressure helium atmosphere. This is performed in a pressure vessel known as a helium bomb. The principle of the test is that, if the package has a leak, helium gas will enter the device. After being pressurized, the device is removed and placed in a spectral analyser. Any helium gas which enters the device through a leak will escape out once the pressure is reduced and can be detected by the spectral analyser. A gross leak test involves subjecting the device to pressurized fluorocarbon gas in a fluorocarbon bomb. The device is then immersed in a liquid. Any fluorocarbon which entered the device through a leak will escape and form bubbles which can be observed.

4.8.4 Yield

In order to determine the costing for an individual die of a particular type it is necessary to have an indication of the number of functional dice which can be made from a single substrate and the processing cost per substrate. The primary measure of the percentage of functional dice from a substrate is that of yield. This is the percentage of functional devices obtained from the theoretical maximum number of devices which can be fabricated from all the substrates which enter processing. The total yield is a function of three separate yield figures:

$$Y = (LY)(DY)(FY) \tag{4.1}$$

LY is the line yield which is the percentage of substrates starting the process which survive until the end. Line yield failures result from breakage, errors and failures in equipment or process reliability. The line yield is in fact the product of the yield for each process. A 50-step process requires a 99.42% yield at each step in order to achieve a 75% total yield.

DY is the die yield which is the number of dice which pass the wafer level electrical testing after processing. This gives the best indication of how successfully a design has been implemented. A major cause of die yield problems is that of area-like or point-like substrate faults. These are areas of the substrate which are defective owing to contamination or damage. Process control failures can also result in point-like failures. A major source of point-like failure is particulate contamination. A single contamination particle which is similar in size to a die's feature dimensions will result in a die being defective. In effect one particle can totally incapacitate one die. The die yield is in fact inversely proportional to the individual die area.

FY is the final test yield and is the percentage of dice which are assembled into packages and pass the final test stages. This factor should be very high provided that the packaging and testing procedures are reliable.

5

Printed circuit board manufacture

The term printed circuit board (usually abbreviated to PCB), which is synonymous with the term printed wiring board (or PWB), is used to describe a substrate which provides mechanical support and the necessary electrical connections for an electronic circuit. Printed circuit boards have become an almost universal medium upon which electronic circuits are assembled. This makes the ability to manufacture high quality printed circuit boards an essential requirement. Printed circuit board technology has evolved relatively little compared with the other technologies used in the rapidly evolving electronics industry. The electronics industry has a distinct resistance to the introduction of alternative interconnection technologies to the printed circuit board. Some of the reasons for this resistance and hence the almost universal usage of printed circuit boards are as follows.

1. A well-designed and proven printed circuit board effectively guarantees the correct routeing of interconnections. This has the additional effect of providing circuit repeatability.
2. The performance of an electronic circuit can be made more predictable as the electrical characteristics of a printed circuit board can be controlled.
3. A typical commercial printed circuit board has all its solder joints created in a single process. This helps to ensure that the soldering quality is consistent across a board. Hand-soldered joints can vary considerably depending on each individual operator's skill.

There are many aspects to the manufacture of printed circuit boards. The term printed circuit board is actually used to describe several different forms of interconnection based on similar principles. Printed circuit boards can be manufactured from a range of materials using a variable sequence of manufacturing processes. This chapter describes the different types of printed circuit boards and the materials which can be used for their manufacture. The range of different processes used for printed circuit board manufacture is described separately, followed by the actual manufacturing process sequences for the major types.

5.1 PRINTED CIRCUIT BOARD TYPES

Printed circuit boards consist of an insulating substrate material upon which electronic components can be mounted. Interconnections between components are achieved by conducting paths running on or through the substrate called tracks. Tracks meet components to which they are to be connected by means of a larger conductor area called a land or pad. The electrical connection between a land and a component's terminal lead is formed by means of a solder joint.

Early printed circuit boards were manufactured by drawing a circuit's interconnections on a piece of fine silk with a conducting ink. Tracks could be made to cross by gluing a silk bridge over each track to be crossed and then drawing the crossing track. These were truly 'printed circuits' as opposed to modern printed circuit boards which are created by a photographic process rather than a printing process.

Another form of early interconnection technology, which formed an intermediate stage between chassis wiring and printed circuit board technologies, was that of circuit boards which consisted of an insulating substrate which had a rectangular array of holes drilled into it. Component leads were inserted through the holes in the board and electrical connections were formed by soldering insulated wires between component leads.

An alternative interconnection method, which is still used for prototyping simpler circuits, is veroboard. This consists of a substrate with a rectangular array of holes drilled into it in a standard pitch spacing, usually 2.54 mm (0.1 in). A series of parallel copper tracks join the holes into rows on one side of the board. Components are mounted on the non-copper side, their leads passing through holes and being soldered to a copper strip. The interconnection patterns required for a circuit can be made by breaking copper tracks and by soldering insulated wires in place to form connections between tracks.

Modern printed circuit boards consist of an insulating base substrate, which is usually rigid, which carries tracks in the form of a thin copper film. The copper tracks terminate in lands which take the form of larger areas of copper. These lands, where connections are made to components and other areas of a printed circuit board, can have a wide range of shapes and sizes and often have holes drilled through them. These holes can either accommodate component leads or be via holes which provide connections through the substrate to other track areas. Figure 5.1 shows a typical printed circuit board's appearance. The copper track and land areas can be created either by a plating process or by etching a complete copper skin laminated onto a base material, the latter method being the most commonly used.

There are three major types of printed circuit board, single sided, double sided and multilayer, which have one, two or multiple parallel planes, or layers, of copper tracking.

Single-sided boards, which have copper tracking on one side of the board only, are the simplest form of printed circuit board. They are also the simplest to manufacture.

Double-sided printed circuit boards have copper tracking on both sides of the substrate. As connections are usually required between the sides of the board, some method of achieving this must be included in the manufacturing process. This usually takes the form of through hole plating which increases the manufacturing complexity.

Multilayer boards consist of a sandwich of individual printed circuit boards which can be either single sided or double sided, or both. Multilayer boards are the most complex as, in addition to interlayer interconnection, there is the added problem of ensuring that the component layers are correctly aligned.

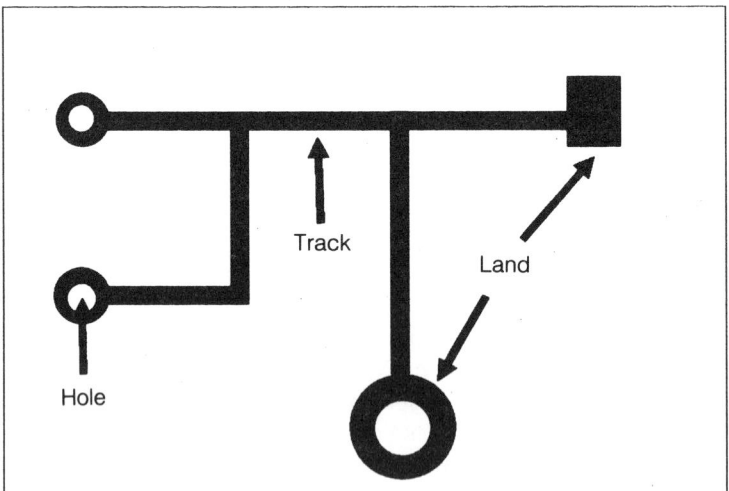

Figure 5.1 Printed circuit board features.

The actual type of printed circuit board which is appropriate for a particular application is dependent on the interconnection complexity of the circuit it is to bear. An indication of the levels of complexity can be obtained by considering the packing density of the printed circuit board types. A good measure of packing density is the number of holes which can be accommodated per unit area of usable board surface. Another measure of density is the number of centimetres of conductor contained within a square centimetre of usable board area. Typical values are between one and two holes per square centimetre for a single-sided board, between two and four holes per square centimetre for a double-sided board, and in excess of three holes per square centimetre for a multilayer board.

Printed circuit boards are usually rigid in construction; however, flexible circuits are in usage. Flexible circuits are described in Chapter 8.

Various different sequences of manufacturing processes can be used for the production of bare printed circuit boards of all types. Typically each manufacturer will have a preferred method. Several of the manufacturing processes, particularly in the final stages, can be interchanged in sequence, or even omitted, and still produce the desired results. Thus the sequences of processes described are typical examples which do not have to be rigidly adhered to.

5.2 PRINTED CIRCUIT BOARD SUBSTRATE MATERIALS

The most commonly used base materials for printed circuit boards consist of a resin material which is reinforced with paper or glass. The main types of resin materials are phenolic resins and epoxy resins. Typically phenolic resins are reinforced with paper and epoxy resins are reinforced with glass. The resin materials are usually flame retardant in order to reduce the fire hazard during printed circuit board manufacture and circuit operation.

Printed circuit board substrates are usually fabricated in a copper-clad laminated form. The board is constructed from a number of layers of reinforced resin which are bonded together with a sheet of copper foil on one or both sides. In addition to the reinforced resin substrate materials, ceramic substrates are used for high performance circuits.

When selecting a substrate for a particular application it is important to consider both its mechanical and its electrical characteristics. The mechanical characteristics must be able to tolerate the environment in which the circuit is to operate. The electrical characteristics are important for correct circuit operation, especially in the case of high speed circuits.

From the mechanical point of view, the actual size of the substrate is important. Substrate materials are available in a range of thicknesses to within a tolerance. A substrate with an out-of-tolerance thickness will cause problems if an edge connector is incorporated into a circuit's copper track layout. In the case of multilayer printed circuit boards, the substrates used for the manufacture of the board's component layers must have the appropriate thicknesses in order to produce a finished board of the correct thickness. A substrate must be sufficiently rigid and resistant to warping in order to prevent problems in later processes such as soldering. A substrate must also be resistant to fungal growth, which can damage a printed circuit board's integrity and cause electrical problems such as short circuiting. Other mechanical factors which need to be taken into consideration are thermal expansion characteristics, mechanical strength and flammability.

From the electrical point of view, two of the most important factors are the substrate's resistance and dielectric constant. The substrate's resistance must be sufficiently high both across the surface and across the substrate's width to provide sufficient insulation between the conducting paths of a circuit. The dielectric constant contributes to the capacitance between conductors on the substrate. In the case of high frequency circuits, the electrical characteristics of the substrate contribute to an electrical parameter called the characteristic impedance, usually designated Z_0, of a circuit. It is important that this characteristic impedance closely matches the impedances of the components used in the circuit. The control of a substrate's electrical characteristics can be crucial to correct circuit operation.

5.3 PRINTED CIRCUIT BOARD SUBSTRATE MANUFACTURE

The commonest type of printed circuit board is the glass-reinforced epoxy resin type with copper lamination. The manufacturing process for such a board is described.

Copper-clad boards need to be manufactured in a clean room environment as dust particles can cause problems. In particular, a dust particle can result in pits and dents occurring in the copper surface.

The board manufacturing process is performed in a heated press which has highly polished stainless steel press plates. The manufacturing process starts by placing a sheet of copper foil onto the lower press plate. The copper sheet will form a copper-clad board surface and forms a base onto which the board structure is built.

The copper sheet can be produced either by rolling out a piece of copper or by an electroplating process. Electroplating is used in preference to rolling for the manufacture of the copper sheets as it produces a more uniform and controllable film thickness and granularity.

Layers of glass cloth which have been impregnated with an epoxy resin are built up on top of the copper foil until the required board thickness is achieved. It is necessary to be able to determine how many layers of impregnated glass are required to produce a board to the correct thickness and tolerance after pressing. Once the resin-impregnated glass layers have been built up a final layer is added. This final layer consists of a second sheet of copper foil for double-sided boards or a material which acts as a release film for single-sided boards.

The entire assembly, as shown in Figure 5.2, is placed in a steam-heated hydraulic press which bonds the layers into a completed board.

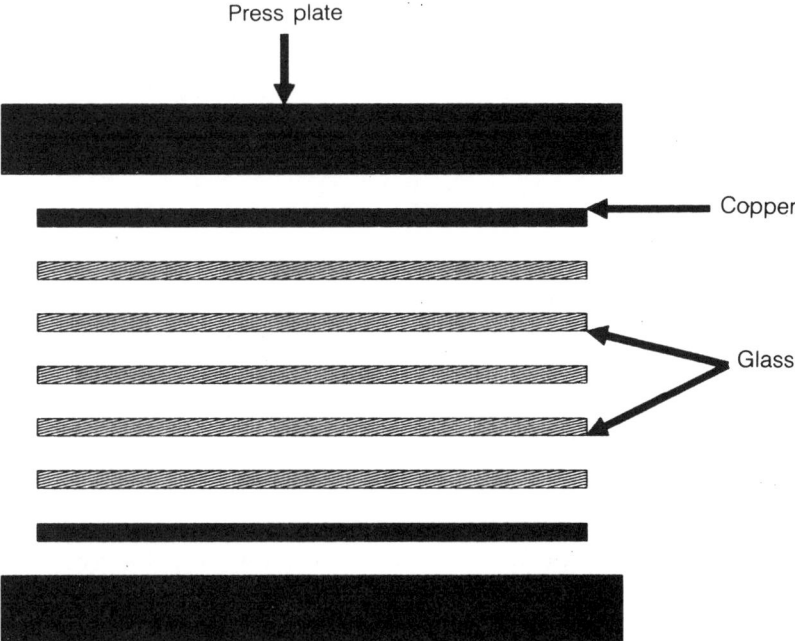

Figure 5.2 Bare board lamination.

A typical press has multiple press plates and is capable of pressing several hundred boards simultaneously. The pressing operation proceeds by applying pressures of over 7 000 000 Pa and steam heating the press plates to the resin curing temperature. Once the required curing time has elapsed the plates are then water cooled to about 25 °C and the boards removed from the press. After pressing, the boards are trimmed to remove any extruded resin material. British Standard BS 4584 (British Standards Institute, 1972) defines the standard specifications for metal-clad printed wiring boards.

5.4 PRINTED CIRCUIT BOARD FABRICATION PROCEDURES

There are a number of different processes which are used to manufacture a printed circuit board which is ready for component assembly from a copper-clad substrate material. These processes include board preprocessing, photolithography, etching, drilling, various plating processes, testing and finishing. Each of these processes is described individually. The actual processes used for the manufacture of a printed circuit board are dependent on the board's complexity and the application for which the board is intended. For example, a simple single-sided board will only use a subset of the processes whereas a complex multilayer board will use all the processes.

5.4.1 Preprocessing

The preprocessing of a printed circuit board involves the initial preparation of a copper-clad board ready for subsequent processing. Copper-clad boards are commercially available in a fixed range of sizes. Unless the final printed circuit board is for an application which uses standard-sized printed circuit boards, such as the eurocard format for computer circuits, it will be necessary to fabricate the board from a larger-sized sheet of copper-clad material. Logically the preprocessing stage is the obvious time to cut an oversized copper-clad board to the required size of the printed circuit board. However, there are several reasons from the manufacturing point of view why this may not be the appropriate time. Many manufacturing processes, such as automatic component insertion and wave soldering, utilize automatic feeding mechanisms. These feeding mechanisms may require particular board widths and special handling features built into boards. It is always more efficient to use standard board widths with feeding systems which need to be mechanically adjusted to accommodate different widths in order to minimize equipment down time. In general it is also more cost effective to manufacture a small number of large boards than a large number of small boards. As a result of these manufacturing constraints it is common practice to fabricate all printed circuit boards from a standard width of copper-clad material. When small printed circuit boards are required, several identical boards are fabricated from a single sheet of copper-clad material and separated after processing.

Once a piece of copper-clad board has been selected, and cut to size if appropriate at this stage, the next stage is to drill or punch tooling holes and any special features into the board. Tooling holes are used to achieve registration between processes. An example where registration is required is to ensure that holes are correctly drilled through land areas. Additional tooling holes may be required to provide mechanical support in order to prevent warping during soldering. Certain features such as tabs may need to be formed into the edges of boards for use with automatic assembly equipment. An example of this is the 'Fuji strip' used in conjunction with Fuji automatic assembly machines. Where multiple boards are being fabricated from a single piece of copper-clad material, slots may be cut out in order to define board boundaries and to facilitate the later separation process. Figure 5.3 shows some typical features which may be cut into a board at this stage.

A board may also need to be marked for identification using a bar code or a stamp. The identification may include a code identifying the type of board for use with automatic assembly and test equipment. A serial number can be included to enable the monitoring of each particular board's progress during manufacture.

The copper surface of a copper-clad board needs to be thoroughly cleaned before processing as dirt and grease will adversely affect later processing. The cleaning operation is performed by passing a board through rollers in an abrasive slurry. When very fine tracks are required on a printed circuit board it is very important to ensure that the board and processing environment are very clean. Dust particles can easily be of a similar size to the required track thickness and hence cause a break in a track or a short circuit between tracks to be fabricated. The definition of very fine tracks may require a clean room environment approaching that required for integrated circuit manufacture.

Tooling holes   Handling strips   Separators

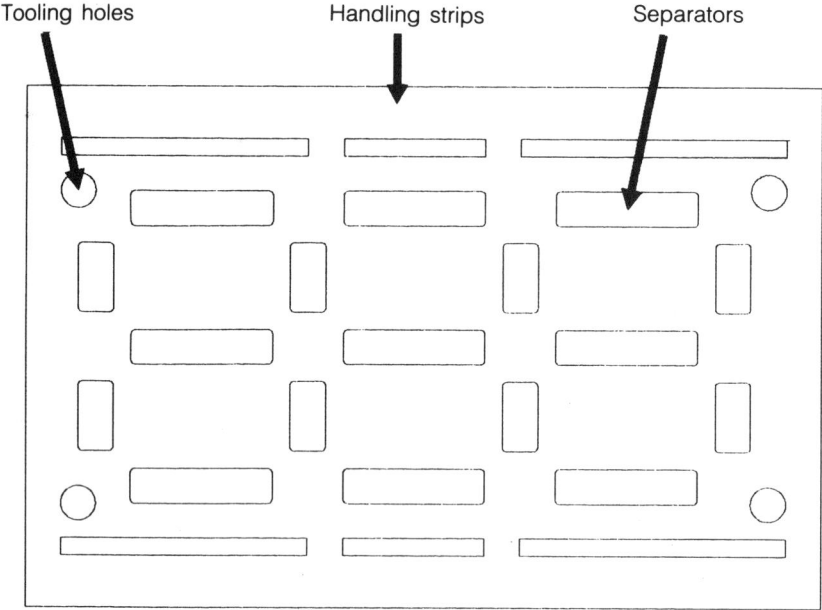

Figure 5.3 Board tooling holes and separator slots.

5.4.2 Photolithography

The copper track and land patterns are defined on a copper-clad board by means of a photolithographic process. Like the related processes used for integrated circuit manufacture, the photolithographic process for printed circuit boards involves the exposure of a photoresist material to light through a mask. Both positive and negative photoresist materials can be used depending on the actual process being used. The use of a negative photoresist, which becomes insoluble on exposure, is almost universal owing to a lack of commercially available positive resist materials. The exposure uses ultraviolet light through a mask which has usually been created and output on a computer-aided circuit layout system. The masks used for printed circuit board manufacture are often full sized and hence require no photographic enlargement or reduction.

A preprocessed board, which is to undergo photolithography, is initially laminated with a photosensitive resist material. The photoresist can be applied either in liquid form or as a dry film.

Liquid resists are the oldest variety and are becoming obsolete. The reason for this is that they are difficult to control, especially when fine track features are to be created. Liquid resists were usually applied by dip coating, spray coating or a roller application process. The major disadvantages of liquid resists are that it is very difficult to achieve a uniform coating thickness and that they require exposures of several minutes.

Dry film resist materials take the form of a photosensitive polymer material sandwiched between polymer films. These cover films allow the resist to be stored in roll form without it sticking to itself. The dry film is applied to a board by removing a cover film and allowing the photosensitive polymer to adhere directly to the board's surface. The second cover film may be removed after application to the board or at a later stage during processing.

The exposure part of the photolithographic process involves the exposure of the photoresist-coated copper-clad board to ultraviolet light through an artwork mask. The mask can take the form of either a photographic positive image or a photographic negative image of the required track layout, as output from the circuit design system. It is vitally important during the exposure stage to ensure that the image is correctly aligned with the board's geometry. This is particularly true in the case of double-sided and multilayer boards.

After the exposure the image needs to be developed. The development process involves the removal of the less soluble areas of resist material. This corresponds to the unexposed areas of resist material with negatively acting photoresist material. The commonest method of development is the chemical removal of resist material. In the case of dry film resists, the developing agent is usually either a solvent such as trichloroethane or a sodium carbonate solution, depending on the actual materials used. Chemically developed dry film resists must have their second polymer film layer removed after exposure and before development. Another form of dry film photoresist is the dry processable variety which does not require chemical development. These resists work on the principle that the exposed and unexposed resist materials have different adhesion properties with the second cover film and with copper. The unexposed resist adheres more strongly to the cover film than it does to the copper board surface. The exposed resist material adheres more strongly to copper than to the cover film. Hence the unexposed resist material can be removed simply by peeling the second cover film away from the copper-clad board. This method has limitations as to the achievable resolutions owing to irregularities introduced by the tearing action which occurs between the exposed and unexposed resist areas on removal.

Although predominantly negative photoresist materials are used in the printed circuit board photolithographic processes, there are certain processes which naturally call for positive resist material. In these cases a negative photoresist can be used if the exposure is made through a photographic negative image of the artwork patterns.

Once the selective processing which required the photolithographic process has been performed, it is necessary to remove the remaining resist material from the board's surface. In the case of dry film resists and, depending on the actual materials used in the resist, this removal process uses either a methylene chloride solvent at a temperature of about 20 °C or a solution containing sodium hydroxide at a temperature of about 60 °C.

5.4.3 Etching

The etching process is used to remove any of a printed circuit board's copper surface which is not protected by a resist material as defined by a photolithographic process. This usually corresponds to the areas of a printed circuit board which are between its tracks and lands. The etching process is performed by exposing the board's surface to an etchant solution which dissolves away the exposed copper areas.

The etchant solution usually consists of a solution of ferric chloride, ammonium persulphate, chromic acid or cupric chloride; however, other etchants solutions are used. The etching process can be performed by simply immersing a board in an etchant solution and agitating. This is rarely used by professional board manufacturers as the process is difficult to control and can result in non-uniform etching.

The commonest commercially used method of etching is spray etching where the boards are subjected to a continuous fine spray of etchant solution. It is important to control the etching process carefully in order to produce good consistent results. Insufficient etching will result in excess copper being present on the board, which can cause short circuiting between tracks. Over-etching will result in the etchant undercutting the track area defined by the resist layer, which can result in tracks which are broken or so thin that they are likely to become open circuits at a later stage. Figure 5.4 shows the different effects of under-etching, correct etching and over-etching. The careful control of the etching process is especially important when fine tracks in the order of 100 μm are required.

The usage of an etchant solution must be carefully controlled as it becomes increasingly contaminated with copper, which adversely

Under-etched

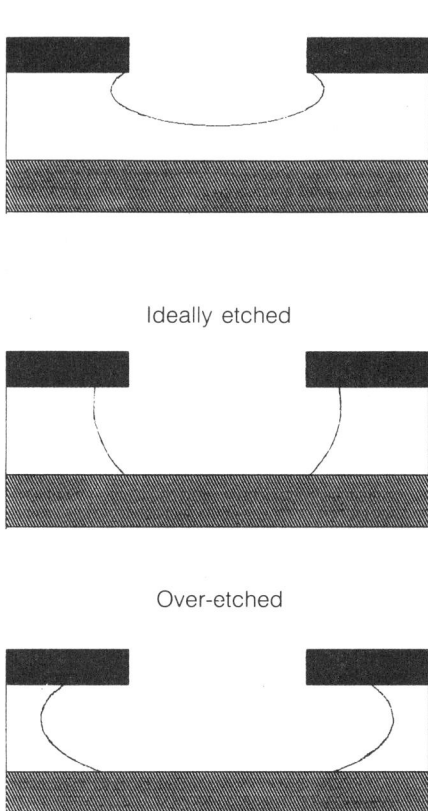

Ideally etched

Over-etched

Figure 5.4 Etching profiles.

affects its performance. The copper contained in an exhausted etchant solution can be reclaimed by chemical or electrochemical extraction methods.

Once the etching process has been completed the etch resist material is chemically removed. This leaves the track and land areas defined in copper on the base material.

5.4.4 Drilling

The drilling process is used to create the component lead holes and via holes in a printed circuit board. These holes pass through land areas and must be carefully positioned. In addition to component lead and via holes, holes may also need to be drilled for providing mechanical connections. These can be holes for bolting heat sinks or connectors onto the board's substrate material. The drilling operation can occur either before or after the track and land areas have been defined, depending on the processing sequence.

The actual drilling process is usually performed using a computer numerical control (CNC) drilling machine. The drilling machine's program can be generated automatically from a computer-aided design system's drill template output. Drill holes may be required in a range of different sizes. Small diameter holes are required for component leads. Larger diameter holes may be required for bolting sockets and heat sinks to the board.

It is common practice for several boards to be drilled simultaneously. Using suitable jigging, boards of the same type are stacked and mounted on a drilling machine. This enables multiple boards to be drilled in a single drilling cycle. The boards to be drilled are sandwiched between two sheets of material in order to reduce drill entry and exit burrs on the actual boards. Careful monitoring of drill bit tool life is required, particularly in the case of small diameter drills. This minimizes the risk of drill bit breakage. Boards are deburred after drilling by passing through abrasive rollers.

5.4.5 Electroless plating

In the manufacture of double-sided and multilayer printed circuit boards it is necessary to provide electrical connections through the board in order to link the interconnection layers. This is usually performed by making the inside surfaces of component lead and via holes electrically conductive in a plating through hole process. As there is initially no conductive path through holes it is not initially possible to use an electroplating process. Instead a non-electrical method is required known as electroless plating.

The objective of the electroless plating process is to deposit a sufficient amount of copper on the insides of holes to make the entire board surface conductive. Once this has been achieved the copper layer can be built up to the desired thickness using the more efficient electroplating process.

Electroless plating is a chemical process where copper is deposited on the entire surface of the board. The process is very sensitive to contamination, temperature and the chemistry of the solutions used.

The first stage in the electroless plating of copper is to clean the board thoroughly of contaminants. This can involve the use of both acid and alkali solutions to remove all surface contaminants and to leave a uniform surface.

The electroless plating operation requires that a copper-containing solution is chemically reduced to elemental copper on a board's surface. This is achieved using a catalyst which usually takes the form of a colloidal metal system such as palladium. A board is initially immersed in a solution which contains the catalyst. This takes the form of a neutral or acidic solution containing palladium and tin. The tin causes the palladium to come out of solution and to be deposited on the board. This is called the activator stage and is anteceded by a post-activator process which removes the tin from the board's surface. The electroless copper process then follows where the board is immersed in a copper-containing solution. This is a mixture of copper sulphate and sodium hydroxide in formaldehyde. This solution is reduced by the catalyst to leave a fine copper deposit on the board's surface. The process must be well agitated to ensure a good flow of solution through the board's holes. This is essential in order to supply adequate quantities of the copper-containing solution to the insides of the holes where it is most required.

There are certain constraints which the electroless plating process places on the geometry of holes to be plated through. One important constraint is that of the aspect ratio of a hole which is the ratio of a hole's diameter to its length. Aspect ratios which fall below a certain threshold cannot be plated as a sufficient flow rate cannot be achieved through a hole to effect plating. This constraint sets a lower limit on via hole diameter for a particular board thickness.

5.4.6 Electroplating

The electroplating process is concerned with increasing the thickness of copper, as applied by the electroless plating process, on the inside of holes to the required dimensions. A board which has been completely covered in a layer of copper by electroless plating forms the cathode in a copper electroplating process. It is important to note that the copper-laminated board surface is also thickened by this process. This may need to be taken into consideration when selecting the copper laminate thickness of the copper-clad board in order to produce a target board to the required specifications.

There are two electroplating processes in common usage, the differences being the chemical composition of the plating solution used. These processes are referred to as 'acid copper' and 'pyro-copper'.

The acid copper process uses an acidic copper sulphate solution. This process is relatively easy to control but is not very efficient at depositing copper.

The pyro-copper process uses a copper pyrosulphate solution. The process is much more efficient at depositing copper but is sensitive to changes in temperature and pH.

The electroplating process described above is known as panel plating as the entire panel surface of a board is plated. This is the simplest plating method and is suitable for boards with relatively large tracks. An alternative method is in use, particularly for very finely tracked boards, which is known as pattern plating.

The pattern plating process works by applying a photoresist layer before the plating process. This results in only selected parts, corresponding to the desired track and land areas, of a board's surface being thickened by the plating process. The thickened areas tend to overlap the resist layer which, in conjunction with the fact that less copper needs to be removed from non-track areas, reduces undercut problems associated with the later etching process. In practice pattern plating is more difficult to control as the exposed board area is more difficult to assess. Figure 5.5 shows a comparison between panel and pattern etch profiles.

5.4.7 Gold plating

Some printed circuit boards which are designed to be plugged into another board or a rack will incorporate edge connectors, or fingers, as part of the track layout. These fingers are often gold plated in order to

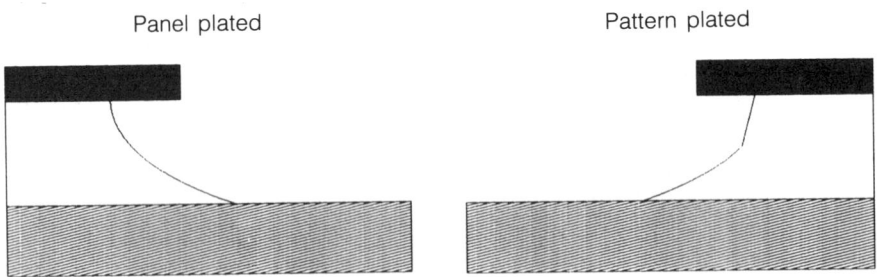

Figure 5.5 Panel and pattern plating etch profiles.

ensure a good electrical connection and to provide resistance to oxidation. The gold plating of fingers is performed by the following processes.

A board is initially masked with tape to leave only the connector area which is to be plated exposed. A chemical etchant spray is applied to remove any tin–lead (solder) layer which may have been applied by a roller tinning or a plating process.

A thin, 1.25 μm thick, layer of nickel is often plated onto the copper fingers as an intermediate layer before gold plating. The reason for this is that gold on copper can produce a poor electrical junction.

A thin, minimum thickness 2.5 μm, layer of gold is plated onto the finger areas. There are a number of different gold plating processes. One of the most common processes is an electroplating process which utilizes potassium gold cyanide in an organic acid as the electrolyte. The gold layer can be made harder and more wear resistant by introducing small quantities of cobalt, nickel or iron to the solution. Gold can also be plated using an electroless plating process.

The gold contacts need to be inspected after plating to ensure that an adequate coating of gold has been applied. A layer of gold which is too thin, or contains pinholes, allows the underlying copper to corrode. A poorly applied gold layer may also peel off the nickel base. An electrograph porosity test is performed which checks for pinholes in the plating layer. The thickness of the gold plate layer can be measured using a Betascope which utilizes β particle backscattering measurements.

5.4.8 Bare board testing

Each board needs to be tested to ensure that the required connections exist, that there are no short circuits, and that the drill holes are correctly placed (i.e. pass through centres of lands and not edges). Testing procedures in common usage are visual inspection and continuity testing. Complex and high value boards will often be tested using both methods.

Visual inspection can be automated by using a machine equipped with an *x–y* moving table which presents areas of a board to a camera. The inspection system is programmed to present all of the track areas in turn for inspection. Any faults, or suspected faults, detected in the tracking will be reported by the system. Automatic visual inspection systems will often mark track areas which have suspected faults with a dye for later manual inspection.

Continuity testing is usually performed on a bed-of-nails test bed. A bed of nails consists of a rectangular array of pointed contact probes which are forced into contact with the track areas of the board to be tested. The contact is usually enforced by using a vacuum to pull the board under test onto the bed of nails. The continuity of a track can then be tested by checking for an electrical connection between contacts. A more detailed description of bed-of-nails test beds is given in Chapter 6.

The commonest faults in printed circuit boards are short circuits or open circuits due to faulty artwork or contamination in the photolithographic processes. Open circuits can also result from over-etching the copper. Other sources of defects are damage due to handling and contamination.

5.4.9 Bare board finishing

Bare copper track and land areas are prone to oxidation and contamination which can cause subsequent soldering problems. To overcome this a protective solder layer is applied to the tracks. Depending on the type of board, this can be applied either by a plating process or by roller tinning.

The final processes are to add a solder resist layer and a legend to indicate component positions. The solder resist layer covers all the copper areas of a board except for the land areas and their immediate neighbourhood. The purpose of this layer is to reduce the area of the board to which solder can erroneously adhere. As its name implies, a solder resist layer resists the adhesion of solder. The legend layer consists of component positional information in the form of a diagram of the components' outlines and identification codes such as R1 for the first resistor.

The resist layer and legend are defined at the design stage alone with the rest of the artwork. These layers are usually applied by silk screen printing after the board has been degreased in a solvent bath.

5.5 SINGLE-SIDED PRINTED CIRCUIT BOARD MANUFACTURE

The single-sided printed circuit board is the simplest type which consists of an insulating base material bearing copper tracks and lands on one side only. Single-sided boards usually have holes drilled through the land areas; however, the use of surface-mounted components can reduce or eliminate this requirement, thus reducing manufacturing costs.

The manufacturing processes for single-sided printed circuit boards are shown diagrammatically in Figure 5.6. Board manufacture starts with single-sided copper-clad board materials. These boards undergo a preprocessing operation which involves cutting the board to the correct size, creating tooling holes and cleaning the board's surface.

Once cleaned, the board goes through a photolithographic process where a layer of photoresist material is laminated onto the board's surface and exposed to ultraviolet light through the required artwork mask. Following the development of the resist image, the remaining

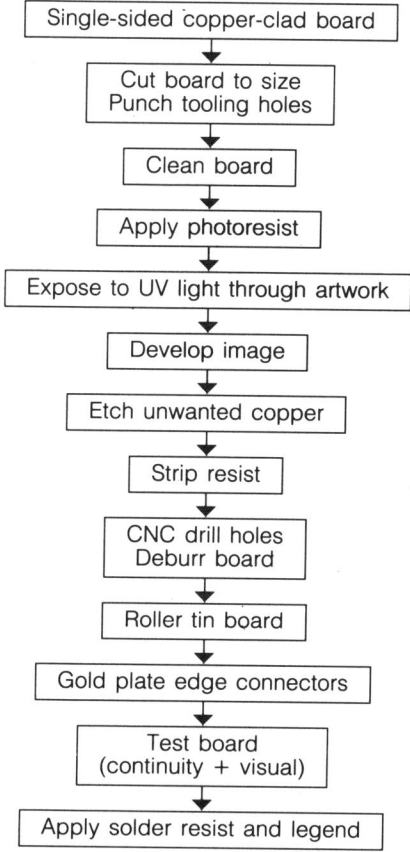

Figure 5.6 Single-sided printed circuit board fabrication.

photoresist material covers the areas which are to form the copper track and land areas.

The next operation is an etching process to remove the exposed copper areas, leaving the copper track and land areas. The remaining photoresist material is removed after etching.

The board, which now has its tracking defined in copper, is placed on a CNC drilling machine which drills component lead holes through land areas and any fixing holes. The drilling program is generated from the artwork. Boards are deburred after drilling. In the case of single-sided printed circuit boards the copper track areas are solder coated by means of a roller tinning process. This involves passing the copper side of the board over rollers which are running in a molten solder bath.

Boards which feature edge connectors will need to undergo a gold plating process on the connector track areas.

The final stages of single-sided printed circuit board fabrication are the testing stages and the application of a solder resist and a legend layer.

In cases where multiple printed circuit boards are manufactured from a single copper-clad board, or where extra board area has been utilized for jigging holes, it is necessary to cut the finished printed circuit boards from the remaining material. The board separation is typically performed by a CNC routing process; this will include the chamfering of any connector areas. The printed circuit board separation process may be deferred until after the components have been assembled onto the board. The deferred separation occurs when automatic assembly machines have special feeding requirements such as standard board sizes with predefined jigging holes.

5.6 DOUBLE-SIDED PRINTED CIRCUIT BOARD MANUFACTURE

Double-sided printed circuit boards require a more sophisticated manufacturing process as they have tracks on both sides of the board which need to be interconnected. The boards typically have additional holes to the normal holes for component insertion. These additional holes, which are usually of smaller diameter, are used to connect tracks on opposite sides of the board and are referred to as via holes.

During the manufacturing process it is necessary to provide an electrical connection between the two sides of a board through the via holes and the component insertion holes. This can be achieved in a simplistic manner by inserting small lengths of wire through via holes and soldering to both sides of the board. This method is rarely used as it increases the assembly costs and is not very reliable. The normal method of achieving via hole connections is by a plating process. This results in a board which is described as having plated through holes.

There are two major sequences of processes used for the manufacture of double-sided printed circuit boards with plated through holes. The first process is commonly used for manufacturing the intermediate logic layers for multilayer printed circuit boards which will be referred to as logic layer processing. The second process is used for stand-alone boards and the outer layers of multilayer printed circuit boards which will be referred to as outer layer processing. The fundamental difference between the two methods is that the latter requires that the copper track areas be covered in a solder layer. The solder layer is incorporated into the board manufacturing process rather than being a later addition. The two processing methods are described separately as complete processing sequences.

5.6.1 Logic layer processing

The manufacturing processes for logic layer double-sided boards are shown in Figure 5.7. Board processing starts with a double-sided copper-clad board. The board is preprocessed by cutting to size and punching any tooling holes and identification marks, and an abrasive slurry cleaning process is performed as for single-sided boards.

In logic layer processing the requirement for plated through holes is met by creating the plated through holes before defining the track patterns. Thus a copper-clad board is first placed on a CNC drilling machine which drills the component lead and via holes, the CNC drilling program being created from the drill template generated by the design system.

After the drilling process it is necessary to plate the holes to provide an electrical connection between the two sides of the board. The plating process is performed in two stages, electroless plating and electroplating. As described for the individual processes (sections 5.4.5 and 5.4.6), the electroless plating applies a thin layer of copper to the entire board surface, including the interior surfaces of any through holes. The electroplating thickens the copper layer to the required thickness.

Once the through holes have been plated a track pattern needs to be created on both sides of the board using a photolithographic process. The board is thoroughly cleaned and a photoresist film is applied to

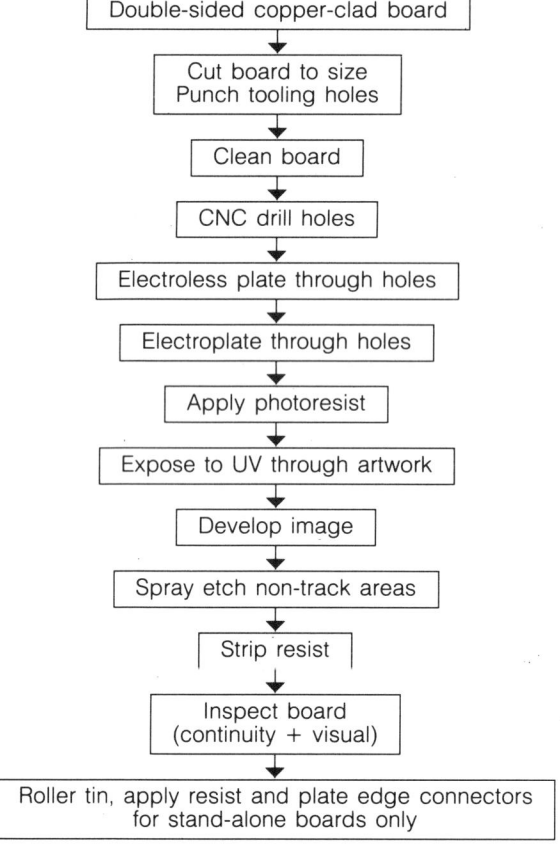

Figure 5.7 Logic layer double-sided printed circuit board fabrication.

both sides of the board. Following exposure to ultraviolet light through the artwork masks, the remaining photoresist material covers the areas of the board which are to form the track and land areas. It is important that the photoresist material be able to cover the through holes of the board in order to prevent the later etching process from removing the through hole plating.

It is also very important at the photolithographic stage to ensure that the correct registration is used such that the two artwork patterns and the holes in the board are correctly aligned with each other. An image inspection stage may be included at this point to check that the resist layer covers the correct areas of the board for higher value finished printed circuit boards.

A developed board is passed through an etchant spray process to remove the surface copper from non-track areas. After etching, the photoresist layer is stripped from the track areas. Additional tooling holes may need to be punched at this stage for use by later processes.

When a logic layer board is to become a component part of a multilayer board a detailed inspection of the track and land areas is required. The inspection process typically involves a visual inspection followed by a continuity test.

Double-sided boards which are not going to be part of a multilayer board need to undergo the roller tinning, solder resist layer and legend layer application as for single-sided printed circuit boards. Stand-alone boards with edge connectors will need to have the connector areas gold plated.

5.6.2 Outer layer processing

The outer layer manufacturing process used for double-sided boards, as shown in Figure 5.8, differs from the logic layer process in the plating and photolithography stages.

The process begins with a double-sided copper-clad board which is preprocessed by punching and cleaning. A CNC machine drills the required through holes defined by the drill template artwork. Following the drilling process, the holes are through plated with copper using an electroless plating process followed by an electroplating process as for the logic layer process.

The outer layer process differs from the logic layer process in the track and land definition stages. The photolithographic process operates in reverse to the corresponding logic layer process. A board is coated with a photoresist material and exposed to ultraviolet light through the track definition artwork negatives for both sides of the board. The image is developed to leave photoresist material on the areas of the board which are to be free from copper. This resist layer is to be used as a plating mask, for a pattern plating process, rather than as an etchant resist.

The developed board is placed in an electroplating bath where a lead–tin layer (solder is a lead–tin alloy) is plated onto the track, pad and through hole areas of the board. This lead–tin layer is actually going to be used as a resist layer for a subsequent etching process, and to leave the copper areas covered with a protective solder layer. The photoresist material is stripped after plating.

The plating quality may be inspected at this stage for higher value boards, particularly in the regions of through holes.

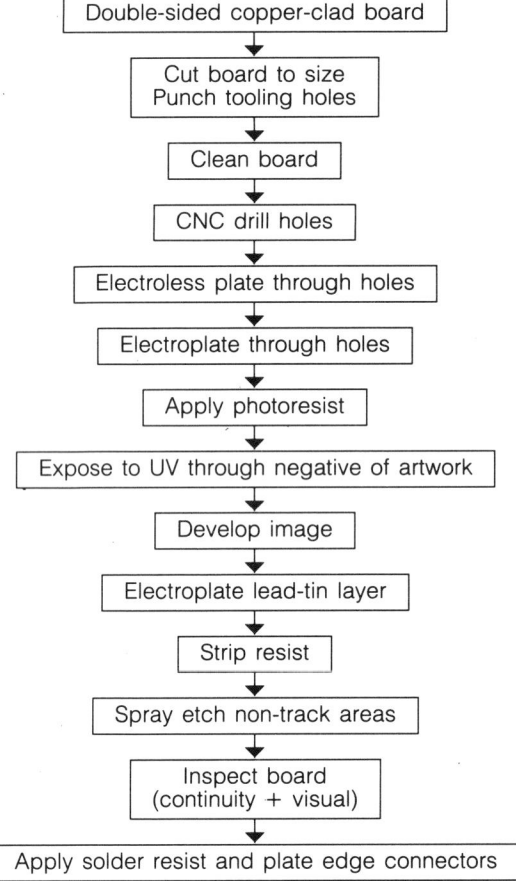

Figure 5.8 Outer layer double-sided printed circuit board fabrication.

The board is spray etched to remove the areas of copper which have not been lead–tin plated. Once the etching process has been performed the board undergoes a reflow process which involves heating the board and passing it through flux-impregnated rollers. The purpose of this process is to melt the lead–tin layer to remove any oxidation and to produce a smooth surface finish. The resultant lead–tin layer obviates the need for a roller tinning process.

After reflowing, each board is cleaned in a solvent degreaser to remove excess flux. Solder resist and legend layers are applied by silk screen printing. When necessary, gold plating will be applied to connectors.

Where multiple boards are created from a single substrate, or a board has complex non-rectangular outlines, a CNC routine process is used to produce the correct outline. Gold fingers need to be chamfered. Finished boards undergo a final visual inspection followed by a continuity test.

5.7 MULTILAYER PRINTED CIRCUIT BOARD MANUFACTURE

Multilayer printed circuit boards consist of a number of thin single- or double-sided boards sandwiched together between layers of epoxy-resin-impregnated glass cloth. Connections between layers are achieved by means of plated through component lead and via holes. All component lead holes and most via holes pass all the way through the board and are through plated. This through plating has the additional role of forming electrical connections to the tracking of intermediate layers through which they pass. In addition to these through board holes, through plated via holes may have been fabricated into component double-sided layers of the board. These are referred to as buried via holes. Figure 5.9 shows an example cross-section of a multilayer board.

When selecting the materials for the manufacture of multilayer printed circuit boards, it is important to pay attention to the electrical characteristics of the finished board. The internal copper tracks of the board all add a component of capacitance to the board. This is important as it adds to the characteristic impedance of the board. This factor is extremely difficult to control as the calculations of the various contributing factors are complex. One method of impedance control is the use of a microstrip which is a signal line of carefully controlled

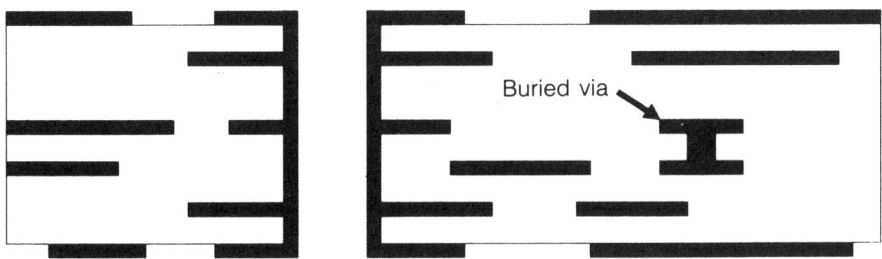

Figure 5.9 Multilayer printed circuit board cross-section.

dimensions. The characteristic impedance of the microstrip signal line can be adjusted by changing its width and thickness. A typical multilayer printed circuit board can consist of a number of different types of constituent boards. The main types of constituent layer boards are typically logic layers, voltage layers and the outermost layers. Interconnections between the various layers are achieved by means of the via holes and component lead holes which pass all the way through the board. Holes may pass through non-track areas of intermediate layers to which no electrical connection is required.

Logic layers carry the electrical signals between devices which are mounted on the board. They are usually double-sided boards with

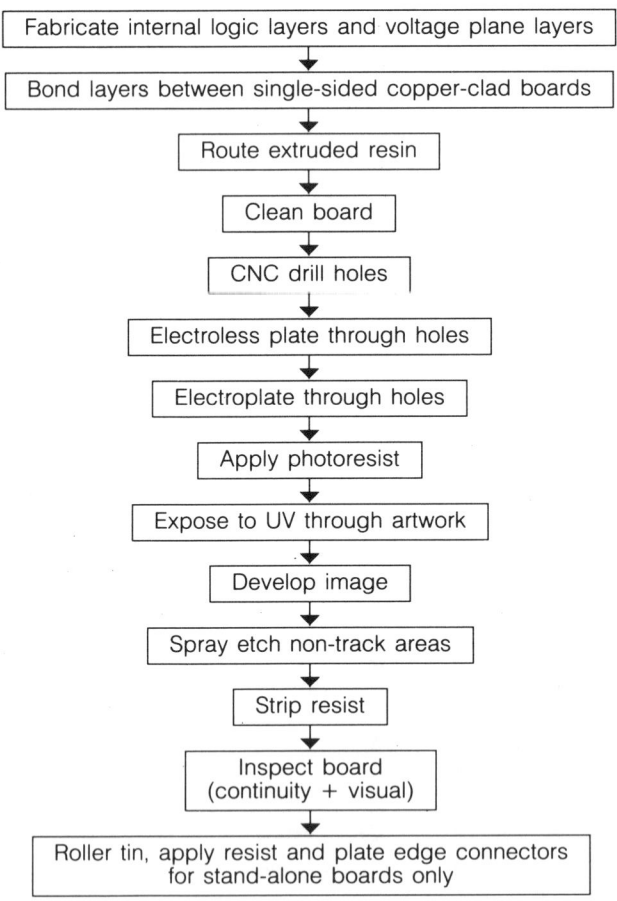

Figure 5.10 Multilayer printed circuit board fabrication.

plated through holes. Voltage layers, which are sometimes referred to as power and earth planes, carry the power supply connections for a board. They are usually single-sided boards which are mainly copper. The etched areas correspond to the sites where plated through holes pass to which no connection is required to the layer. The outermost layers provide connections to devices and to internal layers. These layers are effectively identical to the double-sided printed circuit tracking areas.

The manufacturing process for multilayer printed circuit boards is shown in Figure 5.10. It starts with the fabrication of the individual component layer boards, excluding the outermost layers, using the appropriate single-sided board or logic layer double-sided board processes. Each of the internal logic and voltage layers needs to be fabricated from thinner substrates than for stand-alone boards. The actual thickness of an individual layer is dependent on the number of layers which constitute the board and the desired total board thickness.

The actual processes required for the fabrication of the finished multilayer board are as follows: multilayer bonding; track and through hole creation; testing and finishing.

5.7.1 Multilayer bonding

Following the manufacture of the internal logic and voltage layers which constitute a multilayer board, it is necessary to combine them to make a single board. It is particularly important that sufficient testing is performed in order to eliminate faulty layer boards as the cost of a multilayer board is significantly greater than that of a single-layer board. Thus the constituent layers would typically undergo the full spectrum of tests for a bare board, including both visual and electrical testing.

Each internal layer needs to be thoroughly cleaned in an abrasive slurry to remove any contaminants. The layers are then baked in an oven to drive off any gases which could cause separation of the final board due to bubble formation during bonding.

The layers are built up as a sandwich on a jig which achieves the necessary alignment using jigging holes. The sandwich starts with an outer protective foil followed by a layer of copper foil which forms one of the outermost layers. The various internal layers are then added, each layer being interleaved with a layer of epoxy-resin-impregnated glass cloth. A sheet of copper foil and a protective film complete the sandwich structure and form the second-outermost layer. This assembly process is similar to the construction of the laminated copper-clad substrate. It is vitally important that the jigging ensures the correct alignment of the constituent layers during this process. Some compensation may be required to overcome any movement of inner layers which can occur during the bonding process. Once assembled, the board is bonded together by heating in a press. Three important parameters which need to be monitored after the bonding stage are the resultant board thickness, the degree of adhesion achieved between layers, and the uncured resin component of the board.

Board thickness needs to be within the tolerance required for usage. This is particularly important when gold-plated fingers are to be inserted into a socket. A board which is too thick will not fit into a socket; too thin a board will form a loose fit with poor electrical connections.

The degree of adhesion is a measure of the internal board areas in which resin is present. Poor adhesion results in spaces between layers in which no resin is present. This can be of particular importance with

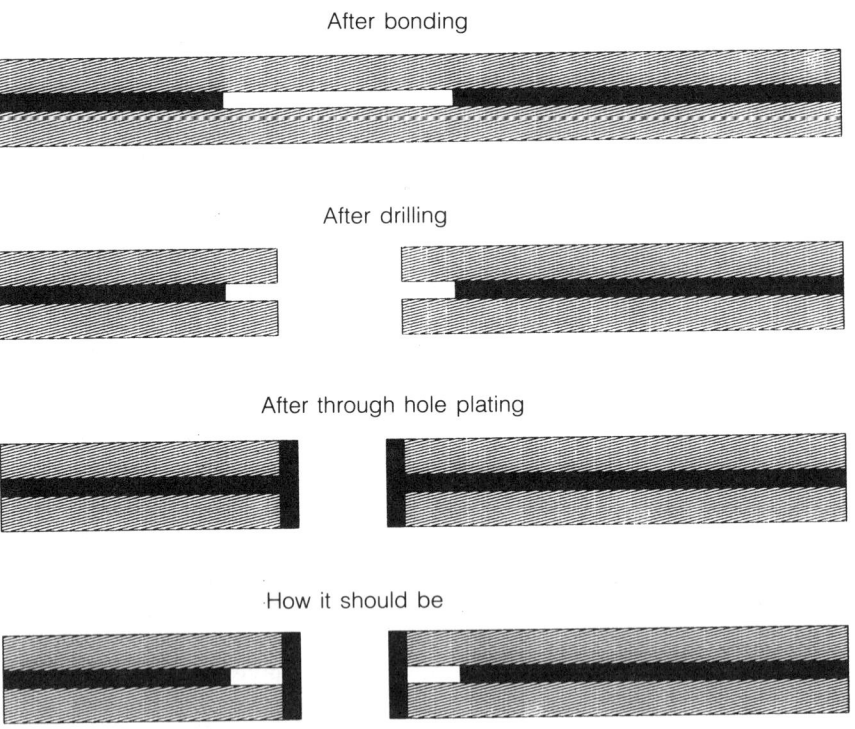

Figure 5.11 Effect of resin gaps on through hole plating.

power and earth planes because, if resin does not fill the non-copper areas where non-connection through holes are to pass, gaps can be left between layers. Plating solutions can penetrate these gaps and create unwanted connections between layers as shown in Figure 5.11.

The percentage of uncured epoxy adhesive needs to be minimized as this will smear in any subsequent drilling stages. The resulting layer of resin on the insides of through holes can prevent effective through hole plating from occurring. The curing rate of adhesive can be monitored by thermal analysis of the board.

After pressing, a routing process is performed to remove any resin material which has been extruded around the edges of a board during pressing. At this stage the board has the external appearance of a double-sided copper clad board.

5.7.2 Track and through hole creation

The multilayer board is at this stage processed as for an outer layer double-sided board with plated through holes. The processing commences with the preprocessing and CNC drilling processes. It is important that the drilling process is carefully controlled so as to produce a smooth hole and to minimize the amount of resin smear. Poor drilling can result in plated through holes which are liable to crack, i.e. the plating layer becomes open circuit, under thermal stress.

A desmear process is required after drilling to remove any smeared resin which can interfere with later plating processes. The desmear is performed using a strong oxidant such as permanganate, chromate or an oxygen plasma. The chemical processes in particular must be carefully controlled as, for example, a permanganate stain can result in through hole plating failing to connect electrically with inner layer copper.

The next process is the through hole plating. This plating process must connect the internal copper layers of the board in addition to connecting the outer copper layers together. This can be achieved using either the logic layer panel plating or the outer layer pattern plating methods, which define the photolithographic, etching, copper plating and tin plating sequences, used for the manufacture of double-sided boards. Connectors are gold plated when required.

A multilayer board is finished by cleaning and the application of solder resist and legend layers as for double-sided boards.

5.7.3 Testing

It is particularly important to perform a comprehensive series of tests on a completed multilayer board owing to its complexity and the high value circuitry which it will usually carry. These tests take the form of a visual inspection followed by a comprehensive bed-of-nails continuity test. X-rays may also be utilized to examine the internal structure of a multilayer board.

Boards which have been diagnosed as faulty may be cut into sections so that the exact nature of the fault can be determined. The information gained from such sectioning can then be used to improve the processes responsible for the fault.

6
Printed circuit board assembly

The ability to assemble a printed circuit board to a consistently high quality is essential to the manufacture of electronic devices. Printed circuit board assembly covers a wide range of different processes which are dependent on the type of component to be assembled, the two major types of components being leaded components and surface mount components. The assembly of leaded components into printed circuit boards has until recently been the main activity associated with the printed circuit board assembly processes. Surface mount component assembly and the assembly of boards containing both leaded and surface mount components are discussed in Chapter 7.

From the assembly point of view, leaded components can be classified as axial lead, radial lead, dual-in-line and non-standard packages. Each of the packaging classes has its own assembly requirements.

Although the high speed automatic assembly of printed circuit boards represents the state of the art, manual assembly is still widely employed. In fact manual assembly is still an essential process as about 6% of components cannot as yet be assembled automatically.

An important aspect of printed circuit board assembly is the soldering process. The production of high quality solder joints is essential for the production of high quality boards.

In order to ensure that an assembled printed circuit board is functional it is necessary to incorporate comprehensive testing procedures during and after manufacture in order to identify and eliminate faults. It is important to be able to identify both design faults and localized manufacturing faults. When justifiable in terms of cost, manual reworking can be utilized to rectify manufacturing faults.

This chapter, which is concerned with the assembly of leaded components into printed circuit boards, addresses the areas of hand assembly, automatic component insertion, assembly faults, soldering techniques, printed circuit board cleaning, testing and reworking.

6.1 HAND ASSEMBLY

Despite the increasing level of automation, hand assembly of printed circuit boards is still an important process. This is particularly the case when non-standard components are used and where low production volumes preclude the use of automatic insertion equipment on economic grounds. It is not yet possible to perform 100% of printed circuit board assembly automatically, mainly because of lack of standardization. This is particularly true in the case of larger components such as transformers, switches and connectors.

The requirements of a manual assembly environment can be functionally divided into operator skill level, support equipment and task regulation. The operator skill level required for a particular assembly task is dependent on the complexity of the printed circuit board to be assembled and the level of sophistication of the support equipment. Skilled operators require much less task regulation than unskilled operators.

The three functional requirements for manual assembly can each vary considerably. Although the requirements are interdependent, a particular task can be completed by operators with differing skill levels provided that the support equipment and task regulation are adjusted to match. These variations are dependent on the complexity of the printed circuit board and the production volume required. A fairly simple, low production volume printed circuit board can be hand assembled by presenting a skilled operator with a parts list, a printed circuit board and an assembly diagram. This approach allows the operator to choose any appropriate assembly sequence provided that a working board is produced.

As the production volume and/or printed circuit board complexity increases, support methods are required which enable a less skilled operator to assemble boards at higher speeds and which reduce the likelihood of error. These support methods can reach similar levels of complexity and rigour to those of automated assembly methods. The main areas where such improvements can be made are in the automation of part preparation and part handling operations.

The principal operations used for manual assembly are lead preforming, component insertion, and lead clinching and cropping. These three operations can be performed either sequentially, by a single operator, or separately, possibly by different operators. The soldering and test operations associated with manually assembled printed circuit boards are discussed in sections 6.4 and 6.7 respectively.

6.1.1 Manual component preforming

The purpose of component preforming is to ensure that component leads are correctly spaced such that they can be inserted directly into holes in a printed circuit board. This process is essential in the case of axial components where the leads are initially collinear. Axial lead and dual-in-line packaged components may need to have their leads shaped even though they are preformed with standard spacings. A further function of lead preforming is to cut leads to a preferred length for insertion. The simplest method of lead preforming is to use a pair of long-nosed pliers. Axial components need to have their leads bent at right angles to give the lead spacing required by the target printed circuit board. Component forming without the use of jigging is particularly error prone, the accuracy of lead spacing being a function of operator skill. Radial lead and dual-in-line packaged components in principle require only minimal forming. However, in the case of dual-in-line packaged components, the leads are initially splayed to facilitate handling by automatic insertion machines. This means that, before manual insertion, all the leads need to be closed up to match the pitch of the holes in the target printed circuit board. This is achieved by using an integrated circuit insertion tool. A similar device also exists for removing dual-in-line components from sockets. It is, however, a standard practice to shape the leads in order to ensure that a component's body stands sufficiently proud of the board surface to provide adequate cooling. Figure 6.1 shows typical axial and radial lead configurations after preforming.

Improvements in the areas of component preparation and handling encourage the procurement of components which are available in high level packaging. This enables the use of semi-automatic equipment for preprocessing and feeding.

The preforming of component leads before they are presented to an operator for assembly can provide a significant improvement in assembly time. An intermediate stage between manual lead forming and full automation is the use of semi-automatic die forming devices. The use of die forming encourages the use of standard component lead spacing which simplifies any later implementation of automated assembly.

Axial lead   Radial lead

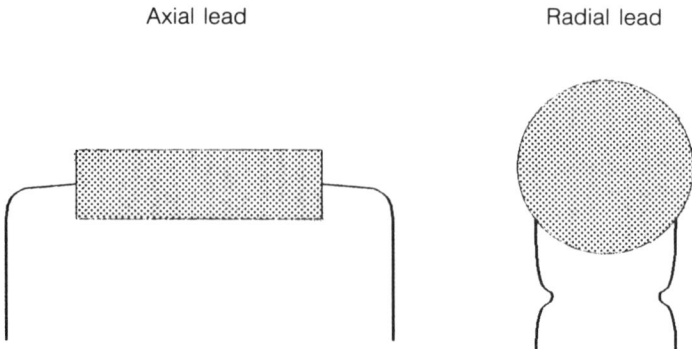

Figure 6.1 Axial and radial component leads after preforming.

Die forming for axial leaded components is performed in a press which bends and cuts component leads. Adhesive tape is applied to axial component bodies whilst they are still in the lead taped packaging as delivered from suppliers. The components are placed in a press which bends the leads to a predefined spacing and crops them to the required length. The lengths to which component leads are cropped is dependent on later processes. The shortest length to which leads can be cropped is that which just leaves a sufficient length for soldering protruding from a board after insertion. Leads which are to be clinched prior to soldering need to be left sufficiently longer.

Die forming devices for radial leaded components need to provide the correct lead spacing and crop leads to the appropriate lengths as for axial components. They also need to shape component leads such that the component body stands clear of the board's surface after insertion. This is achieved by forming an indentation into the lead's profile which will not pass through the hole in the board. Radial components, such as transistors, which have more than two leads have the same lead forming requirements as two-leaded radial components but require their own die forming devices.

6.1.2 Manual component insertion

Component insertion in its simplest form can be performed with a board-holding jig, sequenced components, a pair of pliers, and optionally a pair of wire cutters.

The target printed circuit boards need to be initially mounted in fixtures in order to ensure that there is sufficient space under the board to accommodate component leads before they are cropped. The simplest form of fixture consists of a frame onto which a printed circuit board can be placed. A more ergonomic design consists of a frame which holds a board by its edges and can be angled to suit an operator's comfort.

The components to be assembled into a printed circuit board are numbered in the sequence in which they are to be inserted. The component assembly sequence is typically in increasing order of component complexity. Resistors, capacitors and diodes are inserted first and complex integrated circuit components are inserted last. An exception to this is when integrated circuits are socket mounted in which case the sockets are placed first. The position and orientation in which a component is to be inserted into a printed circuit board are indicated by means of a screen-printed legend on the board's surface. A paper copy of the board layout showing component positions without the accompanying track layout may be provided to reduce confusion.

The simplest form of manual assembly involves an operator picking components up with a pair of long-nosed pliers and pushing the leads into the appropriate holes in a board.

The sequential insertion of components into a printed circuit board does not allow an operator to learn the task as each consecutive operation is different. A greater operator efficiency can be achieved by assembling in batches of identical boards. Inserting the same component type into the same position on a number of boards enables the task to be learnt, which increases operator speed. This is achieved by placing a number of boards on a rotary table. The operator places one component into each board in turn before passing on to the next component. Some of the more sophisticated aids for manual assembly leave very little scope for human error. Such machines utilize a fixture into which a board to be assembled is fastened. A light beam is then directed onto the board to indicate the position in which the next component is to be inserted by the operator. Components are delivered to a slot in the form of a tray containing components of the same type, the component trays being delivered to the operator's slot in the correct sequence for assembly. The operator's task is thus reduced to taking a component from the currently available tray and inserting it into the position on the board marked by the light beam.

6.1.3 High volume manual assembly

When large volume manual assembly is to be performed the task is broken up into subassembly operations for use in an assembly line type of operation. High volume assembly can be performed in line or using discrete operator stations.

An in-line assembly line would typically take the form of a conveyor which can either be manually powered or electrically driven. Boards are presented to each operator in turn, each of whom inserts a small number of components from numbered trays. As with all assembly line applications it is important to ensure that the line is well balanced in that each operator's activity should take a similar amount of time in order to avoid bottlenecks.

The use of a rotary table where an operator performs the same operation on a batch of boards before proceeding to the next operation is also a means of obtaining high volume assembly. Each method has its own individual merits and factors such as availability of floor space and personnel need to be taken into account when selecting a system.

Successful medium volume manual assembly operations have been implemented using the flexible manufacturing system (FMS) and just-in-time (JIT) approaches normally used by advanced automation systems. A flexible manufacturing system type of operation can be implemented by having manual assembly stations in place of machine tools. The assembly stations are served by a materials handling system utilizing conveyors or automated guided vehicles. Individual boards are identified by means of a bar code which is read, using a bar code reader, by each operator who performs an operation on a board. A central computer system is thus able to track the progress of each individual board throughout assembly and to provide information on the performance of the manufacturing facility.

Just-in-time manufacturing can be implemented by using a Kanban system for component delivery and demand-driven assembly. This prevents a stock of partially completed boards from accumulating.

6.1.4 Manual component lead cropping and clinching

Once inserted, component leads need to be cropped to prevent them from protruding too far from a board's surface if they were not previously preformed to the required length. Component leads which are too long are liable to form short circuits with adjacent leads. Conversely, if leads are too short an adequate solder joint cannot be

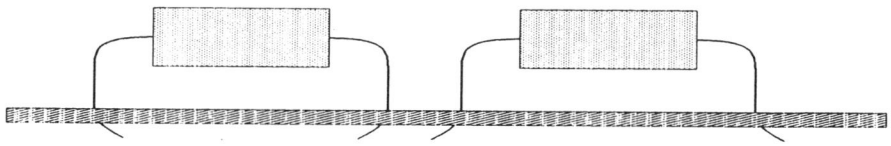

Figure 6.2 Clinched leads.

formed. The cropping operation is often combined with a clinching operation. Clinching involves bending leads, usually towards or away from each other for two-leaded devices, in order to prevent the component falling out of the board before being soldered in place as shown in Figure 6.2. Clinching is particularly important if the component assembly is performed in stages as component displacement can easily occur whilst a board is being transported.

In order to achieve a clinching and cropping operation it is necessary to invert the printed circuit board. It is therefore essential to constrain components mechanically in order to prevent them falling out of the board on inversion. This is achieved by placing boards in a fixture which places a layer of foam rubber and a restraining plate on top of the board before inversion.

The clinching and cropping operation can be performed in a single motion using a pair of diagonal wire cutters. This is achieved by grasping the lead at the point to be cut in the pliers and applying a bending motion whilst cutting the lead.

6.2 AUTOMATIC COMPONENT INSERTION

The automatic insertion of leaded components into printed circuit boards needs to address the three major categories of components: axial lead; radial lead; and dual-in-line packaging. The widely differing requirements of these component categories have caused automatic insertion equipment to have been developed separately for each. Recently, integrated computer control and materials handling equipment has enabled the three insertion processes to be integrated in a similar form to that of flexible manufacturing systems.

The development of early insertion machines was limited by the lack of standardization in handling mechanisms and packaging. This problem has recently been overcome as a result of cooperation between manufacturers. The automatic insertion of leaded components consists of two processes, a presequencing process which delivers components to the insertion machines in the correct order for insertion, and the actual component insertion process.

6.2.1 Axial component sequencing

Early axial component insertion machines had to work with reels of pure components, i.e. all components were of a single type per reel. This severely limited the number of components which could be inserted into a printed circuit board in a single operation. The practice of using multiple break-away boards, where several identical printed circuit boards are constructed as a single larger board, improved the efficiency of the insertion process by the multiplying factor. The break-away board approach still left scope for improvement, which led to the development of the axial component sequencer.

The sequencing of axial components takes the form of creating a single lead-taped bandolier containing all the axial components required for a circuit in the order in which they are to be inserted. Dedicated program-controlled sequencing machines are available which perform this function. A sequencing machine is fitted with a large number of reels of lead-taped component bandoliers. Each bandolier contains a single type of component as purchased from the suppliers. The sequencer is programmed to assemble the components in the correct sequence for insertion into a particular printed circuit board design. Components are removed from their original bandolier by cutting the leads close to the tape. The components are then optionally transported to a test station which performs simple electrical tests. Resistors and capacitors are checked for value. Diodes are checked for polarity, forward voltage drop and reverse leakage current. The verification process is designed to detect missing components, out of sequence components, faulty components and reversed-polarized components. Faulty components can be discarded at this point.

Having passed the electrical tests the components are lead taped into a bandolier in the correct sequence and at the correct pitch spacing ready for input into an insertion machine. The sequenced bandoliers are often gap spaced, i.e. a component position is left empty, to delimit repetitive, i.e. individual board, sequences.

Axial component sequencing machines can either be stand-alone units or an integral part of an insertion machine. Off-line sequences are available with capacities of over 200 input stations which could typically hold a company's complete stock of axial leaded components. Modern insertion machines, which are tending towards integrated automation, utilize integrated sequencing devices. The use of integral sequencing mechanisms eliminates the need to create an intermediate sequenced bandolier. Components can be taken from their original bandolier and delivered directly to the insertion head, optionally via a verification process. Modern automatic axial component sequencer–inserter machines have capacities of between 20 and 160 component reels of the standard 52 mm variety, and optionally the smaller 26 mm variety, of edge-taped axial components.

6.2.2 Axial component insertion

The automatic insertion process for axial components has been developed since the late 1950s. Axial components were the first variety of component for which automatic insertion machines were developed as they were the first type of component to be available in a standardized form. The sequence of operations required for the insertion of an axial component into a printed circuit board is as follows: remove component from lead-taped bandolier; preform component leads; insert component; crop and clinch leads. Early axial component insertion machines were semi-automatic bench-mounted devices which were functionally similar to a stapler. The principle of operation of these early devices is still used in today's more sophisticated devices. The components are fed into a cutting position where their leads are cut from the edge-taped bandolier in a similar manner to the way in which they were removed from their original bandolier. The leads are formed into a staple-like shape by means of grooved formers. Typically the cutting and forming operations are performed in a single operation by arranging a shear point to occur on each lead as the formers descend onto the component. Once the leads have been formed the component is pushed down so that its leads are inserted into the prelocated destination holes in a printed circuit board. A successfully inserted component finally has its leads cut and clinched. These operations are again performed in a single operation by a cutter which severs the leads at a predefined length below the board and then continues on to bend the leads. The clinching operation can bend the leads either inwards or outwards (again this is similar to a stapler). The reason for the clinching operation is to prevent a component from falling out of the board before it is soldered into place. A typical device for the automatic insertion of axial components is shown in Figure 6.3.

Early machines could only insert components at a fixed insertion

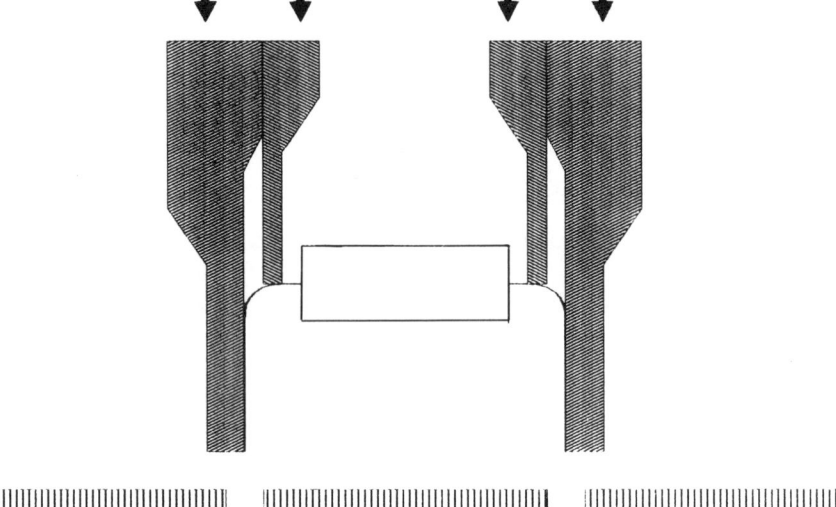

Figure 6.3 Axial component insertion head.

span, the distance between hole centres. The range of body sizes supported by the RS296 standard added a requirement that components be inserted at different insertion spans. This led to the development of the variable centre distance (VCD) insertion head machines which have since become almost universal (Figure 6.4). Variable centre distance machines can also be programmed to accommodate a range of different component body and lead diameters. A modern axial component insertion machine can typically insert components with insertion spans from 7 to 22 mm under program control.

Some axial component insertion machines have a facility to insert wire links, wire link insertion being a similar process to axial leaded component insertion. Wire link insertion is performed by removing lengths of wire from a continuous spool. The wire is then cut, inserted, cropped and clinched as for axial leaded components.

6.2.3 Radial component sequencing

Radial components are typically sequenced on-line rather than using the off-line formation of an intermediate sequenced packaging. A radial

Figure 6.4 Axial component insertion machine.

component insertion machine is equipped with a feeder station containing typically between 20 and 80 reels of sprocket-taped components, the 5 mm standard spacing being the usual configuration. The use of standard lead spacing allows a range of non-standard radial components to use the same packaging; this includes axial leaded components which have been formed into a radial lead form for vertical mounting.

6.2.4 Radial component insertion

The automation of the insertion process for radial components was developed much later than that for axial components. The main reason for this was the lack of standardization of component packaging and of lead spacing. In the early 1970s a cooperative programme to standardize radial component packaging was undertaken. This resulted in a standard tape format and a standard 5 mm lead spacing. Radial components are now readily available on sprocket-feedable standard tapes.

The standard spacing of radial component leads simplifies the insertion head as little lead preforming needs to be performed. Once removed from the sprocket tape, radial components can be picked up by a comb-like arrangement which can make small adjustments to the lead spacing. Optional on-line component verification can be performed at this stage as for axial components. Two approaches are used actually to push a radial component into a board's holes. The first approach applies a downward force directly to the body of the component after the leads have been accurately positioned over the holes. The second approach involves holding the body of the component and pushing it into a comb-shaped tool. The insertion force is then applied directly through the component's leads. A typical device for the automatic insertion of radial components is shown in Figure 6.5. Modern radial component insertion machines can insert components at 0°, +90° and −90° orientations from the standard position, which improves board density.

The success rate of radial component insertion is related to the quality of the components which are to be inserted. The purchasing of cheaper, poorer quality components can be a false economy as variations in lead spacing, due to poorer quality control, can lead to a high failure of insertion rate. Poor quality components are also more susceptible to damage during handling.

6.2.5 Dual-in-line component insertion

Dual-in-line component insertion includes both dual-in-line packaged components and integrated circuit sockets. The capability also exists for automatically inserting dual-in-line packaged components into their sockets. Typically dual-in-line package sizes which have between 6 and 42 pins with widths of 7.62, 10.16 and 15.24 mm can be inserted by a single automatic insertion machine.

Components are gravity fed into the insertion machines from the high level stick packaging. A typical capability is 72 stick inputs. The capability to replenish stick component magazines automatically and to provide an on-line inventory of components has recently become available.

Automatic verification testing of dual-in-line packaged components

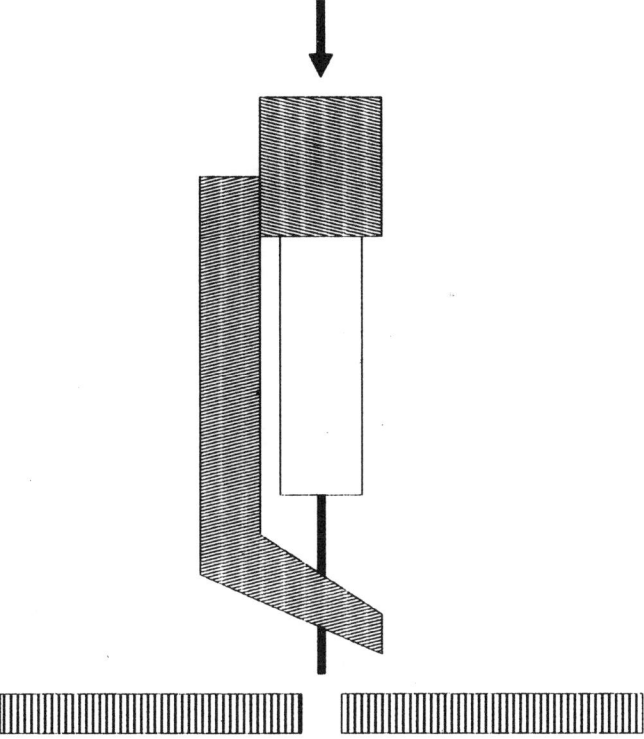

Figure 6.5 Radial component insertion head.

can be performed as for axial and radial components. Obviously the testing is limited by the complexity of the components used. SSI and MSI components, which include the standard TTL and CMOS ranges, can be tested for type, functionality and orientation before insertion.

The insertion process uses a similar process to the lead gathering stage of axial component insertion. The component leads are clinched after insertion as for axial and radial components. Figure 6.6 shows a typical device for the automatic insertion of dual-in-line components.

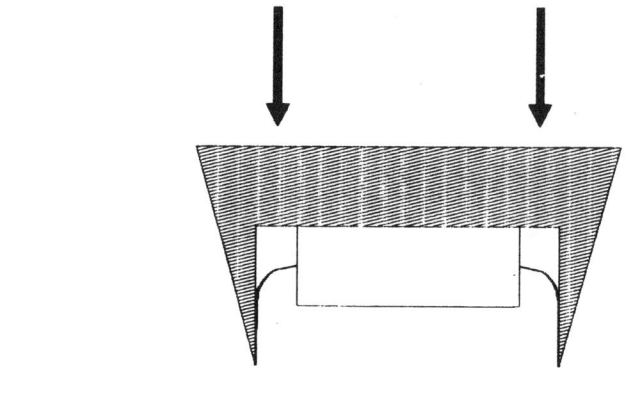

Figure 6.6 DIL component insertion head.

6.2.6 Integrated component insertion systems

The axial, radial and dual-in-line packaged component insertion machines can be integrated into a complete insertion system by means of a suitable materials handling system for transporting boards between machines. The materials handling system typically takes the form of a series of conveyor belts. This materials handling capability, when coupled with an integrated computer control system, forms a flexible manufacturing cell for component assembly.

As with all integrated systems, it is necessary to be able to compensate for different production rates of the individual machines. This can easily be achieved by utilizing buffer stores where partially completed boards can be placed while waiting for the next insertion machine to become available.

Today's sophisticated design tools, such as the Racal Redac Visula design system, can be integrated with a wide range of manufacturing equipment. Design systems can produce much more than hard copies of printed circuit board layouts. The facility to generate a CNC drilling machine tape, which integrates the design process with the board drilling process, is well established. In addition, design systems such as Visula can be integrated with automatic and semi-automatic component insertion machines using numeric control technology. Design systems can also generate test programs for direct use with automatic test equipment.

The machine interfaces are achieved by incorporating user-configurable post-processors into the design systems. This allows new types of automatic production equipment to be supported.

6.2.7 Robotic assembly

The flexibility of industrial robots makes them applicable to a wide range of applications including the assembly of electronic devices. A robot can be considered as a general-purpose machine which is customized to a particular application by attaching application-specific tooling. In a typical application an industrial robot will use techniques that are more related to manual assembly techniques than to automatic assembly techniques. This means that robotic systems need to be provided with components which have been previously sequenced and formed ready for insertion.

The flexibility of industrial robots offers a solution to the problem of automating the insertion of non-standard components. A robot cannot compete in terms of either speed or accuracy with dedicated insertion machines for standard component forms. The non-standard components, however, form perhaps 10% of a printed circuit board's population but may account for up to 80% of assembly labour costs.

A wide range of tooling has been developed to enable a robot to perform electronic assembly operations. This usually takes the form of fingers which may be equipped with tactile sensing. In order to be effective a robot component assembly station will need to be equipped with vision system support in order to overcome the inherent accuracy problems associated with industrial robots.

6.3 ASSEMBLY-RELATED FAULTS

There are a number of different faults which can occur in the assembly operation. These also include component damage which can occur during handling. Thus assembly-related faults can be divided into the categories of insertion failure and component damage.

6.3.1 Insertion failure

Insertion failure faults cause components to be either missing from a printed circuit board, in the worst case, or incorrectly aligned with respect to the overall board geometry. The simplest and worst-case form of insertion fault is that a component failed to be inserted into the holes of a printed circuit board. This reflects the go–no go nature of the insertion process. Insertion failure can be caused either by a misalignment of insertion heads or by incorrect spacing of component leads. Printed circuit board manufacturing faults such as missing holes and holes of incorrect size can also cause insertion failure. Radial leaded components are particularly susceptible to insertion failure due to incorrect lead spacing. A common cause of the lead spacing problem is the use of poor quality components. A company's purchasing department may purchase poorer quality components on economic grounds. The lower quality components can have wider lead spacing tolerance and significantly increase the insertion failure rate. This increased failure rate can result in poorer quality components being more costly than higher quality devices.

Successfully inserted components may still be considered at fault if they are offset from the perpendicular to a board's surface. A typical tolerance for most axial and radial components is that their leads are no more than 15° from the perpendicular. In the case of axial components which are mounted in a vertical configuration, a similar tolerance will be placed on the maximum angle to which the component body makes with the board's perpendicular. Figure 6.7 shows examples of acceptable and unacceptable component body angles. A typical value for vertically mounted axial component bodies would be 25°. Angular deviations from the perpendicular are due to component leads being bent during or after insertion. This effect can also occur during soldering if the holes are significantly larger than component leads.

A further tolerance which may be placed on inserted components is that of the distance of a component's body from the surface of a printed circuit board as shown in Figure 6.8. The placing of components too close to the board may result in part of the component body entering a hole, which can adversely effect soldering. Components mounted too proud of a board are more easily damaged during handling and may cause later clearance problems when packaged. High power devices, such as resistors over 3 W, may need to be mounted at a greater distance above the board surface in order to effect adequate cooling.

The spacing of a component body above the board surface can be established by preforming the component's leads before insertion. The preforming takes the form of crimping the lead such that it is too wide to go into a hole at more than a preset distance.

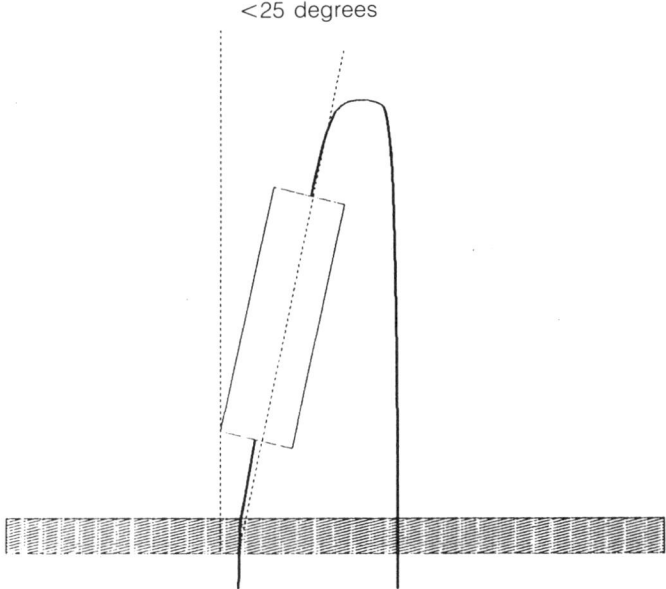

Figure 6.7 Vertical axial component acceptance angles.

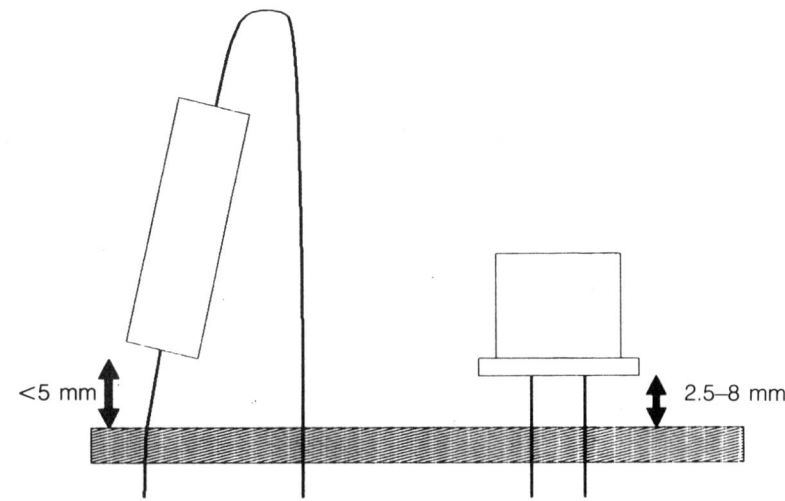

Figure 6.8 Acceptable component–board spacing.

6.3.2 Component damage

Component damage usually takes the form of a crack or a chip in the insulating material surrounding a component. Minor damage does not necessarily constitute a serious fault unless the internal structure of the device is exposed. The target environment of the finished printed circuit board will dictate the maximum tolerable component damage.

Axial leaded components and in particular radial leaded components are easily damaged at the points where the leads enter the component body. This damage takes the form of cracked or chipped insulation which is usually caused by excessive bending of the leads close to the body of the component. Chipped insulation is usually only considered a serious fault if the damage extends to the actual component body, or in particular if the underlying layers are exposed.

In the case of dual-in-line components, particularly when ceramic encapsulation is used, a common form of damage is a break in the encapsulation near to an edge or a corner of a device. This again need not constitute a fault unless the underlying layers are exposed. In the case of ceramic-encapsulated devices, an internal glass layer provides a hermetic seal. Provided the glass layer remains intact, the hermeticity of the device is preserved.

6.4 SOLDERING TECHNIQUES

The soldering process is where all the electrical connections between component leads and their corresponding printed circuit board land areas are made. It is therefore very important that a consistently high quality of solder joint can be made. The soldering process involves the application of a molten solder and a flux material to the board areas where connections are to be made. There are two major soldering processes in common usage, hand soldering and bulk soldering methods such as wave or dip soldering. Soldering operations can be enhanced by using technologies such as hot air knives and solder–cut–solder techniques.

6.1.1 Solder materials

When metals are combined to form an alloy, there exists a ratio of the parent metals, called the eutectic composition, which has a lower solidification temperature than any other ratio. The melting point of a eutectic alloy is always a discrete temperature rather than a temperature range. This is always less than the melting point of both of the parent metals. Solder normally consists of a lead and tin alloy which is close to the eutectic composition. The eutectic composition corresponds to 63% tin, 37% lead, which has a melting point of 183 °C (Coombs, 1988).

Solders are commercially available with a range of compositions around the eutectic composition. A tin content less than the optimal eutectic may be used for economic reasons owing to the high price of tin compared with lead.

It is important to minimize the amounts of impurities present in solder alloys which can be detrimental to the quality of the resulting solder joints. The metals copper, gold, iron and zinc are known to have adverse effects on solder performance. This is important as gold and particularly copper are commonly used in the electronics industry. The presence of non-metallic contaminants such as oxygen and sulphur is also detrimental to solder performance.

6.4.2 Flux materials and application

The function of a flux is to remove, and to prevent the re-formation of, any metal oxides, sulphides or any other contaminants present on the metal surfaces to be soldered which may be detrimental to the formation of a good solder joint. A flux must be a good conductor of heat so as to allow all areas of a joint to reach soldering temperature uniformly. It must also be readily removable so that its corrosive properties do not damage a finished board's integrity.

Fluxes are usually composed of an activator, which is usually a hydrochloride compound, in an alcohol-based solvent. Resins, which are themselves weak activators, are used as less corrosive fluxes. The hydrochloride activators reduce at soldering temperatures to hydrochloric acid which readily dissolves any oxide layers. The activator strength required is dependent on the properties of the metals to be soldered.

Another property which is required of a flux is that of its density, sometimes referred to as its solids content, which affects the coverage properties of a flux. The higher the flux density, the greater the amount of flux which will be deposited on a board's surface by an application process. The density is defined by the ratio of the resin and activator materials to the solvent material. High density fluxes are required when a larger amount of flux is required, for example with printed circuit boards which have high component densities and small holes. High density fluxes are much more difficult to remove after soldering and hence complicate the subsequent cleaning processes.

The two properties of activity and density must be closely matched to the properties of the printed circuit boards in order to achieve a good wetting and hence good quality solder joints. The flux density needs to be selected to match the component packing density and hole size of a board. The activity needs to be selected according to the solderability of the metal base areas to be soldered.

The application of flux to a board to be soldered must be performed in a very efficient manner in order to achieve high quality results. Flux must be applied uniformly and must in particular thoroughly cover the metal areas which are to be soldered. If too little flux is applied, poor solder joints will result. Too much flux presents a potential fire hazard owing to the solvent content, and significantly increases the amount of cleaning required after soldering. It is always advisable to use an air knife or a squeegee to remove excess flux after application.

In a typical bulk soldering application, printing circuit boards pass through a fluxing station immediately before soldering. The simplest method of flux application is to apply flux manually using a brush. This method is not suited to high speed and high volume applications.

More sophisticated fluxing stations make use of a flux bath and a method of applying the flux to board surfaces. It is important to maintain a flux bath in order to ensure correct flux application and performance. Because fluxes are usually alcohol based, flux baths continually lose solvent by the process of evaporation. This evaporation has the effect of increasing the density of a flux. It is therefore necessary to thin the flux periodically to restore the lost solvent content. The rate of solvent evaporation can be monitored by periodically measuring the specific gravity of the flux. In addition to solvent replenishment, additional flux needs to be added periodically to maintain the level of the bath. A flux bath should also be completely emptied at regular intervals so as to prevent the buildup of contaminants which have been added by boards passing through the bath.

Fluxing stations usually operate on the foam fluxing, wave fluxing or dip fluxing principle.

Foam fluxers consist of a flux bath which has a submerged nozzle containing a porous stone material. Air is pumped through the stone to produce a flux foam. Printed circuit boards pass over the foam which deposits a uniformly thin layer of flux on their surfaces. Foam fluxers are particularly effective at depositing flux in plated through holes as the effect of bubbles bursting sprays flux into the holes. With foam fluxers it is important to filter and dry the air supply in order to remove water and other contamination. The air pressure needs to be carefully controlled in order to produce a uniform foam consistency.

A wave fluxer makes use of a flux bath and a nozzle through which flux is pumped to produce a standing wave of flux. Printed circuit boards are passed over the top of the wave which deposits flux on their surfaces. The actual amount of flux which is deposited is less controllable than that of the foam fluxing method.

Spray fluxing, which sprays flux onto board surfaces, offers very good control of the amount of flux deposited. This method suffers from the problems that it requires very volatile solvents and is very messy.

Fluxes only become active when heated to a sufficient temperature to cause the chemical breakdown of the activator material. Although this heating can be made to occur in the actual solder, it increases the amount of time which a board needs to be in contact with the solder. This problem can be overcome by having a preheating process between the fluxing and soldering processes. The preheating process raises the board temperature to about 90 °C which is sufficient to activate the flux. Excess volatiles such as alcohol solvents and water are driven off during preheating. This reduces effects such as spattering and blow holes in solder joints which can result from the rapid vaporization of volatiles which come into contact with molten solder. The preheating also has the effect of reducing the thermal shock when a board enters the soldering bath. This minimizes warping, mechanical damage and damage to heat-sensitive components.

The preheating process is achieved either by the use of radiant heat from electrical heating elements, or by directing hot air at the boards. Excess flux can present a fire hazard with radiant heat sources as the solvents can ignite if they drip onto a heating element. The heated air approach is more suited to multilayer boards as the air is able to penetrate plated through holes, ensuring uniform heating. Through holes are often shielded from radiant heat sources by the nature of their geometries. A combination of the two techniques uses hot air to eliminate volatiles followed by a radiant heat source.

6.4.3 Hand soldering

Hand soldering is only really practical for small batches and for the reworking of faulty printed circuit boards. By definition, each solder joint is created separately which means that the quality of soldering can vary considerably across a board.

Hand soldering is performed using a fine-tipped soldering iron with a power rating under 30 W. The soldering operation takes place by applying solder and a heated soldering iron simultaneously to the joint to be made. Solder is available in a wire form which simplifies the handling and application for hand soldering. Solder wire is commercially available in reels from 10 m in length upwards. Solder wire is available in a range of thicknesses including 18 and 22 SWG.

The application of flux for hand soldering can utilize a separate flux or a flux-cored solder. When flux is separate, it needs to be applied to the joints to be soldered with a brush before soldering. Many of today's solder wires are available with integral flux cores running through the length of the solder wire. This obviates the need to apply flux separately.

When hand soldering is used for reworking it is often necessary to unsolder defective joints prior to resoldering. The reworking aspect of hand soldering is described in section 6.7.5.

6.4.4 Solder baths

Bulk soldering methods, such as dip soldering and wave soldering, utilize a solder bath and a method of solder application. The process name is derived from the actual application method. The requirements of a solder bath are common to both bulk soldering methods.

A solder bath consists of an electrically heated reservoir which maintains solder in a molten state. It is important that the bath is able to maintain a uniformly consistent solder temperature. Good thermal insulation is required to maintain uniformity and reduce heat loss into the local environment. The heating system must be sufficiently powerful to maintain the required operating temperatures. The functions of initially melting solder on startup and maintaining working temperatures have different heating requirements. The initial heating needs to be rapid but does not need to be accurately controlled. The temperature maintenance needs to be carefully controllable but only involves small temperature changes. Many solder baths overcome these two differing requirements by utilizing two heating systems, a powerful heater for initial melting and a smaller thermostatically controlled heater for working temperature maintenance.

It is very important to ensure that the heaters are positioned such that uniform heating occurs. This is particularly important if a high powered bulk heater is used for initial solder melting. If a bath is only heated from the bottom, the solder will initially melt at the bottom leaving a top layer of solid solder. This can result in large pressures being generated as the molten solder expands. In the worst case the top layer of solid solder can rupture and eject a geyser of molten solder a considerable distance – a very hazardous occurrence. The positioning of the temperature maintenance heaters is also important so as not to generate localized hot and cold spots at the surface of the bath which would result in non-uniform soldering characteristics.

Once established, the level of solder in a bath should be monitored and additional solder added when the level falls.

A working solder bath has a surface layer of metallic impurities which is usually referred to as dross. Dross consists primarily of oxides of lead and tin which result from the chemical interaction between molten solder and atmospheric oxygen. The rate of dross formation is a function of the surface area of molten solder and of the amount of agitation applied to the solder. The presence of dross is detrimental to the soldering process and the dross should be periodically removed. This is usually performed using a dross skimmer. Wave soldering machines are particularly sensitive to the amount of dross as it has an abrasive effect on the pumping mechanisms used to create the solder wave. This is a particular problem as strongly agitated solder waves have the effect of increasing the rate of dross formation.

Dross formation can be reduced by applying a blanket of a soldering oil to the solder surface, thus reducing the area of solder exposed to the atmosphere. When used, solder blankets should be changed on a regular basis as they quickly become contaminated.

It is well known that solder is easily contaminated, particularly by other metals such as copper. The solder bath and all of its associated equipment should therefore be made of a material, such as stainless steel, which does not wet in or dissolve in molten solder.

6.4.5 Wave soldering

Wave soldering is one of the commonest methods of applying solder to a printed circuit board. The description of wave soldering covers a wide range of different methods which vary by the number of solder waves used and the fluid flow within waves. In its simplest form a solder wave is created by pumping molten solder through a nozzle, which is situated at the bottom of a solder bath, to produce a standing wave of solder.

The characteristics required of a solder wave are dictated by a number of factors, many of which are contradictory and require compromises to be reached. A solder wave needs to be carefully controlled in order to produce the optimal characteristics which minimize soldering defects. The major soldering defects and their causes are described in section 6.5.

The contact time between solder wave and printed circuit board has particularly contradictory requirements. Short contact times are suggested by the desire to minimize board heating and to reduce dross formation. Longer contact times are required to ensure a good metallurgical bond and to maximize the scrubbing motion of the solder

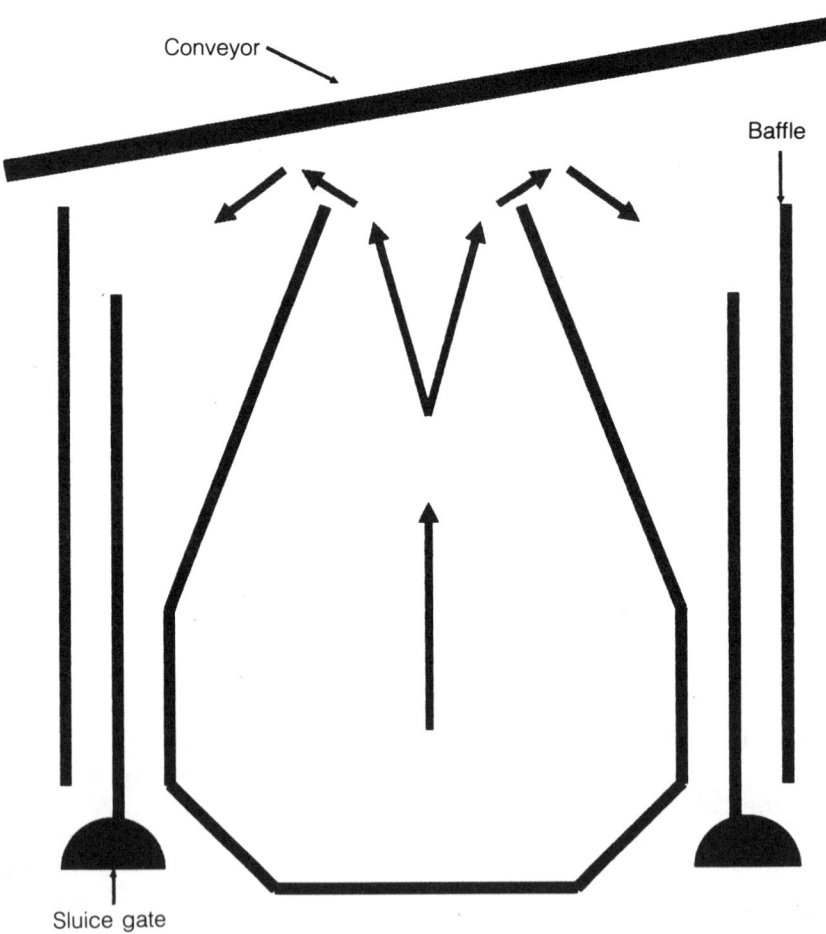

Figure 6.9 Bidirectional solder wave nozzle.

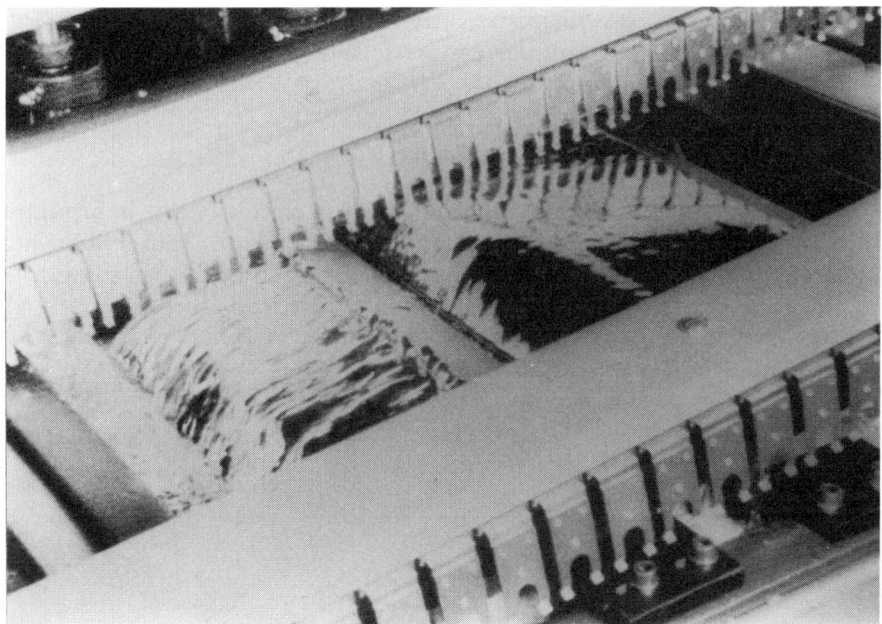

Figure 6.10 Dual-wave solder bath.

wave against the board which improves performance of the flux. In general the fluid flow in a solder wave should be uniform to ensure even contact with boards and to reduce the chance of solder passing onto the top surface of a board.

Ideally a printed circuit board should leave a solder bath at zero velocity in order to prevent the formation of solder spikes. This apparently impossible condition can be met by using a bidirectional solder wave. Bidirectional waves are formed by pumping solder through a shaped vertical nozzle as shown in Figure 6.9. A dual-wave solder bath is shown in Figure 6.10. The central region of the wave can be controlled to give a velocity profile which minimizes solder spike formation. The dynamics of wave soldering are very complex and are in general little understood. Some of the variables which need to be controlled are the number of waves, the wave shape, the solder flow characteristics, solder temperature, and printed circuit board approach speed and angle. The interaction between these variables is very complex and can be difficult to control accurately enough to obtain acceptable results. It is not uncommon for one company to use a technique highly successfully and another company to find the same technique totally unsatisfactory. A more detailed discussion of automatic soldering techniques can be found in Keller (1981).

6.4.6 Dip soldering

Dip soldering is a technique where a printed circuit board is brought into contact with the surface of a molten solder bath, rather than an agitated wave of solder. An effective method of achieving dip soldering is to lower a board into a solder bath as shown in Figure 6.11.

Figure 6.11 Lowering a printed circuit board into a dip solder bath.

6.4.7 Hot air knives

The increasing demand for higher packing densities introduces additional problems into the automatic soldering process. In particular, closely spaced land areas readily encourage the formation of solder bridges during soldering. One successful method of curing this problem is the use of a hot air knife.

The hot air knife is a jet of hot air which is directed onto the underside of a printed circuit board immediately after it emerges from a solder wave, while the solder is still molten. The air jet has the effect of blowing any excess solder, which includes solder bridge material, off the printed circuit board. A correctly installed hot air knife is capable of removing the excess solder which causes short circuits, and also removes excess solder from land areas. It has been found in practice that it is difficult for a hot air knife to remove solder fillets from correctly formed joints; in fact, a hot air knife actually tends to shape solder joints into a uniform geometry – an ideal situation.

A hot air knife consists of a nozzle which directs hot air towards a printed circuit board to make an angle of about 40° to the direction of travel of the board. The air is heated to a temperature which is above the melting point of solder (about 380 °C). The nozzle is situated about 14 mm from the printed circuit board and uses an air speed of about 110 ms^{-1}. Figure 6.12 shows a typical hot air knife configuration (Lambert, 1984).

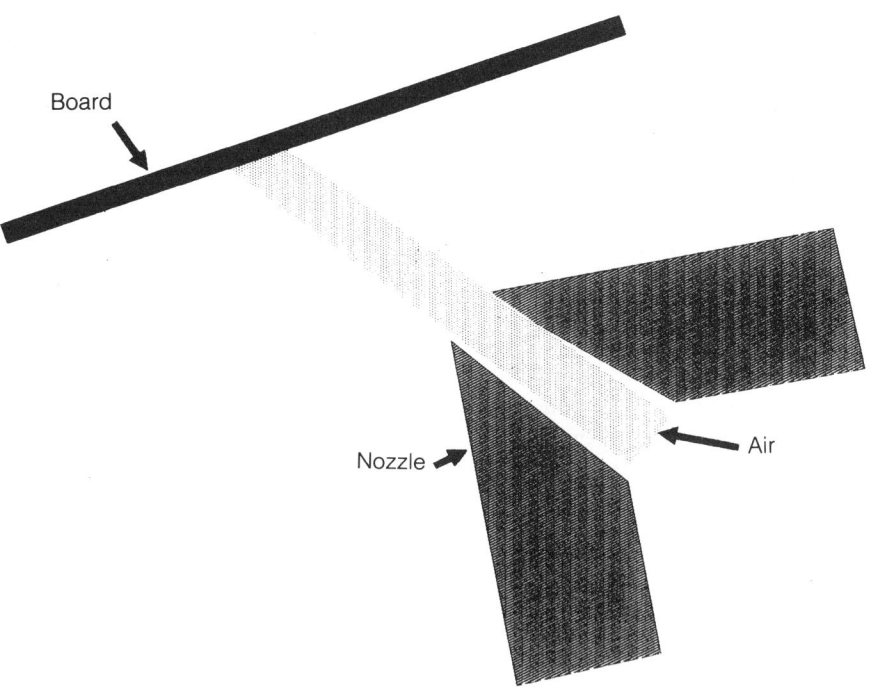

Figure 6.12 A hot air knife.

Figure 6.13 Solder–cut–solder machine.

6.4.8 Solder–cut–solder techniques

A variation on the soldering theme is that of the solder–cut–solder technique. This is used when component leads have not been cut and clinched and need to be cropped after soldering. As the name implies this is a three-stage operation whereby a printed circuit board is initially soldered, the component leads are then cropped and this is followed by a second soldering process. The initial soldering process involves passing the printed circuit board across a static solder bath. The purpose of this operation is to provide the mechanical attachment of components to the printed circuit board. It is not essential to produce a good electrical connection at this stage. A solder–cut–solder machine is shown in Figure 6.13.

After the initial soldering stage the components' leads are cropped by passing the board over one or more rotating blades. The clearance between the board surface and the blades defines the lengths at which the component leads are to be cut. Once the component leads have been dropped the board passes over a conventional solder wave which completes the soldering process.

One of the major problems associated with the solder–cut–solder process occurs in the cutting stage. A common fault is that, instead of cutting component leads, the blade only partially severs the leads and merely bends them at right angles. This results in short circuits occurring as the bent leads come into contact with other leads. This situation is made worse by the subsequent wave soldering operation.

6.5 SOLDER JOINT INSPECTION AND COMMON SOLDERING FAULTS

Visual inspection of solder joints is still the most effective non-destructive test available. Electrical tests such as continuity and resistance measurements only give the current situation. In the case of a recently made solder joint electrical parameters can be misleading as many faults only manifest themselves on ageing. The use of X-rays or ultrasonics is rather limited because solder joints occur in a wide range of geometries. Physical testing tends to be destructive and is therefore only useful for batch sampling or to diagnose a recurring fault.

Although the sole use of visual inspection may be considered archaic in today's manufacturing environment, it has many advantages. Visual inspection can be 100% effective and is non-destructive. In the case of solder joints, visual inspection is particularly effective as most of the common soldering faults have a clearly defined characteristic appearance. A trained inspector can diagnose most fault conditions by the shape and surface texture of a solder joint.

Under ideal conditions a solder joint consists of a smooth, concave fillet which has a bright surface finish. The solder area should also exactly cover the entire land area. In practice solder joints are often less than perfect owing to contamination and process-related faults. Some of the commonest soldering faults are wetting problems, excess solder deposition, solder spike formation, dry joints, joint surface defects and poorly designed printed circuit board layout.

6.5.1 Wetting problems

Poor wetting conditions occur when the surfaces to be soldered fail to form a good metallurgical bond with the solder. For a typical solder joint where a component lead is to be soldered to a copper land, poor wetting can occur between solder and component lead, solder and land, or both.

Some metals require much more active fluxes than others to produce a good solder joint. In particular a flux which is insufficiently active will be unable to remove the surface oxide layers which prevent solder from forming a good bond. Hence a common cause of poor wetting is that the flux material was poorly suited to the metal surfaces to be soldered.

A further cause of poor wetting is if metal surfaces have been contaminated with oil or grease. A grease layer will prevent the flux from removing surface oxides. A common source of grease contamination is human fingers during handling. Poor wetting can also be caused by solder being at too low a temperature, or an insufficient soldering time to allow bonding to take place.

The wetting between solder and a metal base area can be determined by the rise angle which the solder fillet makes with the metal base area. A well wet joint results in a gentle rise angle. An angle of 0° is the definition of ideal wetting, any angle less than 75° being usually acceptable.

Poor wetting can usually be identified by rounded depressions around component leads and convex solder profiles at land areas. Total non-wetting is when the solder fillet makes an angle of 180° to the metal area – it takes the form of a ball on the metal surface. These profiles result from the surface tension of the solder when it has failed to bond with the metal areas. It is important to note that, if too much solder has been applied to a joint, poor wetting can be masked. In particular a component lead can be completely encapsulated in solder but lacking an actual metal–solder bond.

Another wetting-related condition is that of dewetting. This condition occurs when solder initially wets the metal areas and then withdraws. The result of this is that the metal areas have a thin, continuous coating of solder and blobs of solder which are randomly scattered over the metal surface. The solder blobs typically have the convex profiles which are symptomatic of poor wetting. Dewetting is caused by impurities which are present either in the metal areas to be soldered or in the solder bath itself. Examples of contaminants are cleaning residuals in metal areas and metallic impurities in solder.

The two wetting problems described above can occur in isolation or together. A small wetting problem shows up as small holes in a solder layer; this is usually an acceptable defect. At the other extreme, no solder fillet forms at all and no joint connection is formed.

6.5.2 Excess solder problems

Excess solder on a solder joint can be detrimental as it can mask other problems or cause short circuiting. Excess solder is symptomatic of a dip soldering or wave soldering bath operating at too low a temperature. It is a particularly common problem associated with hand soldering.

When excess solder is present on a joint, it often completely obscures the component leads. This makes it difficult to identify other soldering faults such as poor wetting which have a distinctive solder–component lead interface geometry. Excess solder also hides problems such as a component lead being too short to form an adequate joint. The extreme case of this is that it is not possible to see that a component is missing from the soldered side of a board.

Excess solder can also form solder bridges. In their simplest form, solder bridges consist of a web of solder linking adjacent component leads or adjacent tracks. A solder bridge actually spans non-metallic areas, such as an air gap or a bare board substrate area. Thus solder bridges can be very extensive, short circuiting adjacent metallic areas together.

Solder bridges can be formed by low temperatures in solder baths as for the excess solder condition. Insufficient flux and the presence of an oxide film on the surface of a solder bath can also cause the condition. Design factors such as board layout and the shape and approach angle of a solder wave can also have a significant effect on bridge formation.

6.5.3 Solder spike formation

Solder spikes, or icicles, are peaks of solder which stick out either from a soldered board's surface or from the end of component leads. They result from insufficient solder draining as a board is dragged out of a dip or wave soldering bath. They are also attributed to the presence of a surface oxide film on a solder bath as for solder bridge formation.

The presence of solder spikes may not be a major defect provided that they are sufficiently small so that they do not result in short circuits or potential short circuits. In particular, solder spikes formed on the ends of component leads must be sufficiently far apart that they cannot bend into a short-circuit condition. The problems of icicle formation can often be alleviated by causing boards to leave a solder bath at an angle; this facilitates solder drainage.

6.5.4 Dry joints

Dry joints, sometimes referred to as cold or fractured joints, are caused by a component lead moving whilst the solder is in the process of solidifying. The lead movement results in the solder solidifying in a non-uniform manner which causes the joint to be highly stressed. A typical dry joint has a characteristic dull crystalline appearance. A dry joint is highly suspect in terms of its integrity as it is highly liable to fracture and cause an open circuit. Suspected dry joints should always be reworked.

Dry joints are most common in hand soldering operations owing to components or their leads being knocked by an operator's hand or soldering iron. Dry joints which occur in a dip or wave soldering system are usually due to vibrations or excessive accelerations. These can be eliminated by ensuring that boards leave the bath in a smooth motion.

6.5.5 Joint surface defect problems

Joint surface defects are conditions, other than those already described, which result in a dull or rough surface finish on a solder joint. Examples of surface defects are blow holes and metallic contamination effects.

Blow holes are holes in a solder joint due to the escape of gases. If a solder joint is formed which contained entrapped gases or volatile solvents, the escape of these vapours leaves holes in the solder and damages the structure of a joint. The use of too much flux can cause blow holes owing to too much solvent being present. Plated through holes are another potential source of blow holes as moisture and solvents can become trapped.

Solder joints which do not have a shiny surface appearance are usually due to metallic contaminants of the solder. The metals copper and gold are prevalent in the electronics industry and are a common source of contamination. As the shiny surface finish is primarily due to the tin content of solder, low tin solders will have a duller surface finish than high tin solders.

Corrosive flux residues will cause a solder joint to dull if left in contact for extended periods of time. This is due to chemical reactions and is symptomatic of poor cleaning.

Dull solder joints can also be caused by the presence of dross particles in the solder bath. These particles accumulate in the bottom of a solder bath and can be sucked up into solder waves if the solder level becomes too low. It is important to ensure that the solder levels are sufficiently high and to minimize potential sources of contamination. When dross particles become excessive it is necessary to discard the solder bath and to recharge it with fresh clean solder.

6.5.6 Board design problems

The design of a printed circuit board can have a significant effect on the ease of soldering. This is particularly true when surface-mounted components are used, as described in Chapter 7.

The amount of clearance between component leads and the sides of holes can be of particular importance. Holes which are significantly bigger than the component leads can result in solder joints which are incomplete, because the solder is unable to span the gap. Close spacing of land and track areas can cause problems as the formation of solder bridges becomes more likely. Large areas of copper can act as a localized heatsink and produce temperature-related soldering problems such as bridging and wetting problems.

6.6 CLEANING

The cleaning of printing circuit boards after assembly and soldering is of vital importance, particularly for high packing density and high speed applications. Contamination can affect the mechanical and electrical characteristics of a circuit. Materials such as salts and flux activators are ionic and become conducting in the presence of moisture, which affects a circuit's electrical characteristics. Oil-based contamination can cause an insulating layer to form on switches and connectors. Corrosive materials such as flux residues can damage metal areas and affect a board's electrical and mechanical integrity.

When defining a cleaning process, it is important to ensure that the process is effective at removing all types of contamination, but does not damage board and component materials. A common cleaning method is to immerse boards in a solvent. Common solvents are trichloroethane and fluorocarbons.

The effectiveness of a cleaning process can be greatly improved by the use of ultrasonics. There is, however, a reluctance to make use of ultrasonics as there is concern that the fine wires used in integrated circuits could have a resonant frequency in the ultrasonic range and hence could be destroyed.

Recent concerns over environmental issues discourage the use of solvents wherever possible. This encourages the use of water-based cleaning operations. These can be performed in machines which operate on similar principles to domestic dish washers.

6.7 TESTING AND REWORKING

An important aspect of printed circuit board manufacture is testability. Ideally a board needs to be 100% testable; however, this is rarely achievable in practice and a compromise needs to be reached. In particular, a test engineer would ideally want a large number of test points to be made available on a board. This would create difficulties for both design and production engineers in terms of layout complexity and ease of manufacture respectively.

The increasing packing density required of today's printed circuit boards has added to the testing difficulties. Closely packed connections and the use of surface mount devices make it difficult to attach test probes. This necessitates the addition of test lands which are exposed copper areas for the attachment of test probes.

There are a range of test procedures which can be performed on printed circuit boards. Considerations of cost can limit the actual number of tests which can be performed on a particular board type. The full range of tests would typically only be feasible on very complex and high value printed circuit boards. The majority of test procedures are by definition non-destructive. Destructive testing may also be used to give useful information with respect to recurring faults and quality assurance.

6.7.1 In-circuit testing

In-circuit testing involves the testing of individual components after they have been soldered into position on a printed circuit board. The testing procedure involves applying test probes to the leads of a component under test, applying electrical inputs and checking whether the output is within specification. In-circuit testing machines can be extremely complex and expensive devices, particularly if they have functionality testing capabilities.

A typical in-circuit testing machine will utilize a 'bed-of-nails' fixture to form the electrical connections between the tester and the board under test. A bed-of-nails fixture consists of a number of spring-loaded probes which are applied to a printed circuit board's test points and solder joints under pressure.

The individual test probes are available in a range of different tip geometries. The actual geometry used is dependent on the nature of the connection to be made. Connections to solder joints are made with crown-shaped probe tips where the four points are designed to cut into the solder joint. The reason for this is that a solder joint will be covered with a layer of oxides and other contaminants which will result in a high resistance connection. Connections to gold-plated contacts need to be made with soft and blunt probe tips so that the integrity of the gold layer is maintained.

A board to be tested needs to be pushed down onto the spring-loaded test probes by a sufficient force to achieve the desired contact pressure. A probe typically needs to operate at a spring pressure of 200 gf. This pressure is particularly important if a probe is to cut through the surface of a solder joint. Three methods are used to push a printed circuit board onto a bed-of-nails fixture: vacuum, mechanical and pneumatic.

A vacuum fixture pulls a board onto a bed of nails by evacuating the chamber containing the test probes. The board is then pushed onto the probes by atmospheric pressure. Although a vacuum can theoretically exert a pressure of 100 000 Nm^{-2}, a practical system would operate at about half of this value. This limits the probe density to between two and three probes per square centimetre if the desired operating probe pressure is to be maintained. Vacuum test fixtures are the commonest in actual usage.

Pneumatic and mechanical fixtures use pneumatic cylinders or mechanical levers respectively to push a printed circuit board onto the bed of nails. One of the major limitations of these methods is that unpopulated board areas are required for force application. There is also a greater risk of damaging the board under test.

A separate bed-of-nails fixture needs to be available for each type of board to be tested. The drill template created by the circuit layout artwork can be used to define the positions of the test probes on a fixture.

It is important that a good connection can be made between test probes and the board's test sites. Connections can be improved by applying ultrasonic vibration to the contact area. This has the effect of achieving consistently good connections and has the added advantage of keeping the test probes clean – as in ultrasonic cleaning units.

The test program, which typically takes 25 s, produces a printout of any failures which occur, e.g. a 1 K resistor that actually reads 6 M.

6.7.2 Digital function test

A digital function test is a specialized form of in-circuit test in that it checks the performance of circuits and subcircuits rather than just checking whether an individual component is within specification. Digital function testing machines are highly complex and typically cost in excess of £100 000. Genrad and Olivetti are leading manufacturers of such machines.

The digital function test is normally performed using a bed-of-nails testbed as for in-circuit testing. Because of the complex nature of the tests, an operator is required to perform certain actions such as the placing or removal of test links and 'walking through' operations. Digital function testing machines are provided with a circuit definition and a test pattern which is to be supplied to a printed circuit board's test points. The test program is defined in parallel with the circuit design process. A test program typically has to be able to test at least 95% of a circuit's functionality.

In operation a digital function test machine will execute its test program and display the results on a visual display. The test program may need to request operator actions which are also displayed. In the case where a fault is detected it may be necessary to obtain other information from the circuit under test than can be determined using the applied test probes. In this case the test machine may instruct an operator to 'walk' through a circuit with a test probe to find the exact location of a fault, e.g. apply probe to pin 3 of IC9.

A test will take about 10 s using a vacuum test, or 2–3 min if 'walking' is required. A hard copy printout is available which lists the nature and location of any detected faults.

Function testing machines are also available for analogue circuits, and these operate in a similar manner. Some of the more sophisticated test machines may have both an analogue and a digital test capability.

6.7.3 Substitution test

When a printed circuit board forms part of a larger system it is necessary to ensure that it is capable of functioning with the rest of the system. A board can pass all the stand-alone tests but fail to function in a system owing to factors such as timing tolerances. One method of testing how a particular board will function in conjunction with the rest of its system is to perform a substitution test. This test is highly advisable for high cost and performance applications such as large computer systems and telephone exchanges.

A substitution test makes use of a test rig which consists of a stripped-down version of a complete working system. This typically consists of a full system which has not been packaged, or has been modified so as to allow easy access to its component parts. Each board to be substitution tested is inserted into its correct position in the test rig. The name substitution testing comes from the fact that the board under test is substituted for its known working counterpart in the test system. A comprehensive system test procedure is performed to determine whether or not the board functions correctly with the rest of the system. This test should check out each of the systems functions and may need to utilize external test equipment. An example of this is the testing of a telephone exchange where a piece of equipment is required to simulate the making of hundreds of telephone calls.

6.7.4 Soak test

Soak testing is designed to eliminate boards which fail in the 'infant mortality' stage. A soak test is designed to age boards artificially so that they are past the high failure rate section of the failure rate against time curve. Systems under test are powered up and run for 72 h at an elevated temperature of about 40 °C. The systems are monitored twice daily and removed if a fault develops. Some products have a self-test facility which can be invoked during or after soak testing.

6.7.5 Reworking

Reworking is concerned with the correction of minor faults which have been identified by a test procedure. Because of the nature of the operation, reworking is fundamentally a manual operation. The major reworking operations are touching up, placing missing components and the replacement of faulty components.

Touching up is concerned with the correction of faulty solder joints. These can take the form of inadequately applied solder, dry joints and excess solder. Touching up is performed using a soldering iron, typically with a power rating in the order of 30 W. The remaking of poor and dry solder joints is performed using a flux-cored solder wire. When resin-based fluxes are used it is necessary to remove flux residues after reworking. This is performed by applying a solvent with a small brush or a cotton swab.

Care needs to be exercised when performing operations which require the removal of solder, including component removal, in order to prevent damaging the board. In particular, the copper tracking can lift away from the board surface if excessive heating is applied. The use of a suction device in conjunction with a soldering iron allows solder to be removed quickly. A fluxed metal braid can also be used in conjunction with a soldering iron to remove solder.

7

Surface mount component assembly

The demands on the electronics industry towards greater packing densities require that more complex circuits and more sophisticated electronic components are packed into smaller volumes. This has led to demands for small, compact and lightweight components. One of the most successful approaches to this is the use of the surface mount component (SMC). Although surface mount components have been in existence in one form or another for several decades, there have been many technological difficulties associated with the manufacture of very compact and lightweight devices which have had to be solved. Surface mount components have now become almost indispensable, particularly for consumer electronic goods such as music and video reproduction systems. The requirement of an automatic assembly process for printed circuit boards which contain surface mount components has necessitated the development of new technologies in order to meet today's time and quality standards. This chapter addresses the areas of the advantages of surface mount components, surface mount component assembly methods and soldering techniques. The implications of mixing surface mount components with leaded components, and the testing implications, are also discussed.

7.1 ADVANTAGES OF SURFACE MOUNT COMPONENTS

Surface mount components have a number of features which set them apart from leaded components in terms of their manufacturing related attributes. Because of their lack of leads, they can be mounted on a printed circuit board without the need for a through hole connection. Figure 7.1 shows a comparison between leaded component and surface

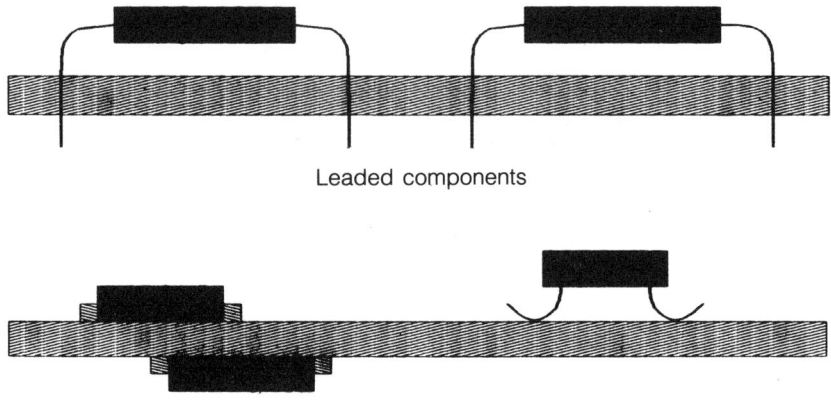

Leaded components

Surface mount components

Figure 7.1 Leaded and surface mount components.

mount component assemblies. Their use also has the effect of reducing spurious inductances and capacitances which can be detrimental to circuit performance. They are physically compact and lightweight, as a consequence of not requiring leadouts, which improves circuit packing density and rigidity. Surface mount components are readily available in a form which can be automatically fed into automatic assembly machinery. This is a consequence of a demand existing for automatically feedable components before their widespread adoption.

Surface mount components offer a number of distinct benefits over leaded components which can be summarized as follows.

1. The mounting of a surface mount component only involves one side of a printed circuit board. Hence both sides of a printed circuit board can be utilized for component mounting. This effectively doubles the working area of a board.
2. The fact that through holes are not required for component leads means that the physical size of land areas can be reduced. This allows track and land areas to be placed much closer together with a resultant improvement of packing density.
3. The improved packing density allows the use of smaller printed circuit boards for the same circuit. This in turn allows the manufacture of smaller, more compact products.
4. Components' terminal leads take up a significant amount of space and place a lower limit on package sizes. Surface mount components can be physically smaller by utilizing a much closer spacing of smaller terminal connections.

5. The lack of leads reduces spurious electrical characteristics such as capacitance and inductance and hence simplifies the manufacture of high frequency circuits.
6. The number of through holes required for a printed circuit board can be considerably reduced. In effect only via holes are necessary through printed circuit boards with only surface mount components. This reduces the drilling costs and hence the overall cost of a printed circuit board.
7. The lack of lead wires simplifies the handling of devices and facilitates the feeding of automatic assembly machines. Components are less liable to damage as they do not have to undergo lead preforming operations.

Although there are many advantages to be obtained from using surface mount components there are also a number of disadvantages which can be summarized as follows.

1. In general the costs of surface mount components are higher than those of their leaded counterparts.
2. The absence of component leads removes the go–no-go advantage from the automatic assembly process. This adds the manufacturing fault of component misalignment on placement.
3. The small physical size of surface mount components makes manual assembly much more difficult and unreliable. Manual assembly requires additional support such as magnifying glasses and tweezers.
4. There are still a significant number of components for which surface-mountable versions are not yet available. This necessitates a mixture of both leaded and surface mount component technologies for most applications which utilize surface mount components.

Although there has been a trend towards the increasing use of surface mount components, their current disadvantages prevent them from rendering leaded components obsolete for the foreseeable future. In particular, 100% surface mount printed circuit boards can only become the norm when all components are available in surface-mountable form.

7.2 SURFACE MOUNT COMPONENT ASSEMBLY

The assembly process for a printed circuit board which contains surface mount components has some fundamental differences from the leaded component insertion process. Leaded component insertion is a go–no-go operation in that, once a component's leads have been successfully inserted into their designated holes in a printed circuit board, they are known to be in the correct position for soldering. The act of inserting a component's leads and then clinching them ensures that the component is mechanically constrained in the correct position. The soldering process then provides electrical connection and additional mechanical support.

Surface mount components, which by definition lack leads, need an alternative method of ensuring correct positioning before and during the soldering process. The solder joint needs to provide the mechanical attachment of a surface mount component to its printed circuit board in addition to the electrical connections. There are two main methods of achieving the positioning and soldering requirements: these are the adhesive and wave soldering method, and the solder paste and reflow soldering method. The actual placement of surface mount components on a printed circuit board is usually referred to as component onsertion to distinguish it from the leaded component insertion process.

7.3 ADHESIVE APPLICATION

Adhesive application is a method of mechanically fixing surface mount components in the required position on a printed circuit board before and during the soldering process. The adhesive application process involves depositing a suitable quantity of a curable adhesive onto appropriate areas of a printed circuit board. The surface mount component devices are then accurately placed on the printed circuit board, each device being positioned over an area covered with adhesive. The adhesive is allowed to cure, which fixes the surface mount component devices to the printed circuit board. Figure 7.2 shows the stages of the adhesive application process for surface mount components.

7.3.1 Adhesive types

There are a number of different adhesives in use for fixing surface mount components to printed circuit boards. The fundamental requirements for an adhesive are that it can be used with automatic dispensing systems, and that it can securely hold a surface mount component in position at temperatures which may be encountered during the soldering process. It is also important that the adhesive material is chemically inert so that it does not damage components and

PCB area for SMC device onsertion

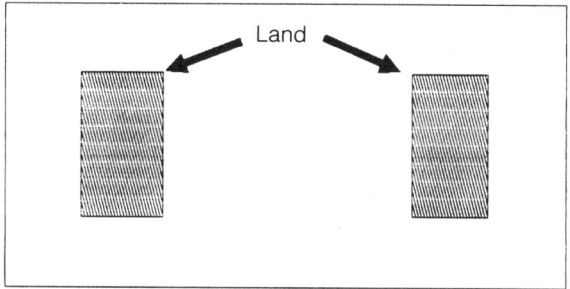

Adhesive bead application

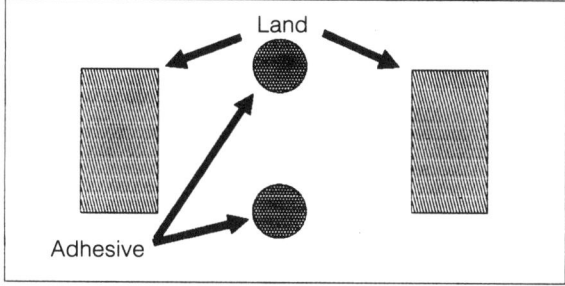

SMC device onsertion

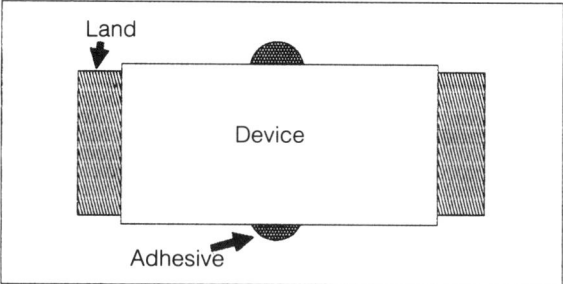

Figure 7.2 Adhesive method of SMC onsertion.

board materials over the life of the product. There are two categories of adhesive in common usage, ultraviolet curable and heat curable.

Ultraviolet-curable adhesives are cured by exposure to ultraviolet radiation for several tens of seconds. They are easy to use and can readily be applied using automatic dispensing systems. Ultraviolet-curable adhesives must be stored at low temperatures and in a darkened place as sunlight and artificial light can start the curing process. They also have a short storage life. A disadvantage of using ultraviolet-curable adhesives is that larger components tend to shield the adhesive from the curing radiation. This reduces the adhesive's effectiveness.

A variation on the theme of ultraviolet-curable adhesives is provided by the acrylic adhesives. These require a combination of ultraviolet and infrared radiation for the curing process. The initial stage is to expose the adhesive to ultraviolet light for several tens of seconds. It is important that part of the adhesive area is directly exposed to the ultraviolet light in order for the exposure to be effective. Following the ultraviolet exposure, an infrared exposure cures the concealed areas of adhesive.

Heat-curable adhesives are cured by exposure to high temperatures for several minutes. An exposure time in excess of 10 min is not uncommon. This puts heat-curable adhesives at a disadvantage over ultraviolet-curable adhesives in terms of curing time. They are, however, easy to use and compatible with automatic dispensing methods. Heat-curable adhesives should also be stored in cool and dark conditions in order to extend shelf life.

Another form of heat-curable adhesive comes in the form of two liquids which heat cure once combined. This form is in principle very simple and low cost; however, it is difficult to dispense automatically owing to the mixing requirement. Poor mixing can produce non-uniform curing and can introduce air bubbles.

7.3.2 Adhesive application methods

Adhesive can be applied to a printed circuit board by either a screen printing or a syringe dispensing process. The actual amount of adhesive applied to a particular area, by either method, must be carefully controlled and is dependent on the size of component to be fixed. Too little adhesive will result in a component being liable to fall off during soldering. If too much adhesive is applied it may cover land areas and prevent a good solder joint from being formed. Adhesive applied to a printed circuit board can take the form of beads or an evenly spread layer between lands. In the case of adhesive bead application, the beads can be of several different sizes to suit the range of components to be fixed. The use of several small beads can give better results for larger components than a single large bead.

Another method of adhesive application is the pin transfer method.

This involves the use of a fixture which has a number of pins, each corresponding to an area of a printed circuit board to which adhesive is required. The process works by dipping the fixture in an adhesive bath and then applying it to the printed circuit board's surface. Adhesive is deposited on the board at the positions where the adhesive-coated pins make contact.

Adhesive dispensing is usually performed automatically using the syringe dispensing method. Screen printing is more commonly used with solder paste application.

7.3.3 Automatic adhesive dispensing machines

An automatic adhesive dispensing machine, or glue station, consists of one or more syringes which can be controlled to deliver various sizes of adhesive beads to areas of printed circuit boards. An automatic dispensing system will typically consist of an environmentally controlled casing, a printed circuit board transport system and a computer-controlled syringe mechanism.

(a) Environmental control

In order to maintain a consistent dispensing performance it is necessary to ensure that the adhesive's viscosity remains constant. An adhesive's viscosity is very temperature dependent, which necessitates that the dispensing system be carefully temperature controlled. This can be achieved by housing the dispensing system in a casing which can keep the internal temperature at a preferred level.

(b) Feeding mechanisms

Automatic dispensing systems require a feeding mechanism to load and unload printed circuit boards. The feeding mechanism is responsible for placing a board at a predetermined position. It is important that such registration can be performed in order to ensure that adhesive is placed in the correct positions. A conveyor adequately provides this function and allows the dispensing to be integrated with a later onsertion process.

The use of a conveyor also allows printed circuit boards which do not require adhesive application to pass through the adhesive application process without being processed in a continuous production environment.

A feeding mechanism works at its most efficient when all the boards to be processed are of a fixed width. Varying board widths necessitate that the feeding mechanism be adjusted for each change – a process which can take several tens of minutes. Some machines require an unused portion of a board along each edge for use by the feeding system and for tooling and registration holes. An example of this is the Fuji FGL-3000 glue station which utilizes 'Fuji strips' of additional board material. The fabrication of several smaller printed circuit boards from a standard size of larger bare board material allows standard board widths and formats to be accommodated without imposing major limitations.

(c) Syringe mechanisms

The requirements of an adhesive dispensing syringe are that controllable amounts of adhesive can be applied to the desired board locations. An adhesive dispensing machine will often have multiple syringes in order to achieve the desired throughput. Component pick and place machines can be significantly faster than the gluing machines. This can create a bottleneck unless the glue station can process two or more boards in parallel. Glue station syringes can also be mounted in pairs in order to be able to deposit two adhesive beads simultaneously for larger components.

The amount of adhesive which is delivered by a particular syringe needs to be computer controllable. This is usually implemented by specifying injection times for each delivery, the injection times being specified as multiples of a predefined injection time, typically 0.01 s. It is also important to monitor the levels of adhesive available to each syringe so that a particular syringe does not run empty during the adhesive application of a board.

The positioning of adhesive syringes over the areas of a board to be glued is achieved by mounting the syringes on an x–y sliding carrier. The carrier is computer controlled to position the correct syringe assembly for the type of adhesive application required. Each syringe can be raised and lowered between standby and adhesive application positions by means of syringe drive cylinders. Figure 7.3 shows a typical syringe dispenser assembly, and Figure 7.4 shows a syringe adhesive application machine.

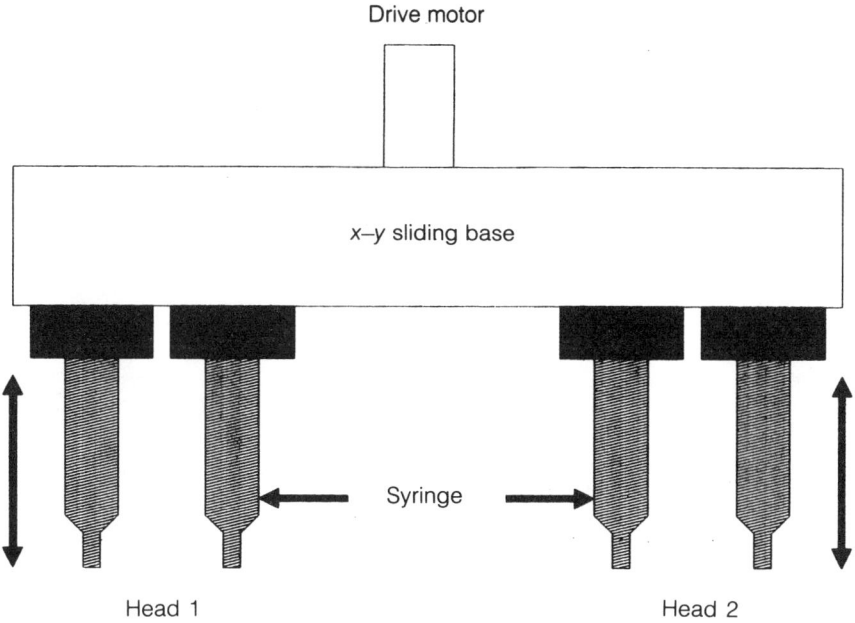

Figure 7.3 Syringe adhesive dispenser assembly.

7.4 SOLDER PASTE APPLICATION

The application of solder paste provides an alternative method of surface mount component assembly to the adhesive application method. The solder paste method hinges on the application of solder in a paste form which can act as an adhesive to surface mount components. The solder paste is later melted, or reflowed, to form a good solder joint. Figure 7.5 shows the stages of solder paste application for surface mount components.

7.4.1 Solder paste

The actual solder paste materials used for surface mount component assembly must have certain properties in order to produce results of the required quality. Some of the properties which a solder paste must have are as follows.

Figure 7.4 Syringe adhesive application machine.

1. The solder paste must have the correct physical properties such that it can be screen printed or syringe dispensed in a predefined quantity, thickness and shape.
2. The paste must not significantly spread on heating, so that it remains in the locality for which it is intended.
3. The solder must have the wetting properties required to form a good solder joint between component electrodes and their corresponding circuit board conductors.
4. The paste must not leave any potentially corrosive flux residues on a board after reflowing which cannot be easily removed.
5. The paste should have sufficient adhesive properties on application that surface mount components can be placed onto a board and that they stay in their correct positions before and during reflow soldering. This requires the use of high viscosity solder pastes.

Solder paste consists of a suspension of a powdered solder in a flux material. The constituents can be adjusted to produce a range of properties which can be selected depending on their suitability for the application processes in which the paste is to be used.

The shape of the individual particles in the solder powder is

PCB area for SMC device onsertion

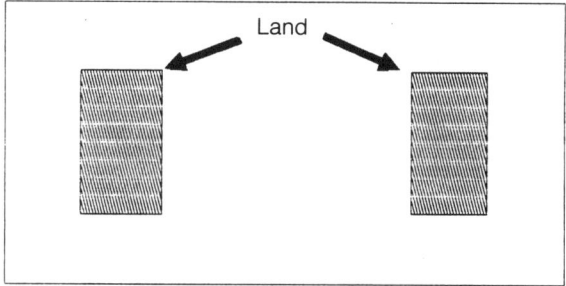

Solder paste application

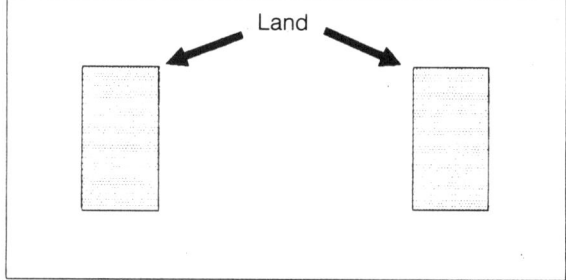

SMC device onsertion

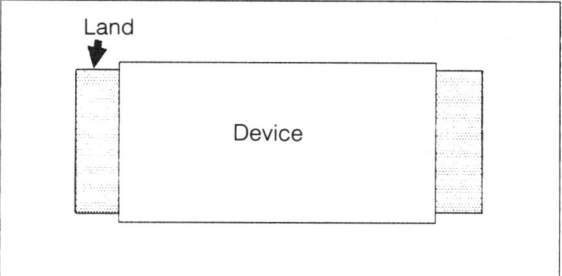

Figure 7.5 Solder paste SMC onsertion.

important with respect to the properties of the resultant paste. Solder powders can consist of randomly shaped or ball-shaped particles. Randomly shaped particles produce a solder paste which has a good viscosity but is difficult to apply correctly. Ball-shaped particles produce poor viscosity pastes with good application properties.

The chemical composition of the flux used in a solder paste can have important consequences, particularly with respect to the corrosive properties of any residues after reflowing. The chlorine content of a flux needs particular attention as fluxes normally contain between 0.1% and 0.5% chlorine by weight. Any flux residues left after reflowing and cleaning will degrade the solder joint quality and reliability if the chlorine content is high.

7.4.2 Solder paste application methods

Like adhesive application, solder paste can be applied to a board by either a screen printing or a syringe dispensing process. Screen printing methods are preferred by many companies. It is important to ensure that the solder particle shapes are compatible with the application method to be used. In particular, it is essential to use ball-shaped particles, or a combination of randomly shaped and ball-shaped particles, if a fine mesh is used for screen printing or if a dispensing process is used.

Screen printing is performed by covering the board with a screen which has small holes aligned with the land areas to which solder paste is to be applied. A quantity of solder paste is applied to the screen and spread across the screen using a squeegee. The squeegee forces solder paste through the holes in the mesh and onto the land areas as required. The squeegee is typically made of a plastic such as polyurethane or neoprene. It is important to inspect and clean the squeegee regularly in order to maintain a good tip surface and profile. A worn squeegee tip can adversely affect the accuracy of the printing process.

There are two methods of screen printing in common usage, mesh screen printing and metal screen printing.

Mesh screen printing uses a mesh which is positioned approximately 0.3 mm above the board to be printed. The squeegee deforms the screen by pushing it down onto the surface of the board during printing. Figure 7.6 shows both mesh and metal screen printing methods. The thickness of the deposited solder layer is dependent on the mesh thickness and the geometry of the mesh with respect to the board surface during printing.

Metal screen printing uses a metal template screen which is placed in contact with the board surface. The screen is manufactured to the thickness required of the solder paste layer after printing. On application, the solder paste fills the holes in the screen and hence is deposited in the desired positions and shapes.

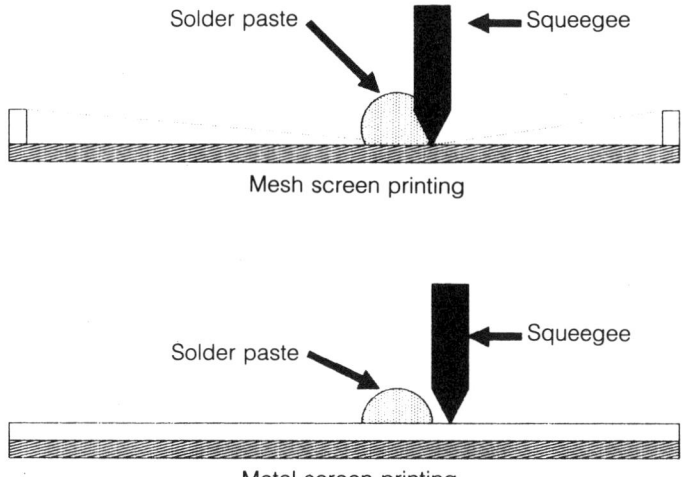

Figure 7.6 Screen printing operations.

7.5 COMPONENT ONSERTION

A fundamental difference between surface mount component onsertion and leaded component insertion is that the latter is a go–no-go operation in that a component misalignment will result in the insertion failing. The surface mount component onsertion process therefore needs to ensure that components are correctly aligned with respect to the printed circuit board before placement.

Automatic pick and place machines are available which are computer controlled with a capability of several thousand programmed placements per board. The computer programs can be generated from the output of printed circuit board layout computer-aided design packages. A surface mount component assembly line may utilize two separate pick and place machines owing to feeding constraints, the two machine types being a high speed machine for small tape-fed components, and a slower machine for the larger stick-fed integrated circuit packages. A typical automatic surface mount component onsertion machine will consist of feeding mechanisms, pick and place heads, and a method of ensuring correct component alignment.

7.5.1 Feeding mechanisms

An automatic surface mount component onsertion machine will require feeding mechanisms for the delivery of circuit boards and components for pick and place operations. It is important that any feeding mechanisms operate at a sufficiently high speed so as to keep up with the pick and place operation which may operate at speeds of 0.25 s per component. Feeding mechanisms can be functionally divided into board feeders and component feeders.

(a) Board feeding and positioning

Board feeding and positioning is concerned with the receipt of boards from a materials handling system and their presentation to pick and place heads for component placement. The materials handling system at its simplest would be a manual operator placing boards by hand. At its most complex a materials handling system would be a fully automated system linking assembly machines in a flexible manufacturing cell. As boards will have been through an adhesive or solder paste application process before being loaded onto an onsertion machine, they will typically be delivered by means of a feed-in conveyor.

Once delivered to an onsertion machine, printed circuit boards need to be registered so that component placement positions can be determined. A board's component footprint areas then need to be presented to pick and place heads in the correct sequence for component placement.

The registration and positioning requirements can be met by using an x–y indexing table. Registration to ensure correct component positioning is achieved by jigging and tooling holes. An example of this is the 'Fuji strip' extra board area used in conjunction with the Fuji series of onsertion machines. The x–y table also has the function of positioning exact areas of a board directly under the placement head which is to deliver the components. The table must be able to position a board to within the tolerance required by quality assurance; this could be as small as 0.01 mm. In order to achieve the high placement rates an x–y table may have to operate at velocities of up to 100 mm s^{-1}.

(b) Component feeding

Component feeding mechanisms are responsible for the transfer of surface mount components from their component packaging to a pick and place head. Mechanisms need to be able to cater for a range of different component packaging styles. Surface mount components are available in a range of tape widths, which include 8, 12, 16 and 32 mm, and stick packaging.

Taped components are loaded onto a machine in the form of slimline reel cartridges. The cartridges are mounted into a dispensing fixture which has a facility to separate the individual components from the tape. Tape is fed out from the cartridge in increments of one component cell at a time by means of a ratchet mechanism. The top layer of protective film is pulled off the component cell onto a take-up spool. The actual component is then at a known position, to within the tolerance defined by the relative sizes of the cell and component, with respect to the dispensing fixture. Hence component positions are sufficiently well known for removal by a pick and place head. Component tapes, once mounted into a dispensing fixture, are fitted onto a shuttle mechanism which is responsible for delivering the component cartridges in the correct sequence to the component pickup point. Once at the pickup point the cartridge's dispensing fixture presents the next component to a pick and place head for removal. A shuttle mechanism can have the capacity of holding 100 individual 8 mm cartridges.

Stick-packaged surface mount components are usually extracted using gravity feeding. Any other approach would necessitate the use of a plunger or equivalent mechanism to push components out of the end of the stick. The use of a mechanical plunger increases the risk of damaging components during extraction. Stick dispensers for surface mount components are very similar to those used for leaded dual-in-line packages. The requirements for a stick feeder are that individual components can be extracted from a stick and delivered to a pickup position.

7.5.2 Pick and place heads

An automatic onsertion machine's pick and place heads are responsible for collecting components from a feeding mechanism and then placing them firmly into adhesive or solder paste. This must be in the correct position and orientation on a target board. High speed pick and place units have multiple pick and place heads mounted on a rotating drum fixture. A typical number of pick and place heads for a high speed mechanism is 12. The use of a multihead pick and place mechanism considerably reduces the effective movement distances and hence can significantly improve the speed of operation. One problem that a multihead machine can overcome is that removing components from the feeding mechanism in the order in which they are to be placed can result in excessive movement of a shuttle, the worst case being when components which are consecutive in the assembly sequence are stored at opposite ends of the shuttle. The use of a multihead placing mechanism allows batches of components to be removed from the feeding mechanism in an order which involves minimal movement of the shuttle. Multihead mechanisms can also collect batches of components from the feeding mechanism whilst boards are being loaded and positioned. This parallel activity offers a further improvement in speed of operation.

Surface mount components are picked up by pick and place heads either by a claw mechanism or by vacuum suction.

The claw mechanism ensures correct component positioning and orientation but is not as effective at removing components from taped packaging. The mechanical claw may also damage components during handling.

The vacuum suction method is simple and effective but has the drawback of allowing a surface mount component to be held at incorrect positions or orientations for correct placement. The positioning and orientation problem associated with vacuum suction pick and place heads can be overcome using either a mechanical or an optical component alignment system.

(a) Mechanical component alignment

An SMC placement machine is shown in Figure 7.7. Mechanical alignment of components held by a vacuum suction pick and place head is achieved by means of alignment fingers or tweezers which are an integral part of the placement head. The placement head is lowered onto the next surface mount component which is in an open cell of a taped package or has been extracted from a stick package. A vacuum is applied to grip the component. Once the placement head has lifted clear of the component packaging, a set of fingers close. This has the effect of aligning the component correctly. The fingers are opened before the actual placement of the component. The sequence of operations is shown diagrammatically in Figure 7.8.

(b) Optical component alignment

Optical alignment of surface mount components held by a vacuum

Figure 7.7 SMC placement machine.

suction placement head is a more recent development. This is featured in the Fuji CP-II high speed pick and place machine. A gripped surface mount component is imaged by a built-in camera system which determines the position and orientation of the component with respect to the placement head. Any positional and orientation errors are calculated and corrected for by repositioning and rotating the placement head. A visual display monitor may be provided which shows the captured camera images of components during operation. The non-contact nature of an optical system has the advantage of reducing the number of moving parts and their associated potential maintenance problems by making alignment fingers redundant.

7.6 SOLDERING TECHNIQUES

There are a large number of different soldering processes which can be used with surface mount components. The techniques fall into the two categories of wave soldering for components mounted using the adhesive method, and reflow soldering for components mounted using the solder paste method.

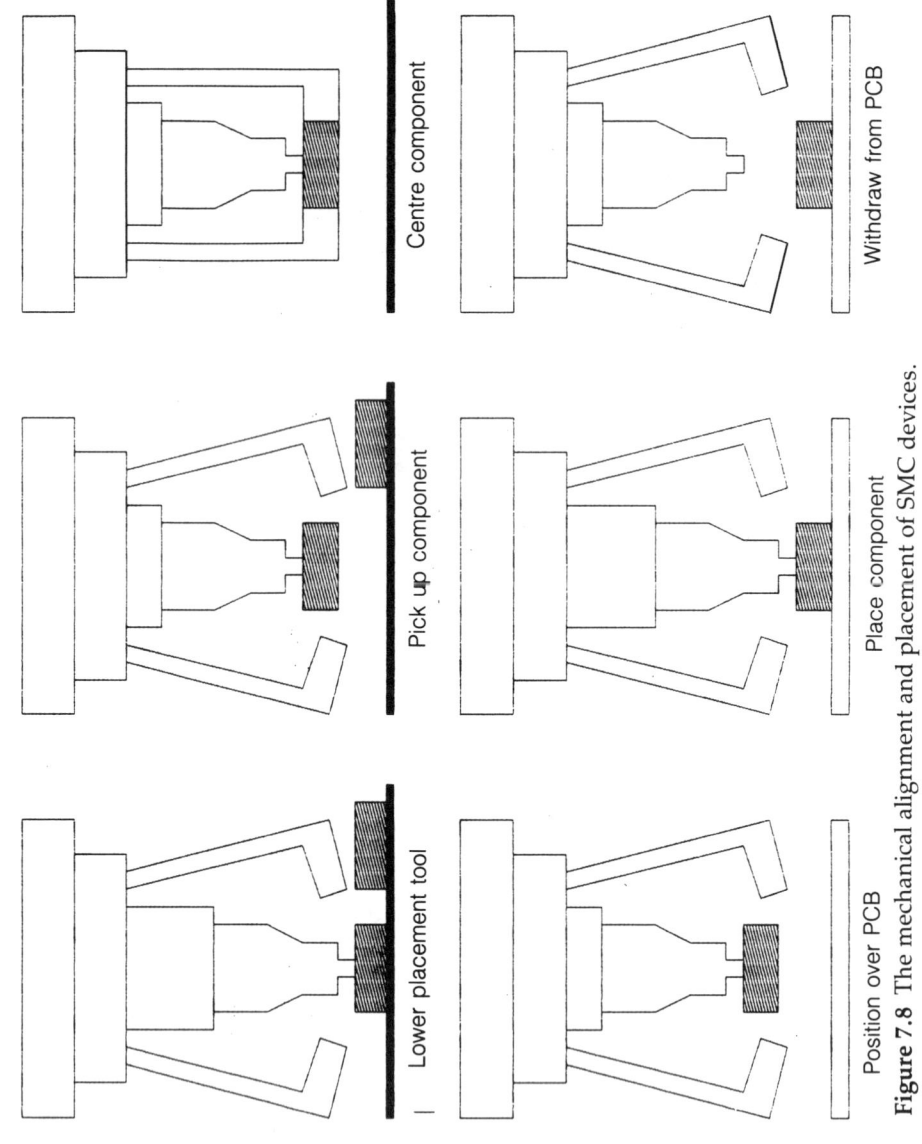

Figure 7.8 The mechanical alignment and placement of SMC devices.

7.6.1 Wave soldering

Wave soldering of surface mount components which have been glued to a board differs from the similar process for leaded components in that the components themselves actually have to pass through the solder wave. Thus the profile of the board surface passing through the wave is dependent on the shapes and sizes of the components mounted upon it. This introduces the possibilities of undesirable effects which include components falling off, tombstoning and shadowing.

The problem of components falling off during soldering is usually symptomatic of problems in the adhesive application process. Adhesive which has been applied in insufficient quantities and incomplete adhesive curing are obvious causes. The temperature characteristics of an adhesive can also cause problems if the adhesive softens at soldering temperatures.

Tombstoning is a related problem to that of components falling off during soldering. A surface mount component is said to have tombstoned if it flipped up into a vertical or near-vertical position during soldering. This problem usually only occurs with two-leaded chip components such as resistors and capacitors. It is attributed to poor land pattern design and occurs when the two component terminals do not wet simultaneously. The result of this is that the surface tension of the solder wave exerts a non-uniform pull on the component, lifting one end off the board.

Shadowing is an effect generated by larger components shielding smaller components, or parts of themselves, from the solder wave. When a large component passes through a solder wave it parts the fluid flow. This leaves an area behind the component where little or no solder passes. This can result in the trailing edge of a large component, or small components behind a large component, remaining unsoldered or being poorly soldered.

The wave soldering process commonly used with surface mount components is dual-wave soldering, or DWS, which utilizes two solder waves each of which has different properties and has a specific function.

The primary wave is usually strongly agitated and has the purpose of wetting the joints and removing flux and adhesive volatiles from the printed circuit board. The agitation is used to prevent larger components creating a solder-free area behind them which can cause the trailing edge and nearby smaller components to escape soldering.

The secondary wave is a more conventional smoothly flowing wave.

This has the function of completing the soldering process and removing any excess solder from the board.

Dual-wave soldering allows double-sided soldering to be performed as it is possible to pass both sides of a board through the soldering process. Provided that the soldering process is carefully controlled, the soldering of one side of a board should not result in the other side becoming hot enough to melt any solder joint. This double-sided soldering provides a means of mixing leaded and surface mount components on the same board. The dual-wave soldering process can also be used for boards containing only leaded components.

The dual-wave soldering process has the disadvantage that it is difficult to set up the correct soldering conditions. In fact some companies do not utilize dual-wave soldering for this very reason. The process by definition requires that the components be fixed in position using adhesive. This effectively adds an additional process, along with its associated problems. Printed circuit boards are subject to a high thermal stress and the wetting characteristics of the waves are dependent on the direction of travel of the printed circuit board with respect to the wave.

7.6.2 Reflow soldering

The principle of reflow soldering is to melt a solder paste in a manner which results in the formation of a high quality solder joint. The flux component of a solder paste must either be carried away by the process or left in a state in which it can easily be removed by a simple cleaning process. The reason for this is that flux residues are often corrosive and cause degradation of a board.

Depending on the actual reflow method used, the main problems associated with reflow soldering result from non-uniform heating. Solder balling is another problem associated with reflow soldering which leaves isolated spheres of solder on the board surface. This is often caused by solvent evaporation ejecting molten solder. Components, in particular two-terminal chip components, can become misaligned or can tombstone if differing surface tensions develop at the two component ends during reflowing. Other effects which are reflow method dependent are described with the method.

Reflow soldering is usually achieved by means of an infrared or a vapour phase process. However, there are other more exotic processes such as laser, hot air and multiple-impulse soldering.

(a) Infrared reflow soldering

Infrared reflow soldering, or IRS, utilizes near-infrared radiation, with a wavelength of about 1 μm, or far-infrared, with a wavelength of up to 10 μm, as a heat source. Near-infrared radiation is produced by halogen lamps and far-infrared radiation is produced by means of panel heaters. The actual wavelength range of infrared radiation used for a particular application is dependent on the absorption coefficient of the printed circuit board with respect to the wavelength of radiation. This is dependent on the colour, temperature and component materials of the printed circuit board. Infrared reflow soldering can be achieved by using a conveyor which carries printed circuit boards under a series of infrared lamps or heaters.

Infrared reflow soldering has the advantages of being low cost and capable of successfully soldering many components at the same time. There is also no component displacement from their placed positions owing to the non-contact nature of the process.

The disadvantages of infrared reflow soldering are mainly due to the difficulty in controlling and maintaining a uniform temperature. Heat absorption is very dependent on the materials of the components of a board – the absorption coefficient. Near-infrared wavelengths are strongly reflected by metal conductors and absorbed by the black plastic packaging used for integrated circuits. Large components can cause a shadowing effect which prevents infrared radiation reaching smaller nearby components.

(b) Vapour phase reflow soldering

Vapour phase soldering, or VPS, utilizes an inert fluorinated hydro-carbon liquid which is heated and vaporized in an oven. The printed circuit board to be reflow soldered is placed in the oven where the hot vapour transfers its latent heat of vaporization as it condenses onto the board, melting the solder paste. This method is a very rapid and efficient means of heat transfer and provides a uniform heating of the board, and hence a uniform melting of the solder paste.

Vapour phase soldering can be performed using a batch process where printed circuit boards are placed in a basket and lowered into the vapour by means of a lifting mechanism. The main problem with batch mode is that large fluid losses can occur whenever the boards are loaded or removed owing to the large opening required in the vapour chamber.

Vapour phase soldering can also be performed in-line using a conveyor which passes through a vapour phase oven. The oven may be preceded by a preheating stage in order to maintain uniform temperatures. Temperature control is the main drawback of the continuous feed systems.

VPS has the advantages of producing a uniform and easily temperature-controlled soldering environment. The use of an inert vapour, which is free from atmospheric oxygen, prevents solder oxidation from occurring. The condensed fluid also carries away unwanted flux residues.

VPS requires expensive equipment and is relatively slow. The fluorinated hydrocarbons are also environmentally undesirable.

(c) Belt hot plate soldering

Belt hot plate soldering uses a conveyor belt which carries printed circuit boards over a series of hot plates which heat the board from underneath, thus melting the solder paste. This process is low cost but its effectiveness is dependent on the thermal characteristics of the printed circuit board base material.

(d) Hot air soldering

Hot air soldering uses a nozzle which directs heated air or nitrogen onto an individual joint which has been applied with solder paste. In cases where higher reflow temperatures are required, helium gas may be used. The equipment is low cost and different-sized areas can be catered for by using a range of nozzle shapes. The process is by definition one joint at a time which limits the speed of the process. There is a tendency for flux to be scattered by the hot air blast which can affect other components.

A variation on the theme of hot air soldering is the use of hot air to unsolder faulty surface mount components. Hot air repair stations are amongst the commonest methods of removing surface mount components. Hot air is directed through a nozzle onto the component leads. The solder then reflows and the component is removed by means of a vacuum tube which runs through the centre of the device. The component is lifted free by being held in place by the vacuum – the reverse of the placement process.

(e) Laser soldering

Laser soldering is a new technique which as yet has only specialized usage. It is an expensive process in terms of equipment but has the advantage of being able to produce very high quality and reliability solder joints. Laser soldering utilizes a laser beam which is directed at the solder joint to melt the solder. Both solid and gas lasers are used. Solid lasers of the Nd:YAG (neodymium-doped yttrium aluminium garnet) variety which emit energy at a wavelength of 1.06 μm are most widely used. The laser energy is absorbed by the metal areas of the joint with a high efficiency. Glass and plastics which constitute the board material itself are reflectors of Nd:YAG laser energy. This makes normal optical glass and fibre optics usable as transmission media.

Carbon dioxide gas lasers, which emit energy at a wavelength of 10.6 μm, are also used for laser soldering. This wavelength is strongly absorbed by glass and plastics and reflected by metals, which would suggest that it would be of little use. Flux, however, strongly absorbs CO_2 laser energy. This fact when coupled with the lower cost of CO_2 laser systems makes it a viable alternative.

As CO_2 lasers cannot be used with normal optics, the laser has to be aimed directly at the target. This is performed by an operator who is assisted by the addition of a visible helium–neon laser for targeting as the CO_2 laser beam is invisible. Nd:YAG lasers can be guided using fibre optics rather than direct targeting. The non-contact nature of the laser soldering process has the additional advantage that it causes no displacement of components.

(f) Multiple-impulse soldering

Multiple-impulse soldering, more commonly known as hot bar soldering, uses a heating tool which is applied to the joint to be soldered under pressure. A high pulsating current is then applied to the tool which rapidly heats up and melts the solder paste. When the current is switched off the tool cools and allows the solder to solidify. The tool can utilize a range of shapes to cater for different joint sizes. This process concentrates the heat to the joint with little thermal infuence on nearby components. The process is liable to displace components owing to the applied pressure. The pressure may however help to avoid planarity problems with fine pitch integrated circuit component terminations. It also subjects the locality of the solder joint to sudden temperature changes.

7.7 MIXING SURFACE MOUNT WITH LEADED COMPONENTS

Printed circuit boards which utilize only surface mount components can be assembled using either the adhesive and wave solder or the solder paste and reflow solder methods, the choice being up to the individual manufacturer. The fact that 100% surface mount component printed circuit boards are a rarity necessitates the mixing of both leaded and surface mount components on a typical board. This mixing of technologies has the effect of constraining the choice of manufacturing methods used and also has implications regarding the testability of a board.

Surface mount components can be mounted on either or both sides of a printed circuit board. Thus a printed circuit board containing both leaded and surface mount components can have the surface mount components on the component side, the lead side or both.

When surface mount components are positioned on the same side of a board as leaded components, it is possible to assemble the surface mount components first and then to assemble the leaded components. This utilizes conventional processes for each component type. Manufacturers often apply the surface mount components using the solder paste and reflow method and then use a conventional leaded component insertion and soldering process. The printed circuit boards can undergo a conventional wave soldering process. This is provided that the component side of the board does not become sufficiently hot to remelt the solder and to cause the surface mount components to move out of position. The solder paste approach removes the necessity of putting a printed circuit board through a wave soldering process twice.

When surface mount components are placed on the opposite side of a board to leaded components the adhesive and wave soldering method is more advantageous. The reason for this is that all the soldering, of both the leaded components and the surface mount components, can be achieved in a single process. This is assuming that the surface mount component's bodies do not cover a hole through which a leaded component's lead has been inserted, as this would prevent soldering. If surface mount components are to cover insertion holes they must be placed after the leaded components and would have to utilize a solder paste process. The reflow method would need to be a process which targets individual joint areas, such as hot air or laser soldering, as opposed to an entire board process which would disturb the existing solder joints.

7.8 SOLDERING QUALITY

There are fundamental differences between the solder joints associated with leaded components and surface mount components. In the case of leaded components an ideal solder joint is described with respect to a component lead protruding from an annular-shaped land area. Surface mount components have completely different geometries and hence different definitions of a good solder joint. Furthermore, the chip form and J lead forms of surface mount components have their own different soldering requirements. One of the fundamental differences between a leaded component's and a surface mount component's solder joints is that in the latter case the solder joint must supply the mechanical attachment of the component to the printed circuit board. It is therefore essential that all solder joints contain a sufficient amount of correctly placed solder to achieve this requirement. Unlike leaded components, surface-mounted components are also prone to be out of position after soldering. Chip surface mount components present a metal face as a solderable surface. The ideal form of solder joint for such devices is the fillet as shown in Figure 7.9. Too little solder will result in poor electrical and mechanical connection. Too much solder may be acceptable provided that the solder does not overhang the land area or the component's body. Chip surface mount devices are unusual in that they are prone to the tombstoning effect, as described in sections 7.6.1 and 7.6.2. An example of tombstoning is shown in Figure 7.10.

J-leaded components, of which the bottom of the J rests on the printed circuit board, are ideally soldered when there is a solder fillet either side of the lead as shown in Figure 7.11. Again, too little solder threatens the integrity of both the electrical and the mechanical connections of the device. In the case of too much solder a significant portion of the J shape may be buried in the solder joint. This may again be acceptable provided that solder does not overhang the land area or cover the actual device's casing.

Figure 7.9 Chip SMC with ideal solder fillet.

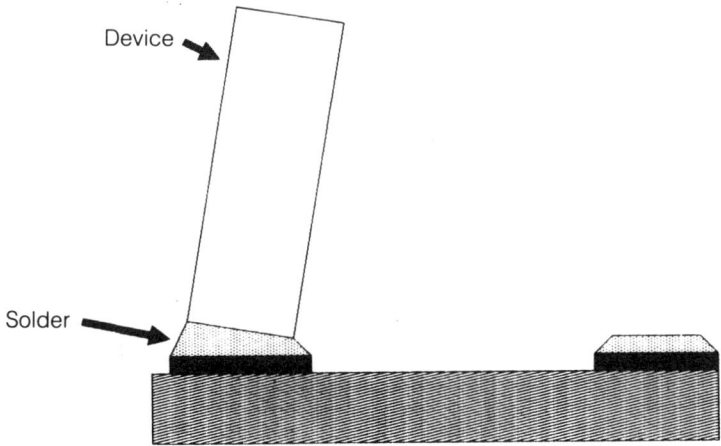

Figure 7.10 The tombstoning effect.

Solder joints created by the reflow soldering methods are prone to certain types of fault which are not always easy to detect. The reason for this is that, unlike poor joints created by wave soldering, solder will typically be present on the land areas and may give the appearance of a good joint. A good example of this is for devices where the solder joint is predominantly under the component body. If the solder fails to wet the component's terminal electrode during reflowing, but wets the land area, no connection will be made. Provided that this does not happen to all the component's leads, in which case it will fall off, the condition can go undetected. An electrical connection may even be present owing to mechanical dry contact.

In cases where a printed circuit board warps as a result of heating at the soldering stage, surface mount components are subject to a lot of stress and can easily be damaged. Leaded components are somewhat immune to this form of damage as their leads can deform and remove some of or all the stress.

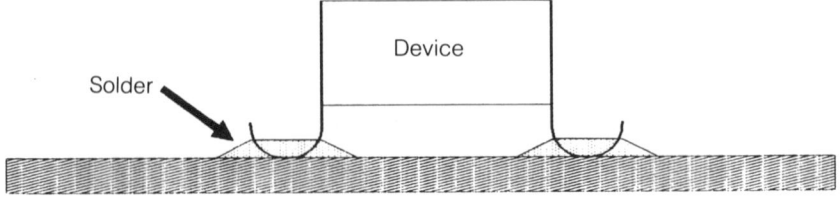

Figure 7.11 Ideal SMC J lead soldering.

7.9 TESTING

The use of surface mount components introduces problems of testability. In particular the use of a bed-of-nails testbed is somewhat restricted.

The small land and terminal sizes associated with surface mount components cause problems when using conventional probes. The number of probes per square centimetre is limited by contact pressure requirements, which may prevent the required number of probes being applied. The physical sizes of probe tips can be similar to that of the land geometry, which can result in shorting between track and land areas, thus invalidating the test. The application of test probes directly to component terminals can result in component damage.

When surface mount components are used in conjunction with leaded components, testing may be restricted. A typical example of this would be when a surface mount component obscures a leaded component's connections from a test probe.

A solution to the testability problem is to incude test lands into a board's track layout. These are bare 'land' areas to which no components are soldered and are purely target areas for test probes. The use of test lands makes the requirements of the test engineer contradictory to those of the design and production engineers. A test engineer would require a sufficient number of test lands to make a board fully testable. A design engineer would prefer to minimize the number of test lands as they are not necessary for functionality and complicate the board layout. Production engineers would prefer minimal test lands as they increase board areas and complexity. A compromise therefore has to be reached to minimize board complexity and to maximize testability.

Another form of testing which is of use with surface mount components is the use of vision systems. Visual testing can detect a wide range of faults including misaligned or missing components. Visual inspection can also diagnose many of the commonly occurring soldering problems. One method of automatic visual inspection is the use of laser systems to determine the positioning of components. A laser beam is directed at the expected component position along with a reference beam. The camera system detects the offset between the main and reference beams and hence can determine the presence or absence of a component. Alternatively, component presence can be detected by a shadowing technique. A bright light is directed at the printed circuit board under test at an acute angle. Each component present on the board's surface will cast a shadow. Each shadow is then easily detected by a camera-based vision system as it will create a high contrast with the rest of the board's surface.

7.10 REWORKING

In the event that a fault is detected in a printed circuit board containing surface mount components, reworking will be required to correct the fault. The manual reworking of surface mount components is particularly difficult owing to the small physical sizes of the devices and their terminal connections. A manual operator will typically need visual assistance such as a magnifying glass in order to be able to see the components adequately. Handling devices such as fine-tipped soldering irons and fine pliers and tweezers will also be required.

The processes required for the removal of surface mount components from printed circuit boards are dependent on the fixing process used and the stage during processing when the fault was detected. The two main cases are when components need to be removed after adhesive application and curing and after soldering.

Surface mount components may need to be removed from a printed circuit board after adhesive application and bonding if they have become displaced from their land areas or lifted from the board surface during handling or processing. A typical method of removing such components is by the application of mechanical force to pull the component away. It is essential to minimize the force used in this operation in order to minimize damage to the component. It may be possible to apply a solvent for the adhesive locally to facilitate removal. Once a component has been removed in this way it is important to test it thoroughly to ensure that it was not damaged during the removal operation before replacing it in its correct position and bonding it in place.

When surface mount components are to be removed after soldering it is necessary to melt the solder. This can be achieved either by using a fine-tipped soldering iron or by directing a jet of hot air at the device. The choice of actual method is dependent on the type of device to be used. In fact the method used for component removal, which works by applying a localized heating source, can be used to solder a new component into position. The replacement part can be soldered by using solder paste with either hot air or a fine soldering iron. Alternatively, a very fine solder wire can be used in conjunction with a fine soldering iron. Although testing has determined that surface mount components can survive several soldering operations without loss of performance, it is common practice to discard all devices which have been removed after soldering.

Poor solder joints can be repaired using a fine-tipped soldering iron. Many faults can be cured purely by the application of a heat source to remelt the solder. In the case where additional solder material is required a fine solder wire can be used.

8
Alternative technologies

Although the vast majority of circuits can be manufactured using standard commercially available devices, there are applications where alternative technologies may be employed. In particular, the packing density of a circuit can be increased by the use of specialized devices and technologies.

The advances in semiconductor technology allow the manufacture of devices with ever-increasing complexity. In order to utilize the full potential of highly complex semiconductor devices the technological problems associated with packaging need to be solved.

It is well known that, the more complex a semiconductor device is, the more pin-out connections it needs. An empirical formula was developed in the 1960s known as Rent's rule which suggests that the number of pin-outs of a device is proportional to the number of gates raised to the power of 0.6. The actual formula is (Laudman and Russo, 1971)

$$P = kC^r$$

where P is the number of pin-out connections required, C is the number of logic gates or cells, k is the number of connections per cell and r is an exponent in the range (0.45–1). For integrated circuits the value of r is typically 0.6 which gives pin-out requirements of 63 pins for a 1000-gate device, 250 pins for a 10 000-gate device and 1000 pins for a 100 000-gate device.

The dual-in-line package for integrated circuits has a natural limit of 64 pins above which the electrical performance of the device becomes unacceptable. This leads to the necessary development of packages which are capable of supporting higher pin counts. Such packages as the surface mount leadless chip carriers (LCCs) and pin grid arrays (PGAs), as described in Chapter 2, support today's more complex devices. The leadless chip carrier and pin grid array packages also have their own limits on the number of pins they can provide. A fine lead pitch leadless chip carrier can probably support 200 pins and a fine pitch pin grid array can probably support 400 pins per device.

Clearly, as device complexity increases still further, the packaging problem poses a serious limitation. One approach to solving the packaging problem is to dispose of the packaging altogether. This is known as hybrid technology. Alternatively, entire circuits can be fabricated in integrated circuit form. This is known as application-specific integrated circuit (ASIC) technology. Alternative technologies to the hybrid and the application-specific integrated circuit are represented by tape automated bonding (TAB) and wafer-scale integration (WSI). A variation on the theme of the rigid printed circuit board is that of the flexible printed circuit board which enables flexible circuits to be produced.

8.1 HYBRID TECHNOLOGY

Hybrid technology has been in existence for some time but until recently has not attracted too much attention. However, with the increasing pressures of packaging pin-out requirements, hybrid technology is gaining recognition.

The basic principle behind hybrid technology is that the bare semiconductor dice are mounted directly onto a substrate and connected to a wiring system built into the substrate. The wiring system includes passive components which are themselves fabricated on the substrate. Hybrid circuits can be formed by the processes of both thick and thin film techniques. Thick film techniques involve the formation of interconnections and components, such as resistors and capacitors, by means of a screen printing process. Thin film techniques use similar techniques to those used for integrated circuit manufacture, as described in Chapter 4, to create interconnections and components. Depending on the fabrication method, the resultant devices are referred to as either thick film hybrids or thin film hybrids. The main advantage of thick film methods over thin film is that they are much simpler from the manufacturing point of view. As thin film hybrids are manufactured in a similar fashion to the actual integrated circuits themselves, this discussion will concentrate on thick film hybrids.

8.1.1 Advantages of hybrids

The main advantage which hybrid technology offers is that of greatly increased component packing density. Although surface mount technology offers up to double the packing density of conventional leaded component technology, hybrid technology offers up to five times the packing density of surface mount.

Hybrids have been considered as an intermediate technology which lies between the printed circuit board and the application-specific integrated circuit. It was considered that the ASIC or wafer level technology would eventually render the hybrid obsolete. The hybrid, however, allows a mixture of different technologies to be integrated. This cannot be done using an ASIC. In fact, modern hybrids are used to interconnect the most complex devices including VLSI and ASICs.

Hybrids offer the following advantages over PCB technology.

1. The number of connections is considerably reduced as the pads of a semiconductor die are soldered directly to the substrate. Traditional packaging requires that a die's pads are wire bonded to the package pins, which are in turn soldered to the PCB. This makes hybrids more reliable as failure rate is proportional to the number of connections.
2. Hybrids have better thermal properties than PCBs as the materials can be closely matched for heat dissipation and expansion coefficients. Hybrids dissipate heat by direct conduct to the substrate material. This allows higher power dissipation for the same operating temperature.

8.1.2 Hybrid design

Modern computer-aided design systems such as the Racal Redac Visula system offer facilities for hybrid design. Such systems contain databases which hold information on the types of pastes which are to be used in the manufacturing process. This allows the system to calculate the sizes and shapes of thick film resistors from the paste's characteristics and the required resistance value. A similar process applies to capacitors, where the correct dielectric dimensions can be calculated. This can be applied to both single- and multiple-dielectric-layer capacitors. Automatic placement and routeing can be performed for hybrids in a similar fashion to that of printed circuit boards.

Hybrids with 250 layers and geometries in the order of 0.01 μm can be accommodated.

8.1.3 Thick film hybrid manufacture

Thick film hybrids have developed more slowly than their thin film counterparts. The rapid developments concerned with the fabrication of integrated circuits have effectively supported the thin film technology. Thick film technology has suffered from commercial secrecy, giving it the reputation of being a 'black art' as opposed to a science. There have also been many problems and misconceptions associated with the material requirements of thick film hybrids.

A thick film hybrid is basically manufactured by silk screen printing conductive and resistive inks onto a substrate material. A glazing layer is selectively applied to the hybrid and the whole assembly is then fired in a furnace. The substrate, conductive inks and glazing layer correspond to the substrate, copper tracking and solder resist layers of a conventional printed circuit board. One of the major advantages of thick film hybrids is that they can be manufactured with relatively low cost equipment and relatively unskilled operators. They are resistant to water and steam; however, they are often adversely affected by the presence of hydrogen.

Although components such as resistors and capacitors can be fabricated directly onto the substrate, many components, and in particular integrated circuits, need to be soldered onto the substrate surface. This can be performed using surface mount procedures, wiring or flip chip techniques.

The discussion of hybrids concerns the substrate materials, conductive interconnection fabrication, the fabrication of passive components and silicon die assembly.

8.1.4 Hybrid substrates

The substrate material used for a hybrid device has to have a dielectric constant, an expansion coefficient and a thermal conductivity which are compatible with those of the devices it is to carry. These parameters are rarely all achievable at an ideal level and a compromise may need to be reached. A low dielectric constant is required for high performance devices. The expansion coefficient should be close to that of silicon in order to reduce fatigue on connections. The thermal coefficient needs to be sufficiently high to keep semiconductor junction temperatures within operating range.

Hybrid substrate materials in use are alumina, beryllium oxide and aluminium nitride.

Alumina is in common usage as it is easy to work with, but it has a poor thermal conductivity. Beryllium oxide is also in common usage and has an excellent thermal conductivity; it is also a very toxic material. Aluminium nitride has a good thermal conductivity and a thermal expansion close to that of silicon; however, it is difficult to work with. The traditional substrate material is 96% alumina. However, demands of circuit performance require the thermal characteristics of beryllium oxide and aluminium nitride for high power applications.

The manufacturing requirements of a substrate are that it has a smooth flat surface. Substrates can be manufactured from alumina to fairly high specifications. However, higher specification finishes can be achieved using machining processes, but these make the substrate much more expensive.

8.1.5 Hybrid interconnections

The interconnection method in hybrid circuits falls into two categories, thin film and thick film. In thin film circuits the metallization is created using methods similar to those used in semiconductor fabrication. Thick film interconnections may be provided by either a subtractive process or an additive process. In the subtractive process, which is similar to fabricating a printed circuit board, a continuous conductive layer is applied to the substrate which is then removed as necessary to leave conductive tracks. In the additive process an ink containing particles of metal and glass is either screen printed or sprayed onto the substrate and then fired in a furnace both sintering the ink particles together and forming a bond with the substrate. Typical metals used are gold, silver, silver-palladium and copper, or for circuits where the metallization is cofired with the ceramic substrate, alloys of tungsten, molybdenum and manganese may be used. In all but the simplest circuits the interconnections must be able to cross. In thick film circuits this is usually achieved by printing an insulating layer over either the whole substrate (leaving windows through which connections may be made) or just over the tracks to be crossed. A further conductive layer is then printed forming a second level of interconnections. This process may be repeated giving a total of up to about 10 layers.

8.1.6 Hybrid resistors

Thin film resistors are formed by a sputtering process. The materials used must have a high resistivity and good temperature stability. The commonest material in use is tantalum nitride. Other materials in use are silicon–tantalum, chromium–silicon oxide and tungsten–silicon.

Thick film resistors are printed like thick film conductors but the ink formulation will usually contain oxides of ruthenium which can be tailored to give a wide range of sheet resistivities.

One of the major problems associated with screen-printed resistors is that the resistance value tends to drift on aging. The resistance drift increases the resistance value for an initial period after which the value starts to stabilize. One of the major causes of undesirable resistance drifts is that the ink firing temperature was too low. It is possible to overcome the effects of resistance drifts by forming the resistor with a lower value than is actually desired and then using a high temperature aging process to cause the resistance value to stabilize at the desired value.

8.1.7 Hybrid capacitors

A capacitor basically consists of a sandwich of conductive film layers with insulating dielectric material layers. This structure can readily be incorporated into a hybrid circuit's fabrication. Thick film capacitors are formed by screen printing alternate layers of conductor and dielectric onto the substrate. This is followed by a layer of an overglaze material which encapsulates and protects the device. The overglaze is then melted in a furnace operating at about 850 °C. It is important to note that the dielectric constant of the dielectric material may change during the firing process. This needs to be compensated for to produce the desired capacitance value.

In addition to fabricating capacitors on the substrate, capacitors can also be in discrete form and soldered onto the substrate's metallization. Surface mount chip capacitors are particularly suited to this type of application.

8.1.8 Hybrid semiconductor assembly

The high packing densities obtainable from hybrids are partly a result of being able to mount integrated circuit dice directly onto the substrate without the use of conventional integrated circuit packaging. This also overcomes some of the limitations associated with the pin-out problem. Hybrids are also very compatible with surface mount forms of integrated circuits such as leadless chip carriers. Conventionally packaged integrated circuit dice have all of their contact pads on the edges of the die in order to facilitate wire bonding. The use of hybrid technologies allows this limitation to be overcome, which results in the flip chip. A flip chip is an integrated circuit die which can have its contact pads anywhere on the die's surface area. It is called a flip chip because it is mounted face down onto the substrate. The relaxation of the requirement for pads to be on a die's periphery gives the silicon designer much more flexibility in terms of both circuit layout and the number of external connections. This gives the added advantage that input and output lines do not have to travel all the way to the periphery of the die.

A flip chip is fabricated with a solder bump on each connecting pad area so as to make it stand proud of the die's surface. The solder bumps can then form solder joints with the interconnect of a hybrid substrate. The one major disadvantage of flip chips is from the testing point of view. The fact that many of the connections to the device are hidden underneath the component's body prevents access to test probes. In addition, it is almost impossible to correct a faulty solder joint.

8.2 TAPE AUTOMATED BONDING

A variation on the packaging theme is that of tape automated bonding as shown in Figure 8.1. This involves the formation of metallized contacts on a plastic tape which often has the same dimensions as standard 35 mm photographic film. The blank film is initially punched to define the outline of the die and any tooling holes. The tape is then metallized by the addition of a metal foil. This foil is subjected to a photolithographic process in order to define the actual interconnections and to remove surplus metal.

This process is applied to lengths of tape to produce a continuous tape of die connections. The tape is then fed into an automatic bonder which bonds the tape to the die pads by means of copper fingers. The tape can then be cut up to form the leads of individual packages.

Figure 8.1 Tape automated bonding: (a) blank polymer tape; (b) punch or mill tape; (c) roll metal foil; (d) apply photoresist pattern; (e) etch metal foil; (f) gang bond leads to IC die.

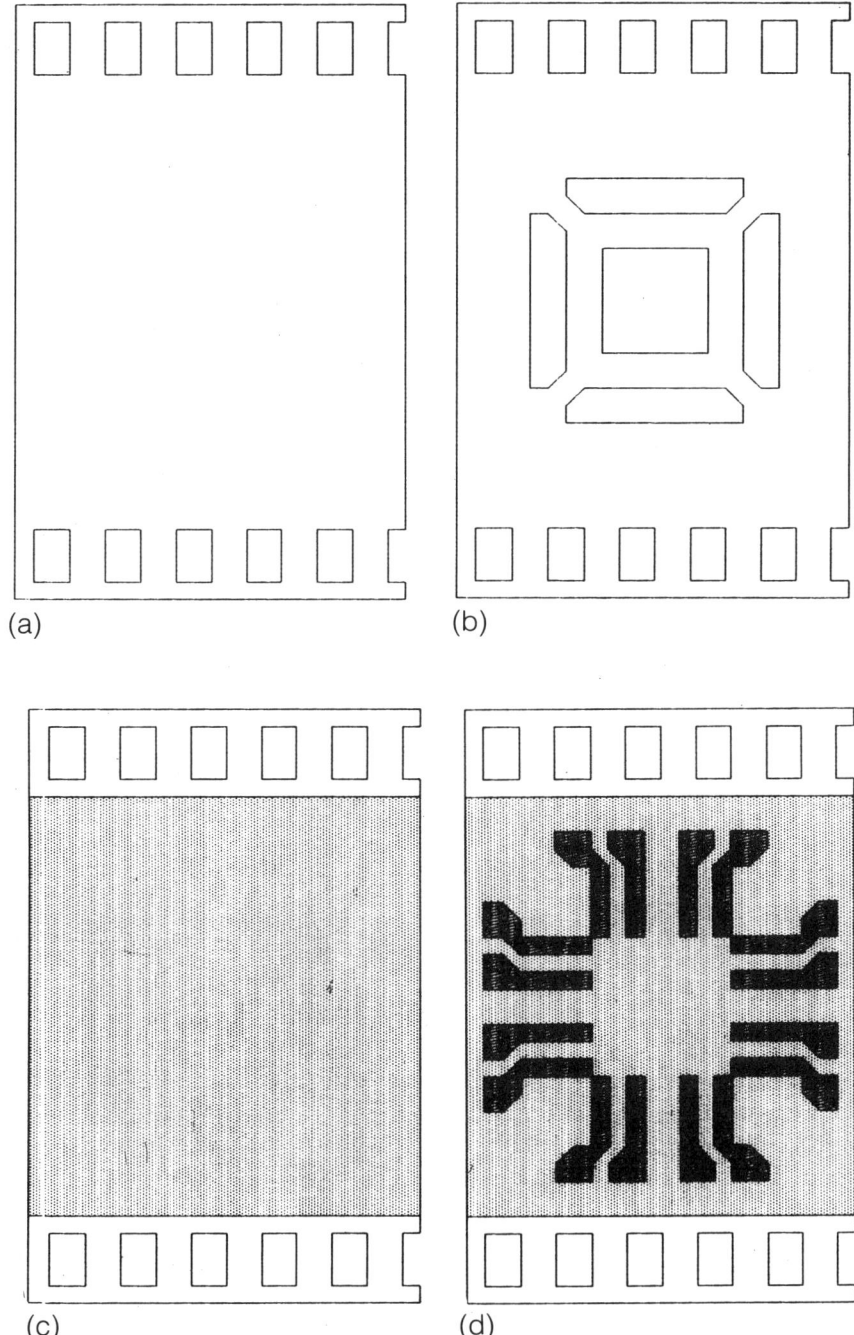

(a)

(b)

(c)

(d)

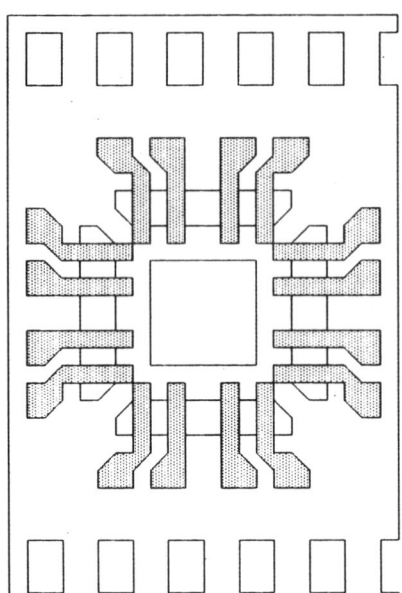 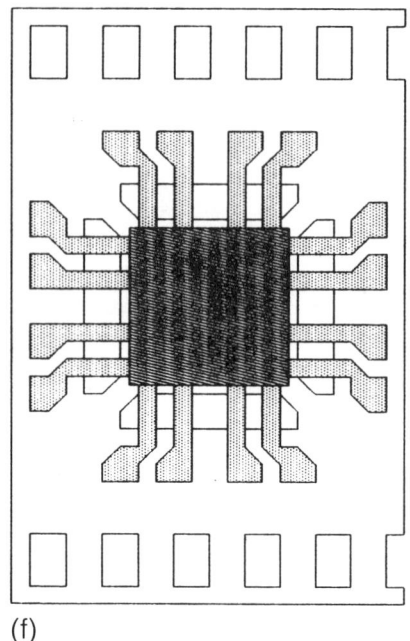

(e)   (f)

Figure 8.1 continued

8.3 SILICON ON SILICON WAFER-SCALE INTEGRATION

Silicon on silicon wafer-scale integration offers a potential doubling of the packing density obtainable from hybrids, at increased reliability. Wafer-scale integration combines the technologies of semiconductor manufacture, multilayer printed circuit board manufacture and hybrid techniques.

Silicon on silicon wafer-scale integration utilizes silicon as a substrate material, as opposed to a ceramic in the case of a conventional hybrid, upon which a high density multilayer interconnect is built using semiconductor-manufacturing thin film techniques. Unlike other approaches which use silicon to obtain multiple devices on a single substrate, the wafer-scale integration method allows a wide range of chip and interconnect technologies to be integrated.

Silicon substrates provide a higher reliability as their thermal coefficients match those of large silicon VLSI devices. Lower junction temperatures can be achieved as silicon has a much greater thermal conductivity than ceramics.

The use of silicon photolithography techniques to create the interconnect layers allows interconnect spacing to be an order of magnitude smaller than with other techniques. This has the effect of reducing signal paths and improving the speed of operation of devices. A very high yield rate is obtained as the interconnect spacing is very much greater than the design specification of the manufacturing techniques. An additional advantage of silicon on silicon wafer-scale integration is that some active devices, including memories, can be fabricated directly into the substrate.

8.4 APPLICATION-SPECIFIC INTEGRATED CIRCUITS

Application-specific integrated circuits are devices which are customized for a particular user application. A good example of this is the microcomputer, in particular those designed for the home market. A microcomputer typically consists of a microprocessor, memory, input and output devices, and various logic circuits to link them together. This logic, which is often referred to as glue logic, frequently consists of a large number of simple devices and interconnections. The implementation of the glue logic using ASIC technology can greatly simplify the printed circuit board and make considerable savings in size and cost. The major methods of implementing ASICs are cellular logic, gate arrays, programmable logic and analogue ASICs.

8.4.1 Cellular logic

Cellular logic takes the form of a library of logic units or cells which can be combined in a variety of ways to implement the customer's functionality requirements. Each semiconductor manufacturer will have a range of logic cells available. This range can be very large and contain functions as complex as processors.

An ASIC is created by placing and routeing the logic cells so as to implement the function – this is analogous to the placing and routeing of printed circuit boards. The fabrication of the device involves the complete processing as for an integrated circuit. The consequences of this are long lead times and high tooling costs. The tooling costs include the manufacture of the masks used for the semiconductor fabrication processes. Hence cellular logic is most applicable to high volume and highly complex applications.

A further variety of ASIC is the full custom device. This is an integrated circuit which is designed from scratch. This may or may not make use of standard cells, although wherever standard cells can be used it is advisable to do so in order to reduce the high manufacturing costs associated with custom devices.

8.4.2 Gate arrays

Gate arrays, sometimes referred to as uncommitted logic arrays or ULAs, are predefined collections of circuits implemented in silicon without the final metal interconnection layer. The ASIC is implemented by defining a customized final metallization layer so as to implement the required functionality. Gate arrays by definition contain a number of redundant circuits as it is rare for an application to utilize all the available gates.

The lead times and tooling complexity are much less for gate arrays than for cellular logic owing to the reduced amount of processing. This makes gate arrays suitable for medium volume and medium complexity applications.

The traditional method of designing a gate array was to have relatively sparsely packed gates with channels running between them. This philosophy was used so that a single metallization layer can be used to interconnect the gates to provide the desired functionality. Recent advances in microelectronic processing allow the use of multiple metallization layers. This has led to a new generation of densely packed gate arrays which do not have channels between devices. The interconnection can be performed directly between devices using several metallization layers if necessary.

8.4.3 Programmable logic

Programmable logic covers a range of technologies of which a common example is the read-only memory, or ROM, device. These programmable logic devices can be either fixed or reprogrammable. Although read-only memories are primarily designed as permanent storage devices for computer systems, they can be used in other applications. A read-only memory works by inputting an address number and then the device outputs a preprogrammed data number corresponding to the address. As the input address does not necessarily have to have been generated by a computer, the devices have other applications. For applications such as decoding switch inputs, a read-only memory can take the place of a considerable amount of discrete decoding circuitry.

Fixed program devices, which include programmable read-only memories or PROMs, often rely on fuses which can be selectively blown to implement the required function. A variation on this theme is the anti-fuse which can selectively establish connections.

Reprogrammable logic devices are typified by the erasable programmable read-only memory, or EPROM, which consists of a number of memory cells which can be set to particular values.

Programmable logic is limited in complexity but very cheap and easy to implement. There are no lead times or tooling requirements, which offers a great deal of flexibility in implementation.

A variation on the themes of programmable logic devices and gate arrays is the programmable logic array. These devices have a number of programmable interconnections between logic gates which can be customized by programming.

8.4.4 Analogue application-specific integrated circuits

Analogue ASICs usually take the form of an analogue version of the digital gate array, although cellular array implementations are beginning to become available. Analogue ASICs are relatively recent arrivals owing to the greater complexity of design and testing than for the digital counterparts. One of the big problems associated with analogue circuits is that computer-aided simulations of circuit operation and performance are considerably more complex and time consuming than digital circuits.

Analogue 'gate arrays' consist of an array of functional analogue circuits such as operational amplifiers and oscillators along with various components such as capacitors for the interconnection of circuits. One of the problems with analogue circuits is that interconnections often need to be via discrete components such as resistors and capacitors rather than direct connections as in the digital case.

Analogue cellular arrays consist of the building blocks from which analogue circuits can be built. These include small subcircuits such as pairs of transistors in a differential amplifier configuration. In addition, a large number of discrete resistors and capacitors are required for circuit construction. Analogue ASICs also offer the possibilities of combining both analogue and digital circuits on the same device.

Examples of this are analogue-to-digital and digital-to-analogue converters. This has important implications for industries such as telecommunications.

Analogue ASICs are somewhat limited in performance as crosstalk can be a serious problem at the small geometries used.

8.5 FLEXIBLE CIRCUITS

Flexible circuits are an innovative form of interconnection technology which allow the fabrication of truly three-dimensional circuits. They differ from wiring systems such as ribbon cables in that flexible circuits can incorporate electronic components. Unlike conventional wiring, a flexible circuit can be tuned to produce an interconnection with specific electrical characteristics. A flexible circuit is basically a highly flexible variant of the conventional rigid printed circuit board theme. There are two types of applications for flexible circuits, which are static and dynamic applications. Static applications utilize flexible circuits by bending them into a particular configuration which remains constant throughout the product life. Examples of static usage are space saving by bending the circuit into a concertina form, and the interconnection of devices with awkward geometries such as disc drives. Dynamic applications of flexible circuits require that the circuit be continuously deformed during operation, for example to interconnect devices which need to be moved relative to each other.

The flexible nature of flexible circuits imposes limitations on the design, materials and fabrication processes. Although these processes are similar to those used for conventional printed circuit boards, they need to be much more carefully controlled in order to produce a working result. A flexible circuit basically consists of a copper film which is sandwiched between a flexible substrate and a flexible cover layer. The substrate corresponds to the conventional printed circuit board substrate. The cover layer corresponds to the solder resist layer in conventional printed circuit boards.

From the design point of view, allowances must be made for lower dimensional stability of flexible circuits. When designing artwork it is necessary to allow for shrinkage of the materials during processing. It is highly advisable to maximize the amount of copper which is to remain on the circuit as this helps to minimize shrinkage of the substrate material. The three-dimensional nature of flexible circuits must also be allowed for in the design stage. It is often possible to determine the major areas of deformation in advance, which facilitates this dimensional allowance. Copper tracking should be designed to run perpendicular to any bends which it crosses wherever possible. It is highly advisable to develop flexible circuit artwork from scratch rather than attempting to modify a rigid circuit layout. The choice of materials for the base and cover films of a flexible circuit is of particular importance. Although there is a large range of potential materials, most flexible circuits are currently manufactured from either polyimide or polyester.

Polyimide film is the best material for most flexible circuit applications. It can readily withstand the temperatures used for soldering and has excellent insulation properties. It also has no known organic solvent. The main drawback of polyimide is its cost.

Polyester has the main advantage of being only a fraction of the cost of polyimide. It does, however, have the major disadvantage that standard soldering temperatures are very close to its melting point. This limitation can be overcome by utilizing a relatively thick base layer and using large copper areas.

The copper foil material can be either electroplated or rolled as for conventional printed circuit boards. The two processes result in different copper grain structures. Each process has its advantages and disadvantages. The general principle is that rolled copper is the best for dynamic flexible circuit applications and electroplated copper is best for static applications.

The manufacture of a flexible circuit starts with the bonding of a copper film onto a substrate material. This is achieved using epoxy or acrylic adhesives with polyimide substrates and polyester adhesives with polyester substrates.

It is important to be able to achieve accurate registration of flexible film materials during the manufacturing process. This is best achieved using accurate jigging and indexing holes. A flexible circuit substrate is typically punched with indexing and sprocket holes which allow accurate materials handling and registration for imaging and drilling operations.

The actual manufacturing processes follow the typical sequence used for the manufacture of conventional printed circuit boards. All the single-sided, double-sided and multilayer technologies can be used. The main differences between the conventional and flexible circuit manufacturing processes occur in the final stages.

The drilling process warrants further discussion as once drilled the holes need to be carefully cleaned in order to produce a very smooth hole with no cracks. Any such defects can result in the flexible circuit tearing during operation, particularly for dynamic applications. The hole is cleaned using an etching process which is typically a plasma etching process. Alternatively, hole etching can be performed using complex chemical processes.

Whereas conventional printed circuit boards are screen printed with a solder resist layer, flexible circuits need to undergo a lamination process. The cover layer is a sheet of adhesive coated film which is typically of the same material type and thickness as the substrate film material. This cover film has been punched before adhesive application with holes which correspond to the tooling holes and land areas of the base material.

The substrate and the cover layer are aligned and placed together on a fixture which performs the necessary registration using pins. The two layers are then heat tacked together in the desired alignment. The complete assembly is then placed in a press which cures the adhesive at a pressure of about 2.5 MN m^{-2} and a temperature of about 180 °C for about an hour. The circuit is then allowed to cool under pressure.

Following the lamination of the cover layer the flexible circuit can be assembled and soldered as for conventional printed circuit boards. Care must be taken when soldering polyester circuit owing to the potential melting problem.

In the case of multilayer flexible circuits, the general rule is to keep the number of layers to an absolute minimum. Once a multilayer flexible circuit exceeds a certain number of layers, problems start to occur when the circuit is bent. A bent circuit will have its inner layers under compression and its outer layers under tension. This can lead to serious problems. One solution to this is to design the circuit in such a way that the areas which are to be bent are not actually bonded together. In addition, outer layers of a bend can be made slightly longer than inner layers so that no stress develops under deformation. It is important not to bond the layers together when this approach is used otherwise the bend in the circuit will become a permanent feature, unless of course this bend is desired.

References

British Standards Institution (1972) *BS 4584: Metal-clad Printed Wiring boards.*

Coombs, C.F. (1988) *Printed Circuits Handbook.* McGraw-Hill, New York, 3rd edn.

Datamation (1988) The Datamation 100 leading worldwide IS companies. *Datamation* (June 15), 29.

Keller, J. (1981) Soldering without shorts – joints are auto ND tested. *Proceedings Annual Reliability and Maintainability Symposium, 1981.*

Lambert, L. (1984) Airknives have an edge on solder defect control. *Electron. Packag. Prod.* (February).

Laudman, W.R. and Russo, R.L. (1971) On a pin versus block relationship for partitions of logic graphs. *IEEE Trans. Comput.*, **20**, 1469–79.

Mackintosh, A.R. (1988) Dr Atanasoff's computer. *Sci. Am.* (August), **259**, 72–8.

Ross, P.J. (1988) *Taguchi Techniques for Quality Engineering.* McGraw-Hill, New York.

Further reading

CHAPTER 4

Ruska, W.S. (1987) *Microelectronic Processing*, McGraw-Hill, New York.

CHAPTER 5

Scarlett, J.A. (1970) *Printed Circuit Boards for Microelectronics*, Van Nostrand Reinhold, London.

CHAPTERS 6 AND 7

Noble, P.J.W. (1989) *Printed Circuit Board Assembly*, Open University Press, Milton Keynes.

Index